Introducing Software Testing

Introducing Software Testing

Louise Tamres

 Addison-Wesley

imprint of Pearson Education

London · Boston · Indianapolis · New York · Mexico City · Toronto
Sydney · Tokyo · Singapore · Hong Kong · Cape Town · New Delhi
Madrid · Paris · Amsterdam · Munich · Milan · Stockholm

PEARSON EDUCATION LIMITED

Head Office:
Edinburgh Gate
Harlow CM20 2JE
Tel: +44 (0)1279 623623
Fax: +44 (0)1279 431059
Websites: www.it-minds.com
        www.aw.com/cseng

London Office:
128 Long Acre
London WC2E 9AN
Tel: +44 (0)20 7447 2000
Fax: +44 (0)20 7240 5771

First published in Great Britain in 2002

© Pearson Education Limited 2002

ISBN 0-201-71974 6

British Library Cataloguing in Publication Data
A catalogue record for this book can be obtained from the British Library

Library of Congress Cataloging in Publication Data
Tamres, Louise, 1961-
  Introducing software testing / Louise Tamres.
   p. cm.
  Includes bibliographical references and index.
  ISBN 0-201-71974-6 (pbk.)
  1. Computer software–Testing. I. Title.

QA76.73.T48 T36 2002
005.1´4–dc21

                                                        2002018347

10 9 8 7 6 5 4 3 2 1

Designed by Claire Brodmann Book Designs, Lichfield, Staffs
Typeset by Land & Unwin, Bugbrooke, Northamptonshire
Printed and bound by Biddles Ltd, Guildford and King's Lynn

The Publishers' policy is to use paper manufactured from sustainable forests.

Contents

8   Reducing the number of test cases   193

9   Creating quality software   213

Introduction

The chaotic testing environment

A project is in panic mode and the deadline is rapidly approaching. Management starts to think about the need to test this product, having already missed some prime opportunities for improving software quality. One unfortunate programmer is assigned the task of software testing, which is often viewed as being transferred to purgatory. Needless to say, this poor hapless soul is given no guidance, and nobody in the organization is capable of providing any help. Despite the poor condition of requirements and other product documentation, the product is being built and it will be shipped. The task given to the tester is to minimize the surprises that could manifest themselves after the product is installed at customer sites. Under extreme pressure, this untrained tester is very inefficient and is at a loss how to begin. A clueless manager may even purchase testing tools, despite there being no useful tests to automate. This is the scenario that gives software testing a bad name.

Software testing is a specialized discipline requiring unique skills. Software testing is not intuitive; one must learn *how* to do it. Naïve managers erroneously think that any programmer can test software – if you can program, then you can test. This is the motivation behind this book: to provide a step-by-step approach for getting started with the testing effort.

Many fine books on software testing are available today. Those that do address test case design describe proven methods such as boundary value analysis, equivalence class partitioning, decision tables, syntax testing, cause–effect diagrams, data-flow methods, and other such concepts. Some novice testers wonder how to weed though poor specifications, before even being able to apply these methods. Many texts state that good requirements are necessary for the test effort – assuming that requirements exist – yet I have not seen any that explain the transition from requirements to test cases. In the chaotic software development environment, adequate requirements are rarely provided, and if they are, their completeness and correctness are questionable. In a situation when no one has analyzed the requirements adequately, the burden falls on the tester to pursue requirements issues prior to defining any tests. It is often impossible to perform thorough testing, given the tight schedules and limited resources. It is possible, however, to make intelligent choices and maximize the effectiveness of the testing effort.

it is possible to make intelligent choices and maximize the effectiveness of the testing effort

The goal is to learn how best to approach the testing tasks and eventually produce a workable test process for future projects.

The author's philosophy

To introduce the ideas on how to begin testing, I will work through several detailed examples, each containing defective "requirements". By definition, good requirements are testable and unambiguous. The fact that the sample requirements are deficient does not prevent useful test activities from occurring. I use the word "requirements" loosely and equate it with some sort of product description. While the sample test scenarios would not be permissible in a mature software organization, the work described will help the lone tester jumpstart the testing process under duress. The goal is to show that some product information, however deficient, can be used to start the testing effort.

I do *not* advocate working from poor requirements. Properly analyzing requirements corrects many deficiencies. Reviews and inspections have been proven to provide the most cost effective method for finding problems early in the development cycle. Many times, I have had to bite my tongue to avoid blurting out to project managers, "The requirements are absolute garbage and there's no way that we can begin a productive testing effort until you clean up your act." Actually, this phrase would contain unprintable language and be uttered under one's breath. We have undoubtedly all shared this fantasy, and the ugly truth is that despite this valid complaint, the product delivery deadline is fast approaching.

a crude list of tests is better than no list

Although I do *not* advocate cutting corners, there are some shortcuts that will help document the testing activities. A crude list of tests is better than no list. The minimum you will have is a documented trail, though rudimentary, that records your testing effort should you need to prove or demonstrate what you did.

Subsequent testing efforts will improve on this initial work, producing test documents and developing a test process that is more in line with accepted practices. Incremental changes lead to successful process improvements.

Just knowing how to get started with testing is a feat in itself. The tester must understand how to transform product information into test cases; this is the book's chief goal. Many existing books do an outstanding job of explaining software testing concepts and methods. Rather than reiterate what others have written, I make many references to their work. This book is a primer on getting started. It supplements currently available literature on software testing by providing an introduction to known software testing techniques.

Intended audience

This book is aimed at several types of readers:

● persons new to software testing who have no guidance or training;

- managers or mentors, who may themselves be experienced testers, seeking ideas on how to provide guidance to novice testers;
- experienced programmers who have been assigned testing tasks;
- knowledgeable testers looking for new ideas.

While readers are not assumed to be knowledgeable about software testing concepts, they should be computer literate and able to use a word processor and spreadsheet.

Job descriptions

The general job description terms used throughout the book are as follows:

- Tester   The person who defines and executes tests.
- Developer   The person who produces the application, including the design, source code, and final product integration.
- Project manager The person with authority regarding schedules and staffing.
- Project authority The domain expert with authority to define and clarify the requirements.

I refer to these descriptive titles without implying an organization structure or employee reporting chain. Project staffing decisions and job responsibilities vary across organizations.

Depending on how the project is staffed, the tester could be either in the same or in a separate group from the developer. Other projects could require that the same person performs both development and testing tasks, thereby changing mindset in mid-project. Ideally, a trained software test engineer performs the testing activities. However, some projects simply assign the testing role to whichever person is available.

The project authority can be the marketing manager, company executive, or customer support liaison, provided that this person has full authority to define the project contents. This role is necessary to prevent further chaos. Someone must be in charge of deciding which features to incorporate into a product; lack of such control is a well-known cause of problems when trying to get bad requirement definitions sorted out.

Your organization may use different job titles than those listed above. The key point is to assign people to perform the necessary tasks – each of which requires specialized skills.

Mature and immature software development environments

The examples cited in this book, with their incomplete product information, are what one could expect to find in an immature software organization. I will refrain from critiquing the work environment and from preaching about software process improvement. The reality is that many companies operate under less than ideal conditions. Despite the lack of suitable software processes, products are still being developed and shipped to customers. Testing, however minimal, can still be done. With poor requirements, the tester spends more time identifying product definition deficiencies rather than proceeding with testing-related tasks.

A mature software organization displays the characteristics listed below. An immature organization often does not understand how the following points can improve product quality:

● provide useful requirements and product descriptions;

● conduct reviews and inspections;

● have signoffs or checkpoints before proceeding to the next step;

● mentor and train personnel;

● schedule adequate time and resources for testing;

● overlap testing and development activities;

● provide defined software development and software testing processes;

● enforce configuration management.

Testing is a responsibility shared with the rest of the development team. The old view of testing as an afterthought – design, code, and then you test – has **a tester often knows more about programming than a developer knows about software testing** never produced good testing results. The adversarial and destructive "developer vs tester" mentality has often resulted from the developers' ignorance about software testing activities – more proof that testing is a unique discipline. It is often the case that a tester often knows more about programming than a developer knows about software testing. A collaborative approach between testers and developers fosters goodwill and good communication.

By working closely with the testers, many developers learn more about software testing, even if all the developers see is how their knowledge about the product filters into the test documentation. Effective software testing requires co-operation among all the members of a project.

Book overview

Chapter 1 deals with the unfortunate "you're new to testing, have no idea where to start, and the product ships Friday" nightmare. Hoping that your next project gives you more time to carry out testing activities, Chapter 2 illustrates the use of outlines, which is also a useful technique for analyzing requirements if no one else has done this task. Chapter 3 transforms the outline contents into test cases. Tables and spreadsheets are an integral tool used by software test engineers, and Chapter 4 shows several table formats and shortcuts for documenting test cases. Chapter 5 shows additional usages of tables. Applications built using object-oriented methods can use many of the same test design techniques outlined in the previous chapters. However, Chapter 6 describes some issues particular to testing object-oriented systems. Chapter 7 lists the challenges faced when testing web applications, although many of the strategies presented apply equally to client-server environments.

No uniform software testing method exists. Each example uses a different approach for producing tests. You may wonder why one method was used in one example instead of another. The answer is simple: I selected a method based on my experience. You may very well try a different approach that will be just as successful in your testing effort. Although the examples cover different types of applications, the core software testing themes apply equally to all examples, and some concepts are reiterated among all chapters. I recommend that you read through each scenario and not dismiss the subject simply because the example does not reflect your type of application.

By following the ideas and methods presented, you will have defined and documented many test cases. Chapter 8 will help you identify the most pertinent tests and thus reduce the necessary number of test cases to execute. Producing a set of test cases to execute is only part of the overall software testing picture. Chapter 9 lists other testing and quality related tasks that are necessary for producing quality software.

If this is the organization's first venture into methodical software testing, you will have established a good baseline. Although the work produced will be a vast improvement over prior chaotic efforts, it will fall short of satisfying, and conforming to, industry standards. Chapter 10 briefly describes some of the more common software engineering standards and how each affects the test case examples. Consider this a launching point for improving the testing effort.

Acknowledgments

The inspiration for this book comes from all the people who had the fortune and misfortune of working with me on software testing projects. I learned to test the hard way: by muddling through it, by watching other testers at work, and by reading well-worn copies of Glenford Myers' and Boris Beizer's books. Eventually, programmers and novice testers would ask me for guidance on how to test. I developed a ritual of pulling out old test documents and showing the steps for defining tests. Seeing an actual example was worth a thousand words. It is time to write down these methods and share them with a wider audience.

Several years ago I met Simon Mills at a software testing conference. He is an accomplished tester who shares the same experiences, passion, and battle scars. We talked, shared and then tried out our ideas by developing and presenting a course to help new testers get started. This was very well received and the participants' feedback was most beneficial. Without Simon's enthusiasm, I may never have set my sights on writing this book.

Many colleagues lent their time, expertise, and editing skills to help improve early drafts. I thank the following people profusely (and alphabetically) for all of their help: James Bach, Jim Brei, Elise Brooks, Kieron Conway, Jerilynn Coulter, Bill Deibler, Brian Forester, Dorothy Graham, Tony Howard, Vladan Jovanovic, Rita Lamport, Arthur Na, Nancy Poma, Lynne Frederickson Rago, Rose Reinhardt, Johanna Rothman, and Irene Ruthven.

I am extremely indebted to Rita Lamport and Jerilynn Coulter for their contributions. Rita generously shared and wrote up her experiences with testing web applications. I appreciated her quick turnaround every time I asked for assistance. Rita also helped me overcome my writer's block with the chapter on object-oriented software. Jerilynn helped develop many of the sections in the web testing chapter, as well as helping to clarify parts of the object-oriented chapter. This was a very productive collaboration.

During many informative conversations, Johanna Rothman conveyed the notion of interviewing the development team to pinpoint potential problem areas. I took her idea and ran with it. The results appear in Chapter 8. I owe her many thanks for introducing me to this concept.

Last but not least, I owe a big one to my husband, Brian Forester, who has been so supportive of this project. He made it possible for me to work from home and was a sounding board for countless ideas. I save the last kiss for my little boy, Justin, who tolerated many babysitters. One day you'll understand why mommy wasn't always available. May you benefit from this book when you write your first computer program!

1 Tackling the Testing Maze

1.1 Introduction

Not all software testing projects start off on a positive note. Maybe you are fresh out of school or you are an experienced programmer whose naïve manager thought would make a good tester – especially when no one is assigned the job of testing. Like other technical disciplines, software testing is a specialized field that requires specific skills. Many managers erroneously assume that a programmer can test software effectively without any training or mentoring.

Here you are with a big testing job ahead of you and no idea where to start – and probably no one else to turn to for help. Just like walking into a maze, a novice tester knows where to end up, but doesn't know how to get there. Oh, and in case you didn't know, the product ships next Friday – and the project documentation is incomplete, inaccurate, or worse, non-existent.

Hopefully, this is an exaggeration of what you may encounter. A good software development environment provides adequate staffing and time for software testing activities, as well as guidance for the test personnel. However, some testers do work under less than ideal conditions, and must learn about and test a new application under unreasonable deadlines. Some organizations have already decided to ship the product by a fixed date and want testers to confirm the product's suitability for use. This is *not* the best way to test, but the tester may have no other choice – other than possibly dusting off the resume and looking for greener pastures.

The focus of this chapter is to guide you through a series of steps that make effective use of your time and provide suitable tests for demonstrating whether the application works as expected. But first, let's look at the application to be tested.

1.2 Sample application

The example used in this chapter is a tax calculator for the 2000 tax year, and it is modeled after the US 1040 federal income tax form issued by the Internal Revenue Service. The ideas presented are for illustrative purposes only and are not meant to implement the complete tax code. Non-American readers may readily associate with testers who are unfamiliar with an application.

The user enters financial information and the tax calculator returns a value representing the amount of taxes due to the taxpayer or due to the Government. The application contains many input screens, four of which are shown below. An output window lists the results. The sample screenshots are:

Figure 1.1 – Taxpayer information and filing status.

Figure 1.2 – Information pertaining to income.

Figure 1.3 – Information pertaining to itemized deductions.

Figure 1.4 – Other taxes and credits affecting the taxpayer.

Figure 1.5 – Tax calculator output.

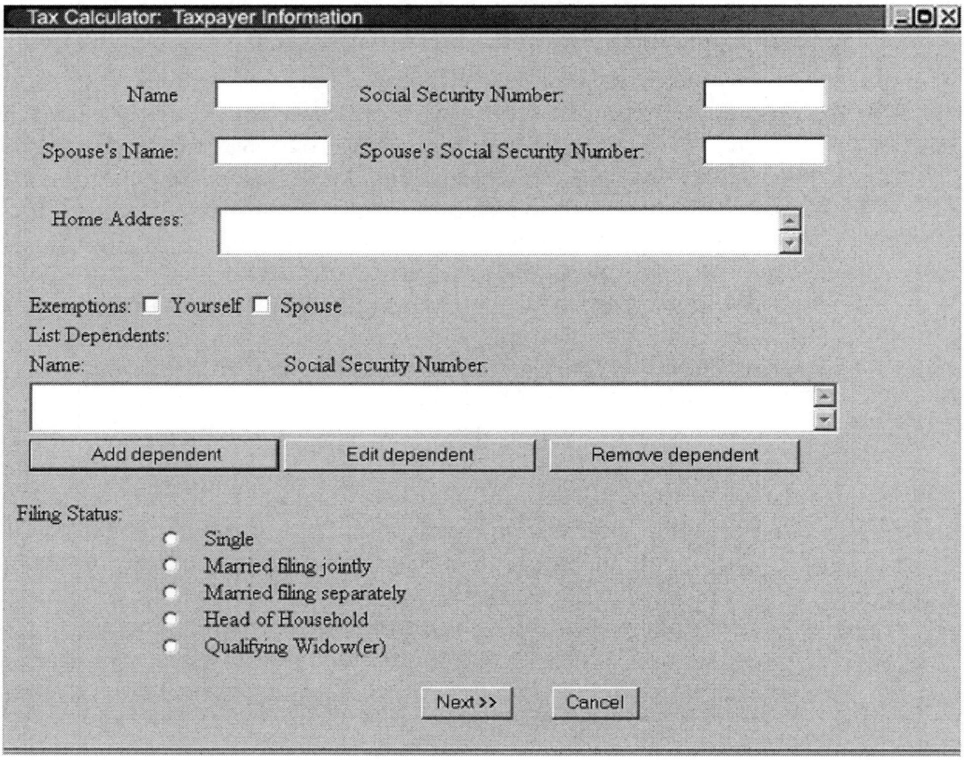

Figure 1.1 Tax calculator – taxpayer information

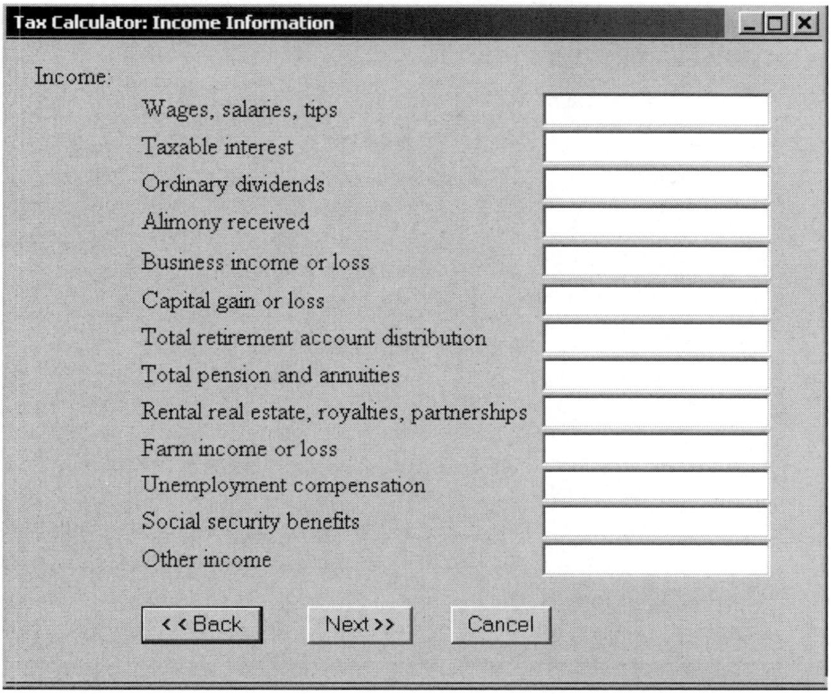

Figure 1.2 Tax calculator – income information

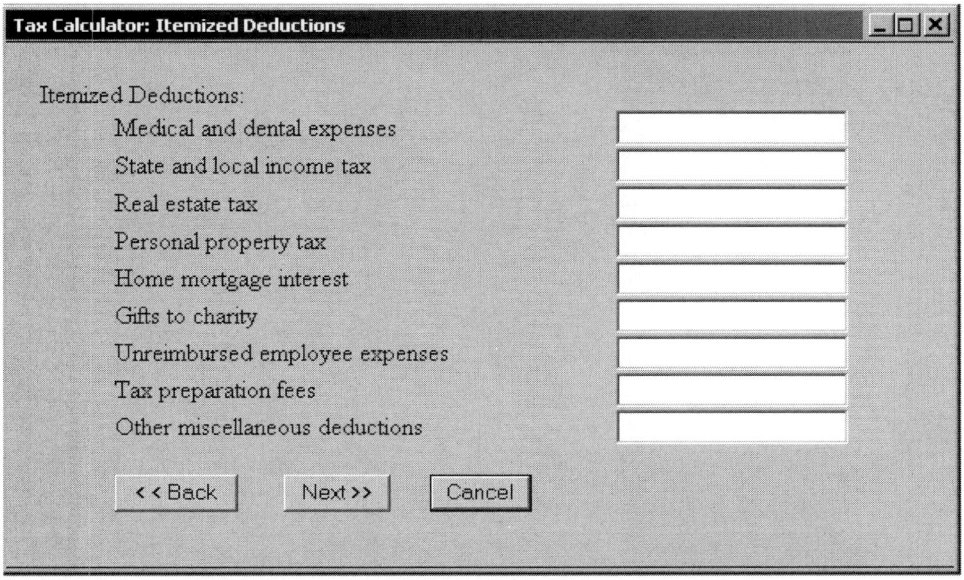

Figure 1.3 Tax calculator – itemized deductions information

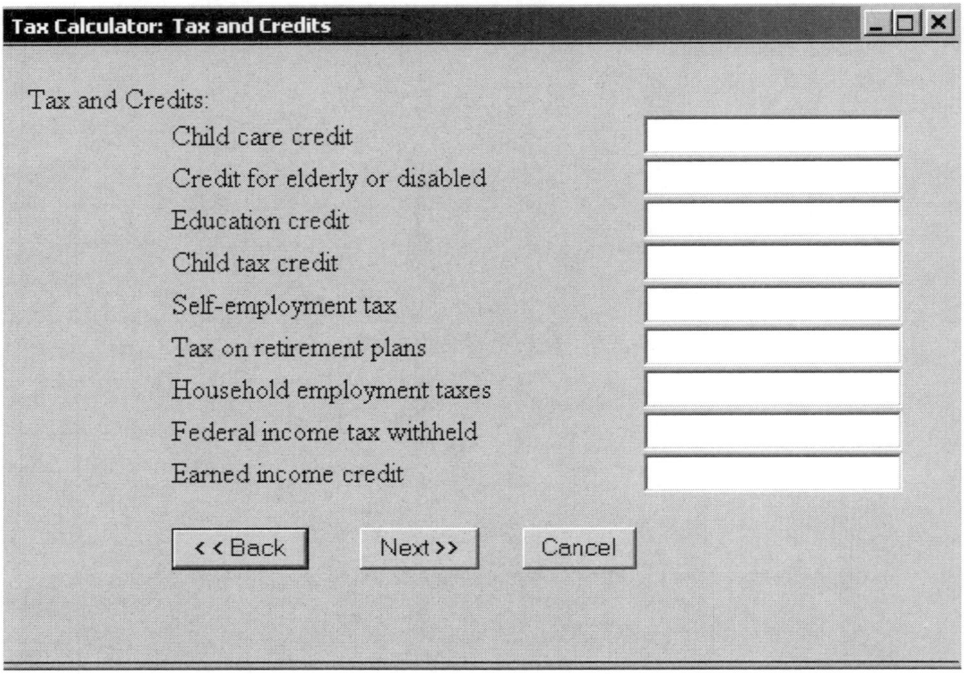

Tax Calculator: Tax and Credits   _ □ X

Tax and Credits:

Child care credit

Credit for elderly or disabled

Education credit

Child tax credit

Self-employment tax

Tax on retirement plans

Household employment taxes

Federal income tax withheld

Earned income credit

< < Back   Next >>   Cancel

Figure 1.4 Tax calculator – tax and credits information

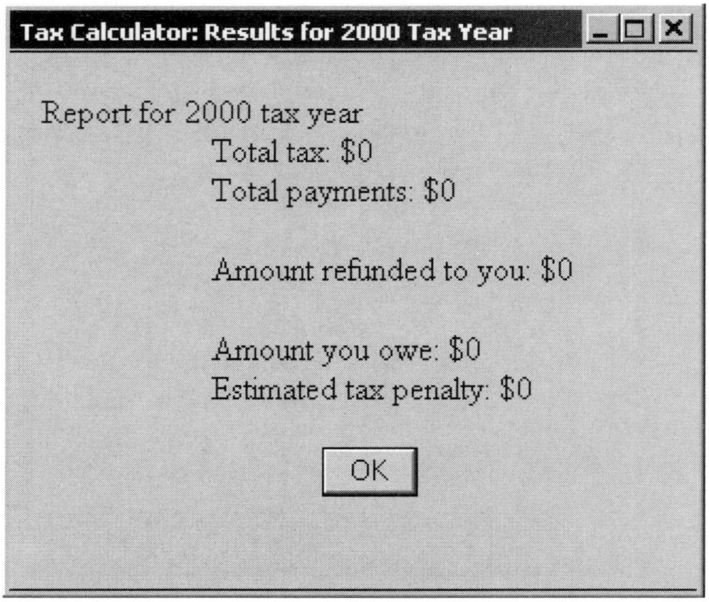

Tax Calculator: Results for 2000 Tax Year   _ □ X

Report for 2000 tax year
        Total tax: $0
        Total payments: $0

        Amount refunded to you: $0

        Amount you owe: $0
        Estimated tax penalty: $0

                OK

Figure 1.5 Tax calculator – calculated output

Our job is to make sure this tax calculator application is suitable for delivery. At this point, we still don't know how to use this application. In terms of documentation, the federal government issues a huge document that describes the tax laws and explains how to calculate tax results, but does not help us understand how to use the software application. When testing other applications or in other situations, we may have very little adequate project documentation, or even no written specification of what the system should do.

We face several challenges:

- a large, complex application;
- limited knowledge, if any, about the application;
- inadequate user documentation;
- minimal knowledge about software testing;
- no guidance or help available regarding software testing;
- an unrealistic deadline.

1.3 The incremental testing approach

To be effective, a software tester should be knowledgeable in two key areas:

1. Software testing techniques.
2. The application-under-test.

For each new testing assignment, a tester must invest time in learning about the application. A tester with no experience must also learn testing techniques, including general testing concepts and how to define test cases. In this chapter, we have the opportunity to do both. Our goal is to define a suitable list of tests to perform within a tight deadline.

To accommodate the very tight deadline, we'll tackle testing of the tax calculator application in eight progressive stages. In the first stages we will determine if the application works under normal conditions by evaluating the output accuracy. In the later stages we attempt to break the system. The rest of this chapter explains the following stages in detail:

Stage 1:   Exploration
Purpose: To gain familiarity with the application.

Stage 2:   Baseline test
Purpose: To devise and execute a simple test case.

Stage 3:   Trends analysis
Purpose: To evaluate whether the application performs as expected when actual output cannot be pre-determined.

Stage 4: Inventory
Purpose: To identify the different categories of data and create a test for each category item.

Stage 5: Inventory combinations
Purpose: To combine different input data.

Stage 6: Push the boundaries
Purpose: To evaluate application behavior at data boundaries.

Stage 7: Devious data
Purpose: To evaluate system response when specifying bad data.

Stage 8: Stress the environment
Purpose: To attempt to break the system.

The schedule is tight, so we may not be able to perform all of the stages. The time permitted by the delivery schedule determines how many stages one person can perform. After executing the baseline test, later stages could be performed in parallel if more testers are available.

Of the ideas presented in this chapter, inventories, pushing boundaries, devious data, and stressing the system readily apply to all testing projects, and these concepts resurface in later chapters.

To illustrate the testing techniques, I'll provide sample test cases for just one input or data field. Defining tests for the other input fields follows in a similar manner. When testing a real application, you may not have sufficient time or other resources to define or execute a complete set of test cases. In such situations, you will have to select which tests are most relevant and which features will not be tested. Applying risk analysis focuses your testing effort on the most important features of the application and helps you to execute the most pertinent tests. Chapter 8 presents risk analysis techniques that you can use even before you create any test cases.

Testers fortunate enough to be assigned to a project that allows sufficient time for proper testing are able to:

- plan the testing tasks;
- design tests by applying the methods described in later chapters;
- build a suitable test execution environment;
- evaluate, acquire, and install automated test tools;
- write suitable test documentation.

Bringing the tester into a project at a very late stage – especially when the deadline is imminent – prevents the application of good testing planning practices and limits the ability to acquire useful testing tools. Under these constraints, the primary focus should be to devise a series of tests to determine if the application functions correctly.

Let's get started with testing the tax calculator application.

1.3.1   Stage 1: Exploration

The tester must become familiar with the application before being able to perform any tests. This exploration can take on many forms:

- following any available tutorial or training materials;
- reading any available end-user or engineering documentation;
- having someone knowledgeable demonstrate the application;
- typing in random data and commands;
- trying out all options;
- taking a curious and skeptical "let's see what this does" attitude.

During the course of exploration, the tester discovers how the application works by observing its behavior. He also acquires a feel for what constitutes good and bad input. When the application displays a result that appears to be different from the tester's expectations, this may flag a potential problem.

Exploring the application and becoming familiar with its features is a necessary step in the learning curve. The tester creates tests on the fly, often influenced by the result of prior tests. This approach, known as Exploratory Testing, is the first step in deciding what to test. Eventually, we want to move into a more formal testing environment where tests are defined in advance. Exploration, although beneficial, does have its pitfalls. First, the results generated by the application may bias the tester's judgment – the tester may believe that the resulting outcome is correct. Second, when the tester encounters an error, a record of prior keystrokes may not exist to identify the application's path or prior state. This can make it difficult to reproduce the error.

For our purposes, the goal of exploration is to learn more about the application by exercising its features. This employs just one aspect of Exploratory Testing. Whenever you create new tests based on your observations while executing current tests, you are using Exploratory Testing. For more information on Exploratory Testing, see [Bach] and [Kaner99].

Another essential task is to identify a person who is knowledgeable about the application and who has the authority to clarify the requirements. We will have many questions throughout this exercise, and we need to find someone who can provide answers. I'll refer to this person as the *project authority*. Any decision or clarification made by the project authority *must* be written down and signed off.

1.3.2   Stage 2: Baseline test

Once the tester is familiar with the application's basic operation, the next step is to create a baseline test case. A baseline test typically is not complicated: it defines the simplest path through the application using default settings or otherwise straightforward input data. With the inputs defined, the tester must then determine the outcome.

The outcome consists of any observable output – or absence of output – that results from a test. Note that some tests are expected to produce no change, which is the correct result if that's what's expected. (See [Beizer90] and [Beizer95] for more discussion on the distinction between output and outcome.) Depending on the application, several sources exist for determining the expected outcome.

1. The project authority or other subject matter expert (perhaps a lead programmer, designer, or project manager) will know how to determine the outcome. In the tax calculator example, an accountant or tax attorney can also assist.

2. The user documentation (if it exists) may contain a sample user scenario.

3. The requirements document (if it exists) may provide the necessary information.

4. Other related documentation may provide clues. In the tax calculator example, a taxpayer instruction guide provides directions for calculating the results by hand.

5. The end user might be available to describe the expected response.

For some applications, the project authority must determine what is the acceptable margin of error. For example, some calculations may vary due to rounding differences. When entering data, the Internal Revenue Service allows the taxpayer to round off currency values to the nearest dollar, rather than carry the cents throughout the calculations before rounding off the final result. In this example, let's assume the project authority declares that the results can differ by ±$1 to account for rounding.

Having defined the baseline test by listing the input and expected outcome, the tester must also prepare to *execute* this test. The tester must create a test environment to run the application with the test data. Creating the test environment involves one or more of the following steps:

● installing the application;

● installing and programming test tools, if needed;

● setting up special files, including populating them with data needed for the test;

● creating utilities that communicate with the application;

● acquiring the appropriate hardware and necessary equipment.

When time is limited and the tester is unable to select, acquire, install, learn, and program a test tool, the tester will have to execute the tests manually.

By executing the test, the tester compares the actual results with the expected results to determine whether the test passed or failed. Executing the baseline test is a significant achievement for several reasons.

1. The tester has explored the application and now knows enough to create an actual test.

2. The tester has had to create a test environment to execute the test.

3. This baseline test becomes the basis for creating future test cases.

4. If the application fails to execute this simple test correctly, then the tester has found a major problem.

An application that fails to execute the baseline test correctly is unfit for use. The developers must correct the problem and create a more reliable application. However, the tester can take advantage of the application to continue to define and execute more tests until a new testable application version becomes available.

In the tax calculator example, the baseline test consists of the simplest type of taxpayer with no complex financial or business transactions. We select these attributes for the baseline test data:

● single person with no dependents;
● one job paying $40,000 a year;
● no other income;
● no deductions.

Based on the above information, this person's expected total tax for the year 2000 is $5,779, ignoring the tax penalty that results from excluding the amount of tax withholding.

We'll use Table 1.1 to track the input data and expected results (or the outcome). Having executed the test, we can record the actual results. Chapter 4 provides many examples of table formats, but for now, let's keep the table simple.

Table 1.1 Baseline test case

Test case ID	Filing status	Wages	Itemized deductions amount	Expected results: tax owed	Actual results
tax-1	single	$40,000	$0	$5,779	

1.3.3   Stage 3: Trends analysis

Trends analysis is an optional stage that is helpful if any of these conditions apply:

● you are barely familiar with the application;
● the input and output data contain numerical values;
● data boundaries are not known;
● calculating the expected results is difficult;
● you have an idea of the range of expected results.

Ideally, we would want to determine the outcome exactly, thus skipping the trends analysis and moving on to Stage 4. Because we know how to calculate expected taxes given different input data, we should skip this stage. However, for the purpose of illustration, let's apply trends analysis to the tax calculator application.

By defining an ordinary taxpayer, the baseline test case becomes the basis for analyzing trends. The trends analysis stage consists of looking for patterns of behavior by modifying the values of one specific numerical variable. We may not know if the actual output data is correct, but we evaluate whether the output values change in the expected direction. For example, if we increase the taxpayer's income gradually, we expect the total tax to increase proportionally. If an output value were to jump considerably when compared to the other values, an issue needs further investigation. This strategy is part of Exploratory Testing, because we do not specify the expected results prior to running the test. However, this approach does provide information about the application's intended behavior.

Table 1.2 tracks the trends information for increasing wages. First we define the input and expected trend and enter that information in the Table. We then enter the data, record the actual output, and evaluate the results. In this example, we decide to increase the wages gradually by $3,000, expecting the resulting tax to increase steadily. Not only does the resulting tax increase, but it jumps by $840 for every $3,000 in increased wages. So far, the tax calculator appears to function correctly. What happens if one output value is out of character as compared to the other values in the series? If test case trend-5 yields a result of $10,500, have we found a problem? We don't know for sure. The project authority will have the answer. Maybe the increased wages places the taxpayer in a higher tax bracket, thus increasing the total tax, or maybe the application generated the wrong value.

Table 1.2 Trends analysis

Test case ID	Filing status	Wages	Itemized deductions amount	Expected results: tax owed	Actual results
tax-1	single	$40,000	$0	$5,779	$5,779
trend-1	single	$43,000	$0		$6,619
trend-2	single	$46,000	$0		$7,459
trend-3	single	$49,000	$0	increasing trend	$8,299
trend-4	single	$52,000	$0		$9,139
trend-5	single	$55,000	$0		$9,979
trend-6	single	$58,000	$0		$10,819
trend-7	single	$61,000	$0		$11,659
trend-8	single	$64,000	$0		$12,499

We can analyze other trends, such as:

● increasing the number of dependents results in a decreased tax;
● increasing other income increases the tax;

- increasing itemized deductions decreases the tax — except that thresholds exist limiting the amount of deductions to apply.

This last case illustrates the tax laws that govern itemized deductions. When the tester observes a big change in a trend, this does not always imply a problem. The project authority will determine if this is the effect of crossing a numerical boundary or if there is a problem in the application.

Although trends analysis does indicate whether the application appears to function properly, it is an inefficient form of testing compared to other test case design techniques. Chapter 4 introduces the techniques of equivalence class partitioning and boundary value analysis, which effectively test ranges of data.

1.3.4   Stage 4: Inventory

The inventory stage consists of identifying the types of data available in the application and then itemizing every state that each data item can have. Testing makes sure that each state is used at least once. Each set of states defines an inventory.

At this point we continue to use the baseline test and modify one value at a time, with the intention of assuring that each item affects the application correctly. Let's look at two inventory examples: *filing status* and *itemized deductions*. We therefore need to know what the expected results will be for every state tested.

The filing status inventory has five possible values, listed below. This is a mutually exclusive category because only one value applies at a time. Each filing status value affects the total tax calculation. Applying the filing status inventory to the baseline test creates the four additional test cases shown in Table 1.3. The varying amounts listed in the Itemized deductions column reflect a specific threshold value associated with the filing status. This threshold is explained later in this section.

Filing status inventory

- single;
- married filing separately;
- married filing jointly;
- head of household;
- qualifying widow(er).

Table 1.3 Test cases applying the filing status inventory

Test case ID	Filing status	Wages	Itemized deductions amount	Expected results: tax owed	Actual results
tax-1	single	$40,000	$4,400	$5,779	
tax-2	married filing separately	$40,000	$3,675	$6,537	
tax-3	married filing jointly	$40,000	$7,350	$4,061	
tax-4	head of household	$40,000	$6,450	$4,616	
tax-5	qualifying widow(er)	$40,000	$7,350	$4,481	

For now, we are concerned with ensuring that each new inventory item affects the results as expected – regardless of whether the state is logical. Three of the filing status conditions would logically require additional information. The filing status "head of household" requires the inclusion of several dependents, and both of the married statuses require information pertaining to a spouse. Still, we can calculate the change in tax. For other applications, a particular inventory item applied by itself might seem an unusual state. However, it is still important to test, because the user is likely to enter that same illogical value. You want to make sure that the application processes the data correctly. This includes any error handling logic and error messages.

Another inventory category is *itemized deductions*. This category is not exclusive because a taxpayer can specify any combination of itemized deduction. Even though we may use multiple itemized deductions, to ensure that each inventory item affects the outcome correctly, we first apply one itemized deduction at a time to the baseline test. Table 1.4 headers have been expanded to track the itemized deductions and show these additional tests.

Itemized deductions inventory:
● medical and dental expenses;
● state and local income tax;
● real estate tax;
● personal property tax;
● home mortgage interest;
● gifts to charity;
● unreimbursed employee expenses;
● tax preparation fees;
● other miscellaneous deductions.

The tax law allows for using either the itemized deduction or the standard deduction – whichever amount is larger. For a single taxpayer, our baseline example, the standard deduction is $4,400. To use the itemized deductions, its total must exceed $4,400. Therefore, this example uses a total of $4,405 for each itemized deduction type. However, not all itemized deduction types are created equal; income-related thresholds limit the amount of some itemized deductions, as listed below.

● Medical and dental expenses must exceed 7.5% of the adjusted gross income. (The adjusted gross income consists of adding up all wages and income, and then subtracting allowable expenses.) In the baseline example with wages of $40,000, the first $3,000 of medical expenses is not deductible. Consequently, only $1,405 is deductible.

● Unreimbursed employee expenses and tax preparation fees are subject to a 2% limit on adjusted gross income. In the baseline example with wages of $40,000, the first $800 of these expenses is not deductible, allowing $3,605 to be deductible.

When the full itemized deduction applies, the expected total tax is $5,765, whereas a deduction subject to a threshold (which in this example does not exceed the limit) results in a tax of $5,779. Table 1.4 shows the itemized deduction types and amounts used, and the additional column indicates whether a limit affects the total.

Table 1.4 Test cases applying the itemized deductions inventory

Test case ID	Filing status	Wages	Itemized deductions type	Itemized deductions amount	Expected results: tax owed	Actual results	*Note*: itemized deduction limit (Tax law)
tax-6	single	$40,000	Medical and dental expenses	$4,405	$5,779		limited to 7.5% of adjusted gross income; $1,405 is deductible
tax-7	single	$40,000	State and local income tax	$4,405	$5,765		applies in full
tax-8	single	$40,000	Real estate tax	$4,405	$5,765		applies in full
tax-9	single	$40,000	Personal property tax	$4,405	$5,765		applies in full
tax-10	single	$40,000	Home mortgage interest	$4,405	$5,765		applies in full
tax-11	single	$40,000	Gifts to charity	$4,405	$5,765		applies in full
tax-12	single	$40,000	Unreimbursed employee expenses	$4,405	$5,779		limited to 2% of adjusted gross income; $3,605 is deductible
tax-13	single	$40,000	Tax preparation fees	$4,405	$5,779		limited to 2% of adjusted gross income; $3,605 is deductible
tax-14	single	$40,000	Other miscellaneous deductions	$4,405	$5,765		applies in full

Inventories provide a checklist of items to test. The tax calculator example contains many more inventory lists that also require testing such as business expenses and other income sources. Isolating the effect of each individual inventory item determines if the application processes each inventory item correctly.

By now, we have defined many tests, by specifying input values and the expected results. Having executed each test, we observe and record the actual results. If the actual results differ from the expected results, then the test has failed and we have an issue. An issue? Is this not a problem? What we really have is a suspicion that something is not right. Several situations could cause a test to fail:

1. The expected results description is wrong. This can happen if the requirements are unclear or misinterpreted, or if the expected results are miscalculated. (A test case review might have found this type of error. See Chapter 9 for a description of reviews.)

2. An error occurred during test execution. Maybe the tester typed the wrong input or the test software is faulty. Test software is not infallible and can have its own bugs.

3. The application does indeed have a bug.

So what do you do? The first step is to make sure that the tester did not cause the problem by typing in the wrong value. The tester must then make sure that the problem does not lie with the test software. Debugging the application is not the tester's job. Make a list of issues and let the project authority decide. The reply may be one of the following:

● a problem exists with the requirements: the requirement may be missing, ambiguous, not well understood, or not communicated to the tester;

● the test is incorrect because it specifies the wrong expected results;

● the problem exists with test execution, such as a problem with the test tool or a typing error;

● there really is a bug in the software;

● the project authority cannot reproduce the problem. If so, suspect a configuration problem in which the tester's environment differs from that of the person trying to reproduce the problem. It is possible that the person trying to reproduce the problem was not provided with detailed or correct instructions, or with the same test data. It is also possible that they did not follow instructions carefully.

Once the developer has fixed a problem and generated a new version of the application, the tester must re-execute tests originally run on prior versions, to ensure that all features in the new application still function as expected. When time is short or other resources are limited, the tester must determine which tests to re-use. Chapter 8 provides several methods for assessing risk and identifying the most important test cases.

In the tax calculator example, keeping track of the application version affects which tests to use, because the expected results will vary from year to year due to changes in the tax laws.

1.3.5   Stage 5: Inventory combinations

The next step in testing is to combine inventory items to determine whether the accumulated effects work as expected. For some applications, it may be beneficial to use an incremental approach that first combines two inventory items at a time, then three, then four, and so on. Another incremental approach is to use the table of test cases where each successive test case has a modification of the prior test.

Thus, the last test listed in the table contains all of the accumulated conditions of the prior tests.

Not all inventories contain simple data values or states. Consider a different application that processes files and handles event-driven interrupts, and where throughput is an issue. An incremental approach would consist of these types of tests:

- process each file individually;
- process one file and generate one interrupt;
- process two files at a time;
- process two files and generate one interrupt;
- process two files and generate two interrupts;
- and so on...

Identifying all combinations tends to create a large number of test cases – more than we could possibly execute in a reasonable amount of time. The key is to use risk analysis to identify the application's most important features, and then determine which combination scheme best addresses the high-priority concerns.

The tax calculator example is data driven and we've already tested each inventory item in isolation, so using an incremental approach for combining inventory values doesn't seem as crucial. We'll use the inventories as checklists and select typical settings used by the majority of taxpayers. At this point, we focus on normal system usage to show that the application works well under typical conditions. We'll look at unusual data combinations later.

Table 1.5 contains tests that use multiple inventories. Column headers marked with an asterisk (*) represent those itemized deductions that are subject to a wage-related limit, and thus may not necessarily be included in the total deductions column. We alter the table format to better track all the different combinations.

1.3.6   Stage 6: Push the boundaries

The tests executed up to this point exercise typical scenarios that reflect general usage. The next step is to push the limits of the application. The application limits – or boundaries – are defined by the data. These limits take on many forms depending on the type of data. Examples include:

- minimum and maximum values of a data range;
- minimum and maximum field size, such as the number of characters;
- minimum and maximum buffer size.

The general rule for testing boundaries is to create three test cases to cover the following conditions:

- boundary value;
- boundary value – 1;
- boundary value + 1.

Table 1.5 Test cases with inventory combinations

| Test case ID | Inputs | | | | | Itemized | |
	Filing status	Wages	Dependents	Medical & dental*	State & local tax	Real estate tax	Personal property tax
tax-15	single	$40,000	0	$0	$2,200	$1,890	$80
tax-16	married filing separately	$60,000	0	$0	$2,200	$1,890	$80

The tax calculator application offers several boundaries to exercise, such as:

● every tax bracket is a defined range, with a minimum and maximum value;

● how to calculate the tax depends on whether the taxable income is above or below $100,000;

● some itemized deductions are limited to 2 percent of adjusted gross income;

● itemized deductions must exceed the standard deduction in order to be used;

● legally, there is no upper limit to how much money one can earn or how many dependents one can have. The minimum, of course, is zero.

For most applications data types have clearly defined upper and lower bounds. It would be obvious to list the boundaries of each tax bracket and then produce tests using these minima and maxima. However, that is not how the US tax code works. With the help of the project authority, let's identify the boundaries that affect the tax calculation for a single taxpayer. The instructions provided by the Internal Revenue Service contain many tables for calculating the tax. Table 1.6 shows the tax rate schedule to use when the taxable income of a single taxpayer is $100,000 or more. The instruction's fine print states that a taxpayer with a taxable income less than $100,000 cannot use this table, but that it is provided so that taxpayers

Table 1.6 Tax rate schedule for a taxpayer filing as single

Schedule X – Use if your filing status is **Single**
Use **only** if your taxable income (Form 1040, line 39) is $100,000 or more.

If the amount on Form 1040, line 39, is: *Over –*	*But not over –*	Enter on Form 1040, line 40		*of the amount over –*
$0	$26,250	- - - - - - 15%		$0
26,250	63,550	$3,937.50	+ 28%	26,250
63,550	132,600	14,381.50	+ 31%	63,550
132,600	288,350	35,787.00	+ 36%	132,600
288,350	- - - - - -	91,857.00	+ 39.6%	288,350

Source: 1040 Instructions, for the 2000 tax year, Internal Revenue Service, US Department of the Treasury.

deductions						Output	
Mortgage interest	Contributions to charities	Unreimbursed employee expenses*	Tax preparation fees	Other misc.	Total deductions	Expected results: tax owed	Actual results
$2,800	$500	$100	$50	$0	$7,470	$4,911	
$2,800	$500	$100	$50	$0	$7,470	$11,073	

can see the tax rate that applies to each level. This tax rate schedule identifies four data ranges:

taxable income < $100,00	use another means to calculate the tax
$100,000 ≤ taxable income < $132,600	taxpayer is in 31% tax bracket
$132,600 ≤ taxable income < $288,350	taxpayer is in 36% tax bracket
$288,350 ≤ taxable income	taxpayer is in 39.61% tax bracket

The data ranges are based on taxable income. Taxable income roughly consists of adding up all types of income and then subtracting all allowable adjustments and deductions. There are many ways of reaching the target taxable income. To keep it simple, let's continue to alter the baseline test case. For a single taxpayer with no dependents or deductions, taxable income consists of subtracting a standard deduction of $4,400 and one exemption of $2,800 from the wages. This holds true provided that the adjusted gross income is less than $96,700 otherwise, this limits the amount of the exemption that can be subtracted. The key issue here is to determine the financial information input that yields the desired taxable income.

With these data ranges identified, the next step is to define test cases that test the boundaries. Because each boundary is closed, meaning that the two consecutive values reside on opposite sides of the boundary, we need only use two test cases for each boundary. (This is an example of *equivalence class partitioning* which is described in Chapter 4.) Consequently, the tests listed in Table 1.7 consist of using the boundary point and the value on the other side of the boundary. Due to rounding, some of the expected results appear identical. These results would differ if calculations are carried out to the penny. The two added columns are for information purposes only. Since taxable income is what defines the boundaries (and the tax bracket) currently under test, let's include this information along with the test case data.

When the taxable income is less than $100,000, a look-up table is used to determine the tax. Table 1.8 shows the look-up table for taxable income in the range $26,000 to $27,000. The Internal Revenue Service provides such tables for every value from $0 to just less than $100,000. Partitioning the look-up table into $50 increments, each of which defines a range with a high and low value, yields 2,000 entries. Since the look-up table is based on $50 increments, which value do we

Table 1.7 Test cases using the tax rate schedule

Test case ID	Filing status	Wages	Dependents	Deductions	Expected results: tax owed	Actual results	*Note:* Taxable income amount	*Note:* Tax calculation method
tax-17	single	$107,200	0	$0	$25,681		$100,000	31% tax bracket
tax-18	single	$139,519	0	$0	$35,787		$132,599	31% tax bracket
tax-19	single	$139,520	0	$0	$35,787		$132,600	36% tax bracket
tax-20	single	$292,749	0	$0	$91,857		$288,349	36% tax bracket
tax-21	single	$292,750	0	$0	$91,857		$288,350	39.6% tax bracket

use to test? The only absolute guarantee that every value in the table is correct is to actually create a test for every range. Given the time constraints, that approach is impractical.

Table 1.8 Tax table for taxable income between $26,000 and $27,000

If line 39 (taxable income) is –		And you are –			
At least	But less than	Single	Married filing jointly*	Married filing separately	Head of a household
				Your tax is –	
26,000	26,050	3,904	3,904	4,437	3,904
26,050	26,100	3,911	3,911	4,451	3,911
26,100	26,150	3,919	3,919	4,465	3,919
26,150	26,200	3,926	3,926	4,479	3,926
26,200	26,250	3,934	3,934	4,493	3,934
26,250	26,300	3,945	3,941	4,507	3,941
26,300	26,350	3,959	3,949	4,521	3,949
26,350	26,400	3,973	3,956	4,535	3,956
26,400	26,450	3,987	3,964	4,549	3,964
26,450	26,500	4,001	3,971	4,563	3,971
26,500	26,550	4,015	3,979	4,577	3,979
26,550	26,600	4,029	3,986	4,591	3,986
26,600	26,650	4,043	3,994	4,605	3,994
26,650	26,700	4,057	4,001	4,619	4,001
26,700	26,750	4,071	4,009	4,633	4,009
26,750	26,800	4,085	4,016	4,647	4,016
26,800	26,850	4,099	4,024	4,661	4,024
26,850	26,900	4,113	4,031	4,675	4,031
26,900	26,950	4,127	4,039	4,689	4,039
26,950	27,000	4,141	4,046	4,703	4,046

* This column must also be used by a qualifying widow(er).

Source: 1040 Instructions, for the 2000 tax year, Internal Revenue Service, US Department of the Treasury.

Testing a table look-up involves two parts:

● making sure the index accesses the correct part of the table;

● making sure that the values in the table are themselves correct.

It seems logical that the application uses the taxable income value as the index into the table. Ask the developers whether assuring that the application accesses the correct table location for one index implies that the look-up portion works correctly for all indices. If so, let's scrutinize the first range in Table 1.8. This gives us two more tests, as shown in Table 1.9.

Table 1.9 Test cases for the tax table look-up

Test case ID	Filing status	Wages	Dependents	Deductions	Expected results: tax owed	Actual results	*Note:* Taxable income amount
tax-22	single	$33,249	0	0	$3,904		$26,049
tax-23	single	$33,250	0	0	$3,911		$26,050

Executing test cases tax-22 and tax-23 demonstrates that the application look-up works – at least for the two specified values. We can assume – but not guarantee – that the other range boundaries work. This just addresses the indexing into the table. What about the integrity of the data in the table? The only real way to verify the data is to create a test to look up every item. Again, time constraints make this impossible. Assuming that the table values are stored in some type of file, the most effective way to verify the table values is to inspect them. Yes, get a copy of the tables and compare them to the tables provided by the Internal Revenue Service. There is no correct answer as to how to approach this. Whatever you decide, make sure that the project authority agrees with your approach.

The taxable income boundary of $100,000 determines whether we use the tax rate schedule or the tax table to compute the tax. We want tests that specify taxable incomes of $99,999 and $100,000, as in Table 1.10.

Table 1.10 Testing the $100,000 taxable income boundary

Test case ID	Filing status	Wages	Dependents	Deductions	Expected results: tax owed	Actual results	*Note:* Taxable income amount	*Note:* Tax calculation method
tax-24	single	$107,199	0	$0	$25,673		$99,999	Tax table look-up
tax-25	single	$107,200	0	$0	$25,681		$100,000	31% tax bracket

If, in test case tax-24, the application mistakenly uses the 31% tax bracket calculation to determine the tax, rather than using the tax table, it returns the wrong tax value of $25,681. This gives us feedback as to whether the application uses the proper method to calculate the tax.

Of course, we also need to test the zero value for different fields, as shown in Table 1.11. We expect the tax calculator application to trap negative numbers and post an error message. Test case tax-30 specifies a wage of $7200 which yields a taxable income value of $0 and hence a final value of $0 in taxes.

Table 1.11 Test exercising the zero boundary

Test case ID	Filing status	Wages	Dependents	Itemized deductions amount	Expected results: tax owed	Actual results
tax-26	single	$0	0	$0	$0	
tax-27	single	$–1	0	$0	Error	
tax-28	single	$0	0	$–1	Error	
tax-29	single	$0	–1	$0	Error	
tax-30	single	$7,200	0	$0	$0	

During the course of defining tests, we made some assumptions about which boundary values to test and which to omit from testing. Applying risk analysis confirms whether the most appropriate tests have been selected.

So far, we have only looked at the data affecting a taxpayer filing as a single. The same scrutiny applies when using the other filing statuses, because the tax rate schedule specifies different boundary values for the other filing statuses, and the tax tables return different values based on filing status. We will also need to define tests that address other types of data boundaries, such as those pertaining to itemized deductions.

1.3.7   Stage 7: Devious data

The next testing stage attempts to break the application by executing conditions that a normal user would probably not perform. Consider creating tests in the following categories:

● not entering data, to see if the application provides defaults or generates an error message;

● entering invalid numerical data, such as negative values and alphanumeric strings;

● entering whatever format is considered illegal for that data type;

● trying unusual data combinations;

● making sure to use the value zero, if not already executed in previous tests.

If possible, get current users to try the new system. See what values they enter and how they interpret the system prompts.

When specifying unusual combinations, the intent is to verify that the application behaves appropriately, even if the test data do not describe a normal taxpayer. Some unusual situations for the tax calculator examples might include:

- very low wages plus a high number of dependents;
- very high wages with no deductions;
- deductions that exceed the amount of total income.

When creating devious test cases, the expected result may often be an error message. We expect the application to trap this data and inform the user of the error. The test passes under these circumstances, because the system returned an error message as expected.

Some testers may bypass the previous stages and focus entirely on breaking the system and finding the really nasty bugs. Although this approach has some merits, the best tactic is to perform risk analysis to determine where to apply your testing effort at the expense of which system features not to test. When several people are assigned to testing the product, one person can devote his time exclusively on finding vicious bugs. Focusing only on finding serious defects poses several drawbacks as many problems do not result in crashes. The tester must know the application well enough to determine whether the resulting output is correct. Attempts to crash a system often consist of typing commands on the fly. It may be difficult to reproduce a problem if input information leading up to the problem is not documented.

Section 2.3.2 in Chapter 2 provides a checklist of valid and invalid data to help you identify devious data.

1.3.8 Stage 8: Stress the environment

The next stage steps away from the application features and evaluates the execution environment in terms of performance and recovery.

Assessing performance typically involves measuring the time it takes to execute specific operations. Performance times vary if the application runs on a dedicated or fully loaded system. Another aspect that affects performance requires stressing the environment in which the application runs. This includes such tests as:

- reducing available memory;
- using all available disk space;
- running multiple instances of the application in parallel;
- running the application while the system is performing a backup;
- generating many asynchronous event-driven processes.

Sometimes the application must recover from adverse situations. Even if the tester reboots the system, once restarted, everything must function correctly. Tests that damage the environment include:

- aborting the application;
- disconnecting cables;
- shutting off power.

Evidence that the application has sustained severe damage includes:

- inaccessible files;
- files locked open;
- corrupted databases;
- inability to restart the application.

The descriptions of test categories in section 2.3.2 identify other methods of stressing the environment.

1.4 Next steps

The sample test cases presented only exercise some of the data values in the tax application. Naturally, additional tests are needed to verify functionality of the other data fields not discussed in this chapter.

Due to a tight delivery schedule, most of the tests in this chapter focus on demonstrating that the application performs as intended. Although the inventories give rise to many test cases, other tests are required to fully exercise the application. Applying the outline methods (see Chapters 2 and 3) and the table approaches (see Chapters 4 and 5) will help identify additional tests.

Graph theory-based approaches generate test cases that identify all the paths through the application. These methods include:

- control-flow testing;
- data-flow testing;
- transaction-flow testing.

[Beizer95] explains these methods and illustrates them in great detail. Unlike the preliminary tests used in this chapter, graph theory approaches result in a thorough analysis of the software.

An entirely different category of tests makes sure the application does *not* do what it's *not* supposed to do. In prior stages, we created some tests that try to break the system, such as entering out-of-bounds data. We still need tests that look for undesirable side effects such as altered memory, corrupted buffers, or other unintended outcomes. Later chapters in this book present ideas for creating these types of tests.

The strategy presented in this chapter is one effective way of tackling the problem of testing a poorly documented application under tight deadline. For other ideas on how to "test in the dark", refer to [Rothman99].

Successful testing – as well as software quality – depends upon many other software engineering disciplines including:

- *Configuration management* to keep track of which version of the application is currently being tested;
- *Problem reporting* to manage the list of issues and problems found by the tester;

● *Change control* to keep track of which problems to correct in this release and to keep a list of those problems that will not be fixed in the immediate future.

Chapter 9 discusses why these topics are relevant to software testing.

1.5   Summary

Even when product delivery is imminent, a tester can evaluate critical parts of the application and verify that key features function correctly. Naturally, the tester can provide better feedback given more time in which to test. The key steps in testing an application under tight deadlines are as follows:

Stage 1:   Explore the application to gain familiarity. Find out who the project authority is.

Stage 2:   Define the baseline test case. Create a test environment to execute the baseline test case.

Stage 3:   Analyze trends if it is difficult to determine expected results.

Stage 4:   Identify inventories. Generate tests cases from the inventory lists.

Stage 5:   Combine data from multiple inventories.

Stage 6:   Push the boundaries of the application.

Stage 7:   Create devious tests to attempt to break the system.

Stage 8:   Stress system resources. Assess how the system recovers from fatal crashes.

Each stage builds on the previous level. The main tactic is to identify the most typical user scenario and use this data as the basis for creating additional tests. By altering one parameter at a time, the tester can ascertain that each change affects the application as expected.

Sometimes, the tester must select which test cases to define and execute, because there is insufficient time to test all features. Risk analysis (see Chapter 8) identifies the most important areas to test – even prior to creating any test cases.

The ideas presented here assist the tester in getting started. More work is required to fully test the system. Subsequent chapters describe methods for planning and creating additional test cases.

2. Test Outlines

2.1 Introduction

The testing part of a project can be overwhelming for many testers. Sometimes the project seems huge, or there is a lot of seemingly unrelated information available. No matter what information is provided, many testers have a steep learning curve to assimilate the necessary information and determine the other information needed to develop test cases.

In this chapter, we'll examine a typical product description, along with its less-than-perfect requirements. Even if your organization works like this, it's possible to proceed with test case developments and identify problems early.

Rather than blame faulty requirements, the testers will provide valuable feedback to the development team and help to improve the product definition. While we examine the requirements, the project authority will provide additional information such as user documentation and answers to our questions. I present this example in a chronological order to illustrate that not all application information need necessarily be available at the onset. You might be fortunate enough to work in parallel with the developers, where test cases and the software are produced concurrently. The key point is that more detailed information about the application becomes available over time, as the tester uses an iterative approach to understand the requirements.

The tester's job will be to:

- learn about the new application;
- list test case possibilities;
- define test cases;
- select which tests to execute;
- create the test environment;
- execute tests.

The example in this chapter uses the outline approach to work through the first two steps. We'll define the test cases in Chapter 3 and then select the best test cases in Chapter 8. Chapter 9 discusses the subsequent steps in the testing cycle.

2.2   Sample application

The sample application consists of an oven controller whose function is summarized in Figure 2.1. Figure 2.2 contains a context diagram, which shows the input and output data for the oven controller. The tester's task is to first analyze the requirements and eventually define a suite of tests.

Application summary

Design a controller for an electric oven that will allow a user to optionally specify cooking temperature, start time and stop time. The oven will heat and turn off according to user input.

Figure 2.1 Application statement

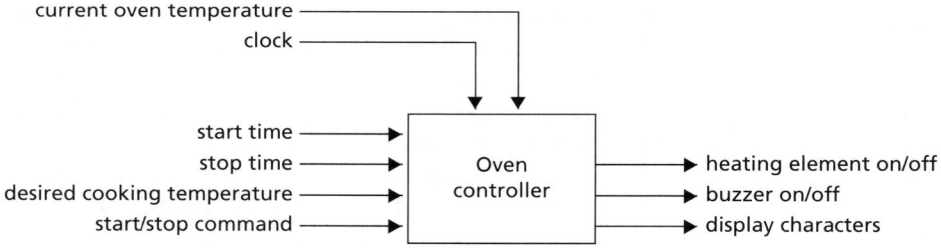

Figure 2.2 Context diagram of oven controller

In addition to the above product information, we are handed a set of so-called requirements. I use the term *requirements* loosely, because the contents do not describe true system requirements. Some projects describe their applications using poor language rather than explicit details.

Despite the fact that these are deficient requirements, there is enough information to proceed with test development. By outlining and defining tests, we will easily pinpoint problems with the given requirements. Ideally, someone would perform requirements analysis to ensure that the requirements are complete, followed by a thorough inspection process to identify any remaining deficiencies. However, not every organization performs these quality-enhancing steps. Despite this serious oversight, we can still identify problems early in the cycle, assuming we have the luxury of starting our work before the developers start designing and coding.

The oven controller will operate at 30 MHz (or more) and control temperatures in the range from 200° F and 500° F, defaulting to 350° and the temperature will be in multiples of 5, as specified by the user on a keypad. The oven temperature and messages can be seen on an alphanumeric display. Operation is automatic or manual and the temperature is kept within 2° of user input. At the end of baking, the oven turns off the heating element and sounds a buzzer for automatic mode. The oven program starts when the user issues a start command, and it will handle broil and microwave cooking in a future release. In automatic mode, the user specifies start time and stop time. Heating starts when the start time is reached and ends when time has elapsed or the user hits the stop command, the latter applying to both automatic and manual modes. The clock can display current time and be able to track elapsed time. Manual mode starts when the user enters the start command and ends with the stop command.

Figure 2.3 The submitted requirements

2.2.1 Extracting the requirements

Those versed in proper requirements may want, at this point, to correct the flaws and improve the information to create good requirements. I will resist this urge in order to illustrate that the test methods will help to find problems. Some testers may not have the luxury of improving the requirements for a variety of reasons, such as the project authority not being knowledgeable about writing requirements, scheduling pressures, and lack of communication between the project authority and testers. However, the prevailing reason is that, for most projects, it's simply too late. While I do not advocate skipping the requirements analysis and inspection steps, some testers may have no choice but to proceed with testing tasks. Some inherent dangers from skipping the requirements improvement step can include:

● building the wrong application;

● not satisfying customer needs;

● difficulty in integrating and merging applications;

● project cancellation.

To learn more about requirements, refer to [Gause89], [Hamlet01], [IEEE 830], [Robertson99], and [Wiegers99].

We start by transforming the overloaded, confusing paragraph into a list of separate sentences or fragments, as shown in Figure 2.4. Because of the ambiguities contained in the application description, we take some liberties in trying to work though the confusion. Naturally, the project authority must tell us whether our interpretation of the requirements is correct. Assigning a number to each item in the list will help us refer to it as we proceed. This facilitates requirements trace-ability, where we can track how each item in the list is used and then identify which test case evolved from that item.

R-1	Oven shall control temperatures between 200° F and 500° F, in multiples of 5.
R-2	Oven controller shall maintain target temperature within ±2° F.
R-3	Oven shall function in manual or in automatic mode.
R-4	The user shall specify a cooking temperature.
R-5	Cooking temperature shall default to 350° F.
R-6	For automatic mode, the user shall specify start time and stop time.
R-7	Automatic mode shall start when user issues the start command.
R-8	Heating in manual mode shall start when user enters the start command.
R-9	Heating in automatic mode shall start at the indicated start time.
R-10	Manual mode shall end when user invokes the stop command.
R-11	Automatic mode shall end when time has elapsed or the user invokes the stop command.
R-12	When done heating, the oven shall shut off the heating element.
R-13	When shutting off automatically, the oven shall sound a buzzer.
R-14	The oven controller shall be able to handle broil and microwave cooking in a future release.
R-15	Processor shall have a processing speed of at least 30 MHz.
R-16	The user interface shall have an alphanumeric display.
R-17	User input interface shall consist of a keypad.
R-18	Oven temperature and messages are posted to an alphanumeric display.
R-19	A clock shall provide current time and shall be able to count elapsed time.

Figure 2.4 Itemizing the application's description

The next step is to partition the requirements into three types: input conditions, expected results, and design constraints. The input information is used to develop the test outline, the output information will be used later when defining test cases, and design constraints are not included in the tests.

Expected results

This is a general term to describe the system's ensuing behavior, including internal state or memory changes not readily observed by a user, in addition to generating a particular value or set of resulting data. When executing tests, it is often necessary to evaluate other transformations in addition to output data values. Five of the requirements listed in Figure 2.4 describe outcomes, and thus we exclude the following statements from the list of input conditions.

Descriptions of expected results

[R-2]   Oven controller shall maintain target temperature within ±2° F.

[R-9]   Heating in automatic mode shall start at the indicated start time.

[R-12]   When done heating, the oven shall shut off the heating element.

[R-13]   When shutting off automatically, the oven shall sound a buzzer.

[R-18]   Oven temperature and messages posted to alphanumeric display.

Design constraints

Although these are sometimes disguised as requirements, they are not the tester's responsibility. Design constraints impose on the system design rather than on the intended system's behavior. Often requirements may call for some future capability or the ability to interface with some feature not yet implemented. The purpose of such a directive is to allow the engineers to adapt their designs accordingly. Design reviews are the proper time to determine how well the proposed system structure would accommodate these future modifications. Otherwise, the resulting product architecture may be inappropriate. Other requirements may list that specific hardware components be included or that the system run on a predetermined operating system. Any issue identified during a design review or inspection is more easily corrected at this earlier stage of the development cycle. If delayed until system testing, the tester would simply confirm that the system failed to meet one of the requirements.

In some instances, having the tester actually modify the product to confirm ease of adding components may be an appropriate test strategy. This is especially true when the end user will modify the product, an example of which includes software applications that allow the end user to add custom modules. In such situations, the tester may need to verify that the instructions for adding user-defined modules are correct. In our example, testing for expandability is not appropriate because the end user will not modify the oven controller to add a broil or microwave feature.

Five of the items listed in Figure 2.4 are design constraints and are best verified during a system design review. Otherwise, the wrong component may be built into the product. Thus, we omit the following design constraints from the list of input conditions.

Descriptions of design constraints

[R-14]   The oven controller shall be able to handle broil and microwave cooking in a future release.

[R-15]   Processor shall have a processing speed of at least 30 MHz.

[R-16]   The user interface shall have an alphanumeric display.

[R-17]   User input interface shall consist of a keypad.

[R-19]   A clock shall provide current time and shall be able to count elapsed time.

By now, we have categorized requirements into input conditions, expected results, and design constraints. Our attention turns to the list of input conditions, because this is the basis for developing the test outline.

2.3   The outline approach

An outline is a method used for looking at the requirements. We convert the requirements into an outline in order to list the various test conditions. The test outline method is process driven, not content dependent. This activity will help identify information missing from the requirements. Each item in the outline will eventually define the input conditions for a test case.

An outline, as shown in Figure 2.5, represents a tree structure, in which a unique path exists between the root and each leaf. Each path in the outline defines a specific set of input conditions, which we then use to define a test case. The outline contains nodes, or branch points, that can designate a prompt, type of value, or input option. The indented portion just below a node denotes a specific input condition of its corresponding parent. The number of leaves in the tree, or paths in the outline, gives an approximate number of test cases needed to test all the features. Depending on how the outline is structured, it is possible to have a one-to-one correspondence between each path in the outline and its associated test case.

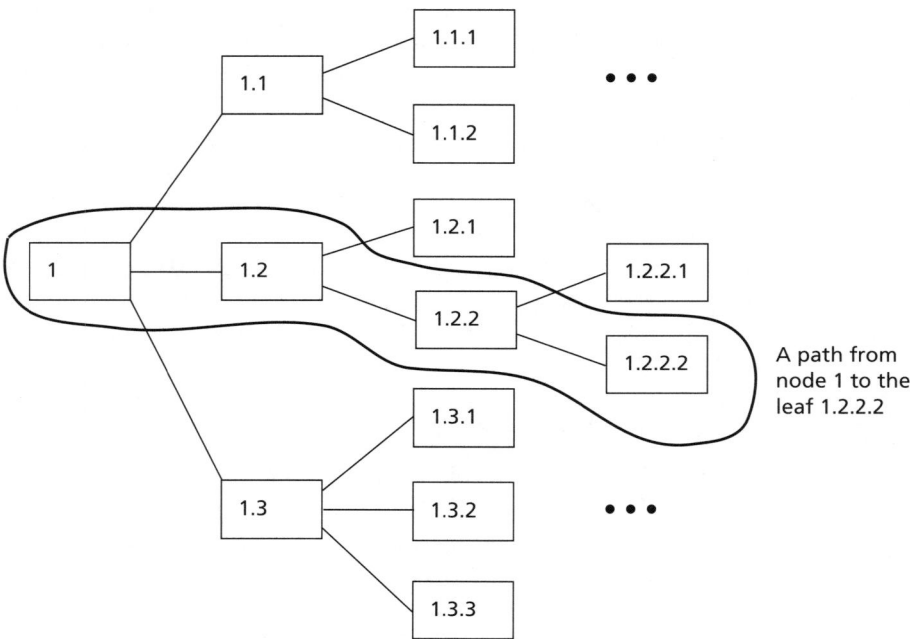

Figure 2.5 A path in an outline

Producing an outline is an iterative process. The initial list is generated from the requirements that have been categorized as input conditions. The requirement number is included to facilitate traceability. Each subsequent outline is a refinement of the previous one. The number of iterations necessary to produce the final version varies among different testers and different projects. Each person proceeds at his own pace. The last iteration is shared with the rest of the development team, because it is from this final version that test cases are derived.

The progression of outline versions is what a tester would develop during one or more editing sessions, each of which could take from two minutes to several days. The intent of the example is to illustrate mental processes. Each iteration of the outline presented in the following example represents an "editing pass" and expansion of the prior pass. The accompanying explanation may seem excessive when describing a thought process that could take less than a minute to execute. No review or inspection is implied between each outline iteration. Perhaps a review would be scheduled upon completion of the final iteration shown in the example. A tester may have to consult the project authority during an intermediate iteration of the outline to get answers about the product's behavior.

The outline approach may seem intuitive to some testers and tedious to others. Its merit is that it is a discussion tool to help extract information from the development team. It is a tool for organizing one's thoughts. An outline highlights the core parts of the requirements documentation by filtering out excess verbiage.

Each item in the outline is grouped in a logical manner, based on the tester's preference. The order or group in which items are specified is not that relevant: the resulting collection of leaves is the important information, because these leaves eventually define test cases. The order in which test cases are defined is not significant provided that all relevant tests are identified.

2.3.1 Test outline development

To create the test outline, we use the indented list of a commercial word processor. The first step, shown in Figure 2.6, is to list all the input descriptions from the list of requirements as separate items and in some logical grouping. The initial groups, in this example, are oven temperature, manual mode, and automatic mode.

To create outline iteration 2, we move the oven temperature items (1.1 through 1.3 in Figure 2.7) to further describe the cooking temperatures for manual and automatic modes. Why do this? The user operates the oven in one of two modes: automatic or manual. The temperature may behave differently depending on which mode is used, thus the outline must have separate paths to differentiate the cooking temperature in manual mode from the cooking temperature in automatic mode. Figure 2.8 shows the modified outline, with the affected items highlighted.

Outline iteration 2 still contains the information from the original requirements. The benefit of an outline approach is to provide a hierarchical structure that groups similar features together. Naturally, different testers will create very different outlines, yet the end criterion is to agree that the outline structure

```
1   Oven temperature
    1.1     [R-1]    Boundaries 200–500° F
    1.2     [R-1]    Multiples of 5° F
    1.3     [R-5]    Default to 350° F

2   [R-3]   Manual mode
    2.1     [R-4]    Cooking temperature
    2.2     [R-8]    Start command
    2.3     [R-10]   Stop command

3   [R-3]   Automatic mode
    3.1     [R-4]    Cooking temperature
    3.2     [R-6]    Start time
    3.3     [R-6]    Stop time
    3.4     [R-7]    Start command
    3.5     [R-11]   Stop cooking
        3.5.1   [R-11]   Elapsed time
        3.5.2   [R-11]   Stop command
```

Figure 2.6 Outline iteration 1

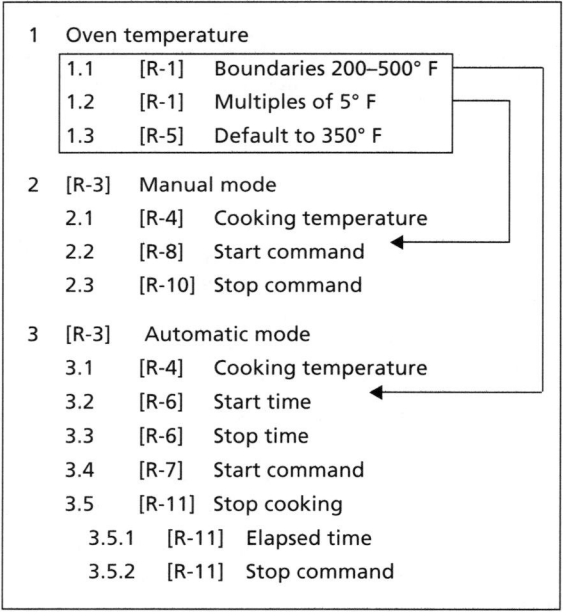

Figure 2.7 The transition from outline iteration 1 to outline iteration 2

```
1   [R-3]  Manual mode
    1.1    [R-4]  Cooking temperature
        1.1.1    [R-1]  Boundaries 200–500° F
        1.1.2    [R-1]  Multiples of 5° F
        1.1.3    [R-5]  Default to 350° F
    1.2    [R-8]  Start command
    1.3    [R-10] Stop command
2   [R-3]  Automatic mode
    2.1    [R-4]  Cooking temperature
        2.1.1    [R-1]  Boundaries 200–500° F
        2.1.2    [R-1]  Multiples of 5° F
        2.1.3    [R-5]  Default to 350° F
    2.2    [R-6]  Start time
    2.3    [R-6]  Stop time
    2.4    [R-7]  Start command
    2.5    [R-11] Stop cooking
        2.5.1    [R-11] Elapsed time
        2.5.2    [R-11] Stop command
```

Figure 2.8 Outline iteration 2

reflects the application's behavior as described in the requirements or other product description. Despite the strong possibility of losing some meaning during translation, our goal is to *identify the core features for testing.*

Although outline iteration 2 lacks complete information for creating test cases, it is a very good intermediate step. Its current form contains the shell in which to add test categories. The test categories contain a standard set of test conditions that flow naturally from the nature of software. Deciding what testing conditions to add comes with experience. I will give you a set of test categories to apply. Let's take a break from the oven controller example and its outline to learn about test categories.

2.3.2 Test categories

Experienced testers seem able to produce ingenious tests off the top of their heads. They're probably thinking about all the devious input states that result from the test categories. Applying the test categories to each possible input condition helps identify tests. For each category, the tester must consider "what is the expected result under this condition?". Often, the tester will not know the answer, because the requirements do not describe the system behavior under that specific condition. Thus, it is the tester's job to compile a list of "what if?" questions and then get answers from the project authority. Of course, not every category applies in every instance.

Test categories to consider when developing test cases include:

- no data provided;
- do it twice;
- valid data;
- invalid data;
- abort;
- power loss;
- stressing the system;
- performance.

The first two categories "no data provided" and "do it twice" are listed separately because, depending on the application, they can represent either valid or invalid data. Let's explore the meaning and interpretation behind each of these categories.

Test category: no data provided

Possible questions:

- How can you *starve* the system?
- What happens if you do *not* provide data?
- What does it mean to withhold data?
- What are the default values or states?

Depending on the type of application, withholding data can mean hitting ENTER on an empty field, sending an empty packet, sending null pointers and null data, failing to initiate a transaction, or any appropriate interpretation of not providing data.

Hopefully, the requirements define the expected outcome. When no data is present, the system can exhibit the following behavior:

- post an error message;
- provide a default;
- reuse the prior value or state;
- prompt user for missing data;
- void the transaction;
- abort execution and enter a message in the log file.

Test category: do it twice

Possible questions:

- What happens if you provide the same data or input twice in succession?

- What happens if you repeat the previous action?

Depending on the type of application, duplicating data can mean entering the same value again, hitting the ENTER key twice in a row, sending the same data packet again, invoking the same command, or any other appropriate interpretation of "doing something twice".

Expected system behavior can include:

- post an error message;
- overwrite the previous value or state;
- prompt user to approve overwriting prior value or state;
- ignore the second incident;
- process the second request as a separate independent event.

Test category: valid data

Possible questions:

- What are valid instances of this data?
- What is the valid input range?
- What are the boundary data?
- What is the format of a valid packet?
- What information is provided in a valid transaction?

Test cases derived from valid data verify that the application processes information correctly. Data values that are not valid fall into the "invalid data" category.

Test category: invalid data

Possible questions:

- What does it mean to exceed the bounds?
- What are the consequences?
- What constitutes bad data for the application under test?

Identify invalid instances of this data. Often there may be more categories for bad data than for valid data.

Examples of invalid data for numeric fields can include:

- values out of range;
- negative numbers;
- decimals;
- leading zeroes or spaces;
- alphabetic characters.

Examples of invalid data for alphanumeric fields can include:

- leading spaces;
- non-alphanumeric characters;
- special keystrokes, such as CONTROL–SHIFT combinations.

Examples of invalid data for pointers can include:

- null pointer;
- bad address;
- uninitialized pointer;
- valid address to garbage memory.

Examples of invalid data for data packets can include:

- bad header;
- bad packet length;
- bad packet format;
- bad cyclic redundancy check value.

Examples of invalid data for signal driven input can include:

- bad timing specifications;
- timeout;
- bad signal;
- missing acknowledge response;
- bad checksum;
- noise.

Possible system behavior under invalid conditions could include:

- post an error message;
- prompt user for correct data;
- reuse a prior valid value or state;
- void the transaction;
- abort execution and enter a message in the log file;
- ignore the incident and try to process the request as given.

Test category: abort

Possible questions:

- What happens if the user hits the ESCAPE key or other type of "halt" key?
- What happens if the user invokes the abort sequence?
- What happens if a communication link is disconnected?

- What happens if processing halts prior to task completion?
- What happens if cables are pulled?

One test to consider is to disconnect and then reconnect a cable and evaluate the system response. Some safety critical systems must provide backup mechanisms to handle such disruptions, while other systems can crash. It may be acceptable for the system-under-test to crash; however, you must be able to restart the application and restore it to an operational state. This leads to further questions:

- What steps are necessary to restore the system after a system abort?
- Are any files left in an open or locked state?

System recovery can take on several forms, such as:

- reboot the system;
- issue a restart sequence;
- alter a status flag or system variable;
- execute a recovery tool;
- reinitialize the application;
- reinstall the application.

Test category: power loss

Possible questions:

- What happens if power is interrupted or lost during processing?
- What happens if power is lost during a start-up or reset sequence?
- What hardware failures are possible?

Power fluctuations and outages are a reality. Some systems mandate a quality power supply, while others may tolerate slight power fluctuations. Certain critical systems have built-in power backups. Power loss can also result from hardware failures or other damaging events. The intent of testing is to assess how well a system recovers from destructive problems.

The possible expected behavior of a system under power loss is similar to the recovery steps listed under the abort category.

Some power loss tests can present a dilemma if there is the possibility of damaging equipment. Be sure to discuss such tests with the systems and hardware engineers who may veto the execution of tests that can potentially damage hardware. For example, a specialized tape drive performing a high-speed rewind could be damaged during a power cycle. If that is your one and only tape drive, this could jeopardize the testing and development environment. Another consideration is to assess the potential harm to prototype hardware. Some "intentional malice" may void an internal component's warranty. The issue here is not whether there is approval for conducting power loss tests: the goal is to raise these issues, document the outcome of the discussions, and hopefully design tests that will assess the potential problem while not damaging critical, expensive hardware.

Test category: stressing the system

Possible questions:

- What does "too much" mean for the system-under-test?
- How can you overwhelm the system?
- What happens when other processes share the same resources?
- What are the limits on processing and on resources?
- Can other processes run concurrently in the background?

Understanding the system's limitations will help the tester formulate strategies for stress testing and load testing. Chapter 9 explains these types of testing. For now, we'll apply the term *stress* in the generic sense.

Possible methods by which to stress a system include:

- reducing available memory space or disk space;
- running multiple instances of the application in parallel;
- creating a massive number of interrupts;
- generating race conditions;
- pressing keys very quickly;
- maximizing or exceeding all boundaries and parameters;
- generating many asynchronous event-driven processes;
- generating the largest possible amount of data (e.g. maximum data packets and buffers);
- providing heavy repetition of certain actions or inputs;
- sending a large complex query to a database system;
- running the application while the system is performing a backup.

A system under extreme stress can exhibit these types of behavior:

- no observable difference;
- slow response;
- suspended tasks;
- system crash;
- deadlock state.

Test category: performance

Possible questions:

- What is the typical user interaction?

- How long should a task take?
- What load can the system handle?

The goal of assessing performance is to check that the system can handle the load and volume that have been specified and to determine at what point the system's response time degrades or fails.

Timing tests evaluate whether the time it takes to complete a task falls within defined time limits. Most of these limits are so small that it is impossible for a person to observe elapsed time correctly. A specialized test tool can monitor execution time. The output of timing tests typically consists of a spreadsheet listing the execution times for various functions. For features with very short execution times, executing each feature repeatedly in a loop achieves better accuracy. Thus, timing is reported as elapsed time per 100 or 1,000 iterations.

Although this is not an exhaustive list, these categories apply to testing most applications I have encountered. Other test categories, such as usability, background, security, installation, reliability and serviceability may or may not be relevant to your particular application. For further information on these other test categories, refer to [Beizer84] and [Kaner99].

2.3.3   Applying the test categories

Returning to the oven controller example, the next step is to apply these test categories to outline iteration 2. The purpose is to question the system's behavior under each unexpected state. The goal is to ask "what if?" and then determine whether a suitable test ensues. When in doubt, add the test category condition to the outline to generate discussion. Not all outline items will become test cases. Having a general knowledge about the oven controller, we'll insert test categories where we feel they are most relevant.

Test category: no data provided

If the user fails to specify cooking temperature, we know from the requirements that the oven temperature defaults to 350° F.

The requirements state that the user specifies a start and stop time, but there is no further information about these two values. We have identified an incomplete requirement.

Questions to ask the project authority:

- How does the user specify start and stop times?
- What happens if the user fails to provide the start time, stop time, or both?

Modifications to outline iteration 2:

- Add placeholders for "no data" under every occurrence of start time and stop time.

● Each instance of cooking temperature already contains a reference to "default to 350° F". This addresses the "no data" condition as it applies to the cooking temperature. Nothing prevents us from adding a separate entry for "no data" which in this particular situation is redundant with the default condition. Although it might look like this clutters the outline, it's important from a logic standpoint to show that the "no data" case is being considered.

Test category: do it twice

The user can enter the cooking temperature, start time, and stop time; however, the requirements do not specify what happens if each parameter is entered twice. Is there a distinction between entering the same cooking temperature twice and specifying two different cooking temperatures? Does the same distinction also apply to the start and stop times? Again, we have identified more holes in the requirements.

Questions to ask the project authority:

● How does the user specify cooking temperature, start time, and stop times?
● What happens if two cooking temperatures are specified?
● Can a second temperature be specified while the oven is heating?
● What happens if two start times are specified?
● What happens if two stop times are specified?
● Can the user enter the times in the order start/start/stop/stop and start/stop/start/stop? If so, how does the system respond?

Modification to outline iteration 2:

● Add placeholders for "enter twice" under every item representing possible data values, which, in this example, would be every reference to cooking temperature, start time, and stop time.

Test category: valid data

We know from the requirements that valid data for cooking temperature are integers from 200 to 500, in multiples of 5. However, it is unclear if this range includes the endpoints and whether all temperatures are in Fahrenheit.

We can assume that after entering valid input, the oven will eventually heat up to the desired cooking temperature. The requirements do not specify a time interval by which the target temperature shall be reached. We can also question whether there must be a minimum elapsed time interval between the start and stop times. What happens if the stop time is reached before the oven reaches its target temperature?

We do not know anything about the start and stop time values, other than the fact that the user provides these values. The requirements do not specify if the user must provide the data in a particular order.

The requirements also state that the user will issue START and STOP commands, without any explanation of how these are achieved. We also need a definition of the user interface.

The requirements mention manual and automatic modes without any clear definition.

Questions to ask the project authority:

- Are all temperatures assumed to be in Fahrenheit?
- Are the boundaries 200 and 500 inclusive? Or is the real range 205–495?
- What is the format and range of start and stop time?
- Are leading zeros allowed?
- What do the assignments *start time = 0* and *stop time = 0* represent? Are these errors?
- Are times based on a 12- or 24-hour clock?
- Do the time parameters also involve the day and date?
- What are the formats of the START and STOP commands?
- Is there a minimum gap between start time and stop time?
- How fast must the oven heat up to reach its target cooking temperature?
- How can the user determine the oven's current temperature?
- Can the cooking temperature, start time, and stop time be entered in any order?
- What is meant by "manual" and "automatic" mode?

Modification to outline iteration 2:

- Add placeholders for valid data under every item representing possible data values, which, in this example, would be every reference to cooking temperature, start time, and stop time.

Test category: invalid data

As determined from the requirements, invalid data for cooking temperature include:

- numbers less than 200;
- numbers greater than 500;
- numbers between 200 and 500 in non-multiples of 5.

What we don't yet know is whether the values 200 and 500 are valid. We also do not know how the oven controller handles other types of values, such as negative numbers, decimals, and other non-numeric characters.

Although we do not yet know the format or the range of start and stop time values, there are some inherent properties associated with time. In automatic mode, it is evident that the current time must precede the start time and that the start time must, in turn, precede the stop time. Such dependencies create fertile ground for new test cases.

Questions to ask the project authority:

- What is the format and range of start and stop time?
- What happens if current time > start time?
- Can the current time be before midnight and the start time after midnight, so that the start time is on the following day?
- What happens if start time > stop time?
- Can the start time be before midnight and the stop time after midnight, so that the stop time is on the following day?

Modifications to outline iteration 2:

- Add placeholders for invalid data under every item representing possible data values, which, in this example, would be every reference to cooking temperature, start time, and stop time.
- Add entries, under automatic mode, that test the relations between current time and start time and also between current time and stop time.
- Add entries, under automatic mode, that account for entering stop time prior to entering start time.

Test category: abort

We do not know how the user invokes commands. We don't even know how the system will behave under an abort command or even if there is an abort command.

Questions to ask the project authority:

- How does the user interact with the oven?
- Is there an "emergency shut-off" procedure?

Modification to outline iteration 2:

- An abort entry under each of the two modes, manual and automatic, has been added as a placeholder. Once the above questions are answered, we may modify the next version of the outline to reflect our new understanding of how the user interacts with the oven controller.

Test category: power loss

The current requirements do not specify what happens if the oven controller loses power. There are three states to consider in our example:

- power loss during the idle state;
- power loss while the user enters values;
- power loss during the oven's heating operation.

Questions to ask the project authority:

● What happens if the power goes out when the oven is idle?

● What happens if power is lost during initialization?

● What happens if power is lost when the user is entering data?

● What happens if power is lost before the start time is set in automatic mode?

● What happens if power is lost while the oven is in heating mode?

● What happens when power is restored?

● What steps, if any, must the user perform when power is restored?

Modification to outline iteration 2:

● A power loss entry under each of the two modes, manual and automatic, has been added as a placeholder. Once the above questions are answered, we may modify the outline to reflect our new understanding of the system's power usage.

Test category: stressing the system

The oven controller only handles the oven's operation, thus requiring few computing resources. If other appliances share this controller, then we need tests that generate additional traffic on the data bus.

   Questions to ask the project authority:

● Is this a single-stream operation?

● What other processes can occur concurrently?

● Can the user enter data very fast?

● What types of interrupts are possible?

● What are the shared resources?

● What are the applicable parameters and their limits?

● What is the available memory and can we limit it?

Modification to outline iteration 2:

● A "stress the system" entry under each of the two modes, manual and automatic, has been added as a placeholder. Once the above questions are answered, we may modify the outline to reflect our new understanding of the system's architecture.

Test category: performance

In terms of the oven controller, the performance aspect affects the time it takes the oven to respond to both user input and to heating directives. There do not appear to be any other features for which measuring execution time is applicable.

Questions to ask the project authority:

- How long does it take the oven controller to process user input?
- How long does it take the oven to heat up and reach its target temperature?
- Is there anything else that can be measured?
- What type of load can the system handle?

Modification to outline iteration 2:

- No changes related to performance testing will be made to the outline. Response time is part of every test case, so test cases that call for heating the oven will state as part of the expected results that the oven will reach <x> degrees within <y> time.

The aim of this lengthy discussion is to call attention to potential problem areas. Applying these test categories significantly increases the outline's size. Figure 2.9 shows a portion of this new outline and Appendix A3 contains the complete outline. The shaded portions show the additions made to the previous outline iteration. At this point, there are many unanswered questions, so we are not ready to define tests. Recall that an experienced tester will probably produce an outline similar to iteration 3 within one editing session. The tester decides on the amount of interaction to have with developers or whether to hold reviews for each new iteration of the outline.

As a result of all the questions posed by the tester, it is evident that the user interface definition is missing. The project authority now provides us with the user interface specification. With new user requirements in hand, the tester processes the information and also identifies new issues to feed back to the development team.

2.3.4 More product information

The project authority answers most of the questions by issuing a user interface specification that describes how the user interacts with the oven controller. This new specification describes how the oven receives user input and what feedback is given to the user.

The oven controller keypad

The user enters commands via a keypad containing 15 keys, as shown in Figure 2.10. Ten of the keys represent the digits 0 through 9. The other five are as follows:

The ENTER key sends the number visible in the display to be processed.

The START TIME key signals the start time entry sequence.

The STOP TIME key signals the stop time entry sequence.

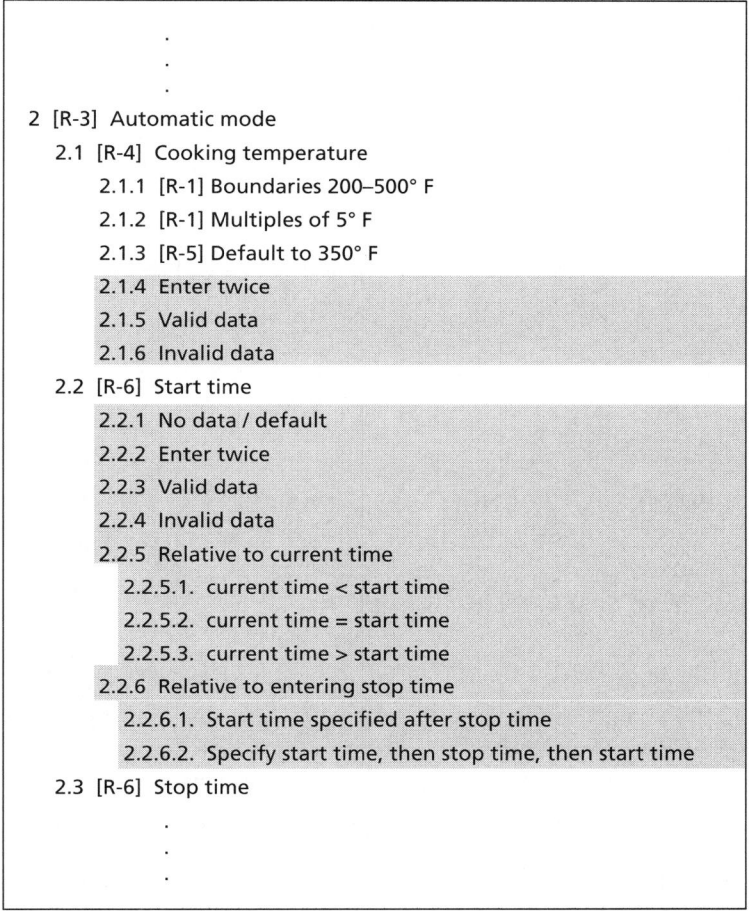

.
.
.

2 [R-3] Automatic mode
  2.1 [R-4] Cooking temperature
      2.1.1 [R-1] Boundaries 200–500° F
      2.1.2 [R-1] Multiples of 5° F
      2.1.3 [R-5] Default to 350° F
      2.1.4 Enter twice
      2.1.5 Valid data
      2.1.6 Invalid data
  2.2 [R-6] Start time
      2.2.1 No data / default
      2.2.2 Enter twice
      2.2.3 Valid data
      2.2.4 Invalid data
      2.2.5 Relative to current time
         2.2.5.1. current time < start time
         2.2.5.2. current time = start time
         2.2.5.3. current time > start time
      2.2.6 Relative to entering stop time
         2.2.6.1. Start time specified after stop time
         2.2.6.2. Specify start time, then stop time, then start time
  2.3 [R-6] Stop time

.
.
.

Figure 2.9 Portion of outline iteration 3

The START key signals the start of manual or automatic cooking.

The CANCEL key aborts the current function, clears the error display, and stops the heating elements. The function performed depends upon the context in which the key is invoked.

Output display

The output display allows for up to 10 alphanumeric characters. The output is left justified. Output formats are as follows:

1. When the user is entering input prior to hitting the ENTER key, the display will echo the user's keystrokes. Time is displayed as "HH:MM" and temperature is displayed as "nnn", where the temperature is in degrees Fahrenheit.

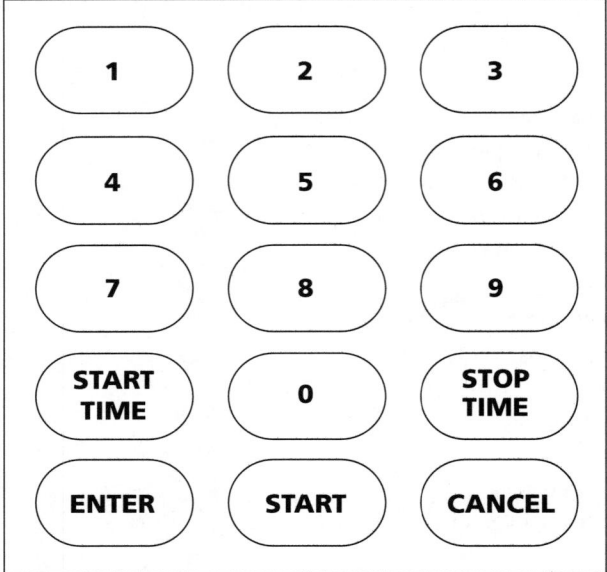

Figure 2.10 User interface keypad

2. If the countdown timer is active, it displays time as "HH:MM:SS".

3. If the countdown timer is inactive, then the display will show the word "BAKE" when the oven is in its heating mode. Otherwise, the display will be empty when the oven is at its target temperature.

4. Error messages have a maximum of 10 characters. These messages include:

   ● "TIME ERROR" when an invalid time value has been entered.
   ● "TEMP ERROR" when an invalid temperature value has been entered.

To clear the error message in the display, the user must hit the CANCEL key.

Input keystroke sequences

To select the cooking temperature, the user must enter the following sequence:

1. Enter the temperature value. Three digits *nnn* represent the target cooking temperature, where *nnn* is 200..500 (inclusive) and *nnn* is a multiple of 5. The temperature cannot have a leading zero.

2. Hit the ENTER key when done. Otherwise, the entry is considered invalid.

3. If no value is entered, the temperature defaults to 350°F.
   If an invalid value is entered, the system displays the "TEMP ERROR" message.

   Note: The user can only specify temperature in Fahrenheit. The current oven controller does not process temperature in Celsius.

To select the start time, the user must enter the following sequence:

1. Hit the START TIME key.
2. Enter the start time value as four digits representing HH:MM, where HH is 00..23 and MM is 00..59.
3. Hit the ENTER key when done. Otherwise, the entry is considered invalid.
4. If a valid value is entered, the start time functions in automatic mode.
    If no value is entered, the start time functions in manual mode.
    If an invalid value is entered, the system displays the "TIME ERROR" message.

To select the stop time, the user must enter the following sequence:

1. Hit the STOP TIME key.
2. Enter the stop time value as four digits representing HH:MM, where HH is 00..23 and MM is 00..59.
3. Hit the ENTER key when done. Otherwise, the entry is considered invalid.
4. If a valid value is entered, the stop time functions in automatic mode.
    If no value is entered, the stop time functions in manual mode.
    If an invalid value is entered, the system displays the "TIME ERROR" message.

Relation between time values.

1. All times must occur on the same day. Thus,

    $$\text{current time} \le \text{start time} < \text{stop time}$$

2. 00:00 signifies midnight, the start of the day. It is a valid value for current time and start time but invalid for stop time.

Preheating condition

The oven reaches its target temperature within the following times:

200–299° F	within 4 minutes
300–399° F	within 5 minutes
400–500° F	within 6 minutes

Although the information provided by the project authority answers many – but not all – of the tester's questions, the user interface description is still incomplete and confusing in some places. Considering the poor state of the requirements, this should come as no surprise. There is no mention of setting the oven's internal clock. For simplicity, let's assume that the internal clock is already set to the real time for the duration of this testing cycle. These new requirements also introduce a new feature. The output display describes that the countdown timer is displayed in "HH:MM:SS" format. This is the first mention of a countdown timer, so pursue this topic with the project authority.

The concept of *automatic mode* and *manual mode* is still unclear. Table 2.1 illustrates how the input sequence determines automatic and manual mode. This table contains the following three sections:

- The first column, line number, contains the prefix "f" to provide a unique identifier that future test cases will reference.

- The second section, user input, contains all eight possible combinations of values that are entered by the user. This table emphasizes which input values a test will specify; this does not detail the keystrokes required to enter the data. For example, line f3 represents the state in which the user provides a value for stop time, but provides no values for start time or cooking temperature.

- The third section, oven controller processing, documents the oven's expected behavior. Again looking at line f3, the start mode is manual and oven heating starts as soon as the user hits the ENTER key. The oven shuts off automatically at the specified time. The oven temperature defaults to 350°F. The display counts down the elapsed time, which is the difference between the stop time and the time when the user entered the commands. In another instance, for example line f5, the user omits the stop time value, so the oven will continue to heat until the user hits the CANCEL key.

We see from Table 2.1 that specifying a start time creates an automatic start condition, whereas specifying a stop time invokes an automatic stop mode. Not only is there an automatic and manual mode, but each applies to both starting and stopping conditions.

As stated before, these are not the best requirements and the user interface design also lacks thoroughness. Testers who design the tests before the start of software development provide valuable feedback to the project team. This is why involving testers at the beginning of a project improves the product definition. However, for this example, this is the state of the product that we must test. Because of the poor condition of the requirements and user interface design, the tester should expect to find a lot of problems.

2.3.5   The last iteration

The user interface specification and the manual/automatic mode description in Table 2.1 answer most of the tester's questions. We can complete the gaps in the test categories as they apply to the oven controller and thus proceed with the outline. To complete this example, let's assume that the project authority has clarified the confusing requirements by providing the information listed below. When working on a real project, you should approach the project authority and discuss any requirement that you consider to be inadequate or inappropriate.

Table 2.1 Manual/automatic mode description

| Line number | USER INPUT | | | OVEN CONTROLLER PROCESSING | | | | |
	Start time	Stop time	Cooking temperature	Start mode	Time to start heating oven	Stop mode	Time to shut off oven	Cooking temperature	Display message
f1	no value	no value	no value	manual	start now	manual	CANCEL key	default = 350°	"BAKE"
f2	no value	no value	valid value	manual	start now	manual	CANCEL key	specified value	"BAKE"
f3	no value	valid value	no value	manual	start now	auto stop	stop time value	default = 350°	timer countdown
f4	no value	valid value	valid value	manual	start now	auto stop	stop time value	specified value	timer countdown
f5	valid value	no value	no value	auto start	start time value	manual	CANCEL key	default = 350°	"BAKE"
f6	valid value	no value	valid value	auto start	start time value	manual	CANCEL key	specified value	"BAKE"
f7	valid value	valid value	no value	auto start	start time value	auto stop	stop time value	default = 350°	timer countdown
f8	valid value	valid value	valid value	auto start	start time value	auto stop	stop time value	specified value	timer countdown

Test category: no data provided

● If the user omits the start or stop time, then a manual mode protocol takes effect. The oven starts heating as soon as the user has entered valid input. The oven stops heating upon hitting the CANCEL key.

Test category: do it twice

● If the oven is idle, any data item entered twice overwrites the prior value.
● If the oven is in heating mode:

   entering another valid cooking temperature overrides the current cooking temperature and the oven adjusts accordingly. The oven controller ignores an invalid temperature;

   the CANCEL key shuts off the oven and returns it to an idle state;

   any other command is ignored.

Test category: valid data

● The temperature boundaries 200 and 500 are valid values.
● Valid time values are based on a 24-hour clock.
● Hour and minute values less than 10 must have a leading zero.
● Current time and start time can have the value 00:00, which represents midnight.
● In this example, there is no way to specify the date.
● While waiting for the oven to start heating in automatic mode, the oven remains in the idle state until the start time specified by the user has been reached. The oven will then turn on and start heating accordingly.
● Although the oven does not display the current temperature, it does display the word "BAKE" to indicate that the oven is in heating mode. The tester needs to supply an auxiliary thermometer to monitor the oven temperature. Even if the oven did post the current temperature, the tester would still have to confirm the accuracy of the displayed information.

Test category: invalid data

● Invalid data for start and stop times are:

   hour portion greater than 24;

   single digit hour portion entered without a leading zero;

   minute portion greater than 59.
● 00:00 is an invalid stop time.
● In automatic mode, the time values must satisfy the following relation:

   current time ≤ start time < stop time.

Otherwise, the oven will not heat up nor will it post an error message.

- A number entry not followed by the ENTER key is considered to be invalid.
- Based on the current user interface, it is not possible to enter a negative value or a non-numeric character.

Test category: abort

- The user aborts processing by hitting the CANCEL key.
- During data input, hitting the CANCEL key causes the controller to return to the idle state.
- During heating, hitting the CANCEL key shuts off the heating elements and restores the controller to the idle state.

Test category: power loss

- If the oven were to lose power, the heating elements would stop heating. Upon power restoration, the oven returns to the idle state.

Test category: stressing the system

- This system contains a single processor controlling a single application, so we assume that there is no other data activity or bus traffic.
- We assume that this system makes no use of memory allocation, external interrupts, system parameters, or other tasks that affect performance.
- We assume that the user has relatively few keystrokes to enter and therefore cannot provide data too quickly.
- We assume that excessive oven usage or extreme temperatures are mechanical issues separate from the software controlling the oven. If there is need to exercise the heating elements for an extended period, we will then define a test to address this issue.

Test category: performance

- Preheating times are defined in the user interface specification. Each test case that directs the heating elements to turn on will state the acceptable preheating duration time.

Applying what we now know about the user interface and oven behavior results in more changes to the outline. We also move a few items in the outline, and the word processor's outline tool automatically renumbers the items in the list. Appendix A4 contains outline iteration 4, a portion of which is shown in Figure 2.11. The shaded portions show the additions made to the outline. The main changes are described below:

1. Combine the items *[R-1] Boundaries 200–500° F* and *[R-1] Multiples of 5° F.* Because of the 5° increments in temperature, boundaries to consider are min ± 1, max ± 1, min ± 5, and max ± 5.

2. Under the item *Valid data*, we add some examples of valid temperatures.

3. Under the item *Enter twice* and for other command keys, we differentiate between an oven in idle and in heating mode, because rules for processing the second input can vary according to the oven's state.

   The Project Authority says that an oven waiting for user input and an oven waiting to turn on automatically are really both in idle mode, so we add the "oven in idle" item to cover these situations. However, this really seems to indicate a whole new category of test conditions. How does the system respond to other commands when the oven is in the "waiting to start heating" mode? Darn! Another set of unclear requirements surface! Maybe restructuring the outline in an entirely different way would better illustrate the application's functionality (more on that in section 2.4). For now, we continue with the current outline, making a note that it does not accurately portray a requirement.

4. We have specified some invalid values under the item *Invalid data*. These include zeros, negative values, alphabetic characters, and other invalid options.

   Since we now know that there is no regular keyboard, thus no way of entering a negative number or an alphabetic character, the tester may be tempted to remove these items from the outline. However, it is recommended to keep such entries in case future product releases undergo significant changes in the user interface, resulting in the possibility of having the user enter negative values. Keep in mind that future enhancements may make a current "impossible" situation possible. This is why seemingly redundant test cases must be retained. For documentation completeness, add a date stamp and a note stating that the outcome is not known or that this test is not applicable at this time.

5. Under the *No data/default* item for start time and stop time, we differentiate between specifying no number and entering a number incorrectly.

   We know from the user interface description that entering the starting time requires hitting the start time function key, followed by a set of numbers and then the ENTER key. Thus outline item 2.2.1 considers what happens when the number entry is missing from this sequence. Two categories of tests exist. Outline item 2.2.1.1 calls for tests where the user hits the START TIME key immediately followed by a non-numeric key. This keystroke sequence voids the start time entry, treating this as a default condition. Outline item 2.2.1.2 first calls for entering a number followed by hitting a key other than the ENTER key, which causes an invalid time entry. Similar changes occur under item 2.3.1. Inserting an explanation within the outline improves clarity and documents the tests' purpose.

6. We will not define tests from the abort, power loss, and stress categories, in order to keep the focus on user keystrokes. The CANCEL key, which is how the user aborts a command sequence, appears within the outline and is therefore already addressed as a test condition. Consequently, we remove these unused

labels from the outline to avoid extra clutter. Some testers may wish to keep these as placeholders for future reference.

```
        .
        .
        .

2 [R-3] Automatic mode
   2.1 [R-4] Cooking temperature
      2.1.1 [R-1] Boundaries 200–500° F / Multiples of 5° F
            2.1.1.1  199 / 200 / 201
            2.1.1.2  195 / 200 / 205
            2.1.1.3  499 / 500 / 501
            2.1.1.4  495 / 500 / 505
      2.1.2 [R-5] Default to 350° F
      2.1.3 Enter twice
            2.1.3.1  oven is idle
            2.1.3.2  oven is heating
      2.1.4 Valid data
            2.1.4.1  350
      2.1.5 Invalid data
            2.1.5.1  0
            2.1.5.2  000
            2.1.5.3  035
            2.1.5.4  non-multiple of 5
            2.1.5.5  negative value (Note: cannot enter a negative value with this design)
            2.1.5.6  alphabetic character (Note: cannot enter a character with this design)
            2.1.5.7  other key (Note: no other key exists with this design)
   2.2 [R-6] Start time
      2.2.1 No data /default
            2.2.1.1  No number given (Start Time key followed by a key listed below)
                  2.2.1.1.1  Hit Enter key
                  2.2.1.1.2  Hit Stop Time key
                  2.2.1.1.3  Hit Start key
                  2.2.1.1.4  Hit Cancel key
            2.2.1.2  Number typed but not followed by Enter key
                     (Start Time key, followed by a number, followed by a key listed below.
                     This aborts the Start Time command, whereas hitting the Enter key
                     accepts the Start Time value.)
                  2.2.1.2.1  Hit Stop Time key
                  2.2.1.2.2  Hit Start key
                  2.2.1.2.3  Hit Cancel key
      2.2.2 Enter twice
                .
                .
                .
```

Figure 2.11 Portion of outline iteration 4

Because the original requirements are marginal, most of the items added to the list are based on test categories and the tester's insight. If complete requirements had been provided, each item in the outline could be traced back to a specific requirement. In this situation, it would be possible to label each item in the outline with a requirement identifier. The ability to link between the product definition and what was tested is required by several industry standards. Chapter 10 discusses such standards compliance issues.

If desired, the tester can also indicate the expected results as part of the outline. Figure 2.12 shows one possible way of modifying the outline to document the expected results for testing the temperature boundaries.

```
1 [R-3]  Manual mode
  1.1 [R-4]  Cooking temperature
    1.1.1 [R-1]  Boundaries 200–500° F/Multiples of 5° F
            1.1.1.1  error at 195°
            1.1.1.2  error at 199°
            1.1.1.3  heat up at 200°
            1.1.1.4  error at 201°
            1.1.1.5  heat up at 205°
                .
                .
                .
```

Figure 2.12 Stating the expected results

2.4   Evaluating the outline

Many may consider the oven controller outline to be disorganized, which is to be expected considering that product information trickled in. Poor requirements beget bad design, and the outline reflects this. We would probably have approached the outline differently had good product information been available at the start of the project. Compare this outline to the one in Chapter 6, which appears easier to follow because of more limited and better-defined user inputs.

Any method that helps the tester understand the application and ask smart questions is valuable. The actual act of building an outline is often more important because of the learning acquired during the process. When the outline becomes too messy or when expanding the outline to incorporate more requirements becomes difficult, several options are available.

Option 1 – Start over and create a new outline

Apply what you now know about the application and restructure the outline accordingly. The oven controller example would benefit from a new outline, in which the top-level items center on the following four features:

- idle (manual mode) – waiting for user input;
- idle (automatic mode) – waiting for oven to start automatically when the selected start time is reached;
- heating (manual mode) – continue heating until user hits CANCEL key;
- heating (automatic mode) – continue heating until oven shuts off at the selected stop time.

The initial requirements do not properly define manual and automatic mode. Even though the project authority says that the above two idle states are the same, enough differences exist in terms of processing user input to warrant separate tests.

Option 2 – Create separate, individual outlines

For large projects, using a separate outline for each feature can help group related information. Otherwise, the number of levels caused by successive indentation will easily overwhelm those trying to understand the outline.

Option 3 – Use a table

Tables often contain the same information as the outline but are presented in a different format. When a particular block of information appears repeatedly throughout the outline, as is typical of menu-driven applications, using a table will help improve the organization of test conditions. Chapters 4 and 5 provide many examples of tables.

Option 4 – Employ use cases

A use case arranges information around a user's actions from start to finish. A possible example for the oven controller could consist of a cook who wishes to program the oven to properly bake a cake. The tester lists the necessary steps and can then list deviations from a successful step. An example of a deviation would be to enter the wrong time or an invalid temperature. Chapter 6 provides examples of use cases.

Option 5 – Continue to use the outline in its current form

The last iteration of the outline does contain information that provides good – though not all – test conditions. Experienced testers know that additional tests will arise during the course of testing. Thus, an incomplete outline is not a drawback. Sometimes, the tester may not know *what* product information is missing. Chapter 3 uses the last iteration of the outline to create test cases.

Except when modeling a very simple application, an outline seldom provides an all-encompassing list of test conditions. Even when using other test design techniques, a tester rarely has all test cases defined prior to executing the tests. As the tester learns more about the application, she will often define additional tests based on information from recent tests. These "what if I tried this input?" ideas are the basis of Exploratory Testing (introduced in Chapter 1). As additional tests become evident, the tester can keep a checklist of these new test conditions or add them directly to the growing set of test cases. Retro-fitting the outline to contain the new test condition is often not necessary, unless it is the sole means of mapping between requirements and test cases. However, tests created on the fly usually imply that requirements are poorly documented.

2.5 Schedule estimation

Let's take a brief respite from creating the outline to address an issue pertinent to management: how much time to schedule for testing. Even before we define the test cases, we can provide a suitable estimate of the number of potential test cases.

As a rough rule, every leaf in the outline translates into at least one test case. Some leaves may lead to more than one. Consequently one option is to count the number of leaves or total lines in the outline. The last iteration of the outline in Appendix A4 contains 135 total lines, of which 44 lines constitute branch points and the remaining 91 lines are leaves. Thus, an initial estimate of 91 or 135 test cases is a good educated guess. Since some leaves result in more than one test case, 91 is the least number of test cases we can expect to have. Experience tells us that we often underestimate schedules and we also create new test cases during test execution. Therefore, the higher figure of 135 is a good start for estimating the number of test cases.

In addition to the estimated number of test cases, the schedule must also allow for other tasks dedicated to the test effort, examples of which may include:

- setting up and configuring a system for executing tests;
- building and installing specialized test tools;
- learning to use the test tools;
- customizing the test tools;
- programming the test cases either as scripts or as data files;
- executing the individual test cases;
- rerunning test cases that have previously failed;
- producing test reports and summary documents.

Even if the organization only provides a bare-bones testing environment, the tester must spend time setting up the test machine. Each test case requires a certain amount of time for its setup and execution. Since each test case in the oven example appears to be quite limited in content, let's say that, on average, we can expect to spend about fifteen minutes on each test case. This translates to setting up and executing four test cases per hour. With 135 total test cases, one can estimate to spend roughly 34 hours on this task.

As is often the case, some tests will fail. The developers will fix the problems and issue a new updated version of the software. The tester will have to re-execute the failed tests to verify the bug fixes. Ideally, even the tests that have been passed initially must be re-executed to assure that the modified software did not alter something that previously worked. With no prior experience in this effort, let's just pick a number out of the air and say that this step will take an additional 50% of the time allocated to the first-pass tests. So if 34 hours are allocated to running the tests cases the first time, then we'll assume that it will take roughly 17 hours to verify bug fixes.

Table 2.2 shows sample schedule information for the test effort. These numbers are an initial estimate; the numbers will be refined as the project progresses.

Table 2.2 A schedule estimate for the testing task

Task	Description	Effort estimate
1	Design and build test program to interface with oven controller.	40 hours
2	Configure the test system.	10 hours
3	Program and execute each test case (135 test cases at roughly 15 minutes per test case).	34 hours
4	Verify bug fixes for failed test cases (50% of Task #3).	17 hours
5	Write a test summary report.	4 hours
	Estimated total effort	**105 hours**

One aspect of project planning is that we won't know how accurate the testing estimates are until the tasks are completed. At the end of the project, comparing actual and estimated task effort provides information that can be applied for the subsequent project. For example, if the initial estimate was low by 35%, then add 35% to the total estimate for the next project in hopes of producing a more accurate schedule. Only by gathering such information over several projects can you then begin to provide more accurate schedules.

Appendix A5, which is explained in Chapter 3, contains 81 test cases derived from the outline. This is far less than the initial estimate of 135 test cases. However, not every outline item results in a test case, while several other outline items point to the same test case. During test execution, the tester will most likely define additional tests, especially since the outline appears to be missing some information about the application. Chances are that when testing is complete, the total number of test cases will be close to – if not exceed – the estimate of 135. We can only guess at the possible number of test cases before actually creating them. Thus, the outline size provides a ballpark figure for an initial estimate.

2.6

Summary

Despite having incomplete requirements, we are still able to start with test development. The first step is to list each requirement individually, and then identify which are input descriptions, expected results, and design constraints.

The test outline approach provides a means by which to organize the requirements. This is a valuable tool for discussing the application requirements with the project authority. As we develop the outline, we identify missing or ambiguous requirements. Addressing the following situations helps identify additional conditions to test:

- not providing data and testing defaults;
- entering data twice;
- valid and invalid data;
- aborting or losing power during processing;
- stressing the system;
- performance issues.

What we produce, with the help of the outline, is a set of test conditions that eventually define test cases.

The number of items in an outline gives an indication of the number of test cases that can be generated. This information is useful for schedule estimation.

3

From Test Outline to Test Cases

3.1 Introduction

In Chapter 2, we developed a test outline by grouping information about the oven controller. Along the way, we identified many questions as we learned more about the application. The next step is to transform the test outline into test cases for later execution.

A test case consists of a test case identifier, an input description, and an expected results definition. In addition, test cases contain a pointer to the corresponding information source to maintain traceability between the test documents. During test case execution, the tester records such information as actual results, pass/fail status, and version number of the software and hardware used for testing. But first, let's get started defining some test cases.

3.2 Creating test cases

The last version of the outline (see Appendix A4) helps us formulate tests. Each path in the outline (from the root to a leaf) identifies an input combination that forms the basis for a test case, and we can then decide whether to define a test using that particular input combination. Once we decide which outline paths become test cases, the next step is to define an unambiguous input state and its associated expected results. A complete set of tests contains one or more test cases for every leaf in the outline. A test case table, as shown in Appendix A5, contains the test case information. For brevity, Table 3.1 shows a few of these same test cases. The table format is as follows:

Test case ID	A unique test case identification number. For simplicity, we select the labeling scheme T-*number*.
Test outline item	The item in the test outline from which the test case is derived. This tracks the traceability between the test outline and the test case.
Prior state	This indicates whether the oven must be in a required configuration prior to executing the test. These preconditions can be:

- the idle state
- successful execution of another test

- requirements on the system clock (current time)
- specific hardware used for testing.

Input	The input sequence to be entered by the tester. Each numerical value, keystroke, or manual action is listed on its own line.
Expected results	The behavior that the tester expects to observe.
Actual results	Space for the tester to record unexpected results or to indicate that the test passed.

Each test case is independent and starts from the initial state, in which the oven is idle. Therefore, you cannot run these tests sequentially without first reverting to the initial state. Tests that depend upon successful completion of another test are indicated as such. For now, our goal is to define test cases, so we will have each test start from the initial state.

The first test case in Table 3.1 and in Appendix A5 is labeled T-1. This test case is derived from line 1.1.1.1 in the test outline, and it corresponds to the portion of the outline shown below.

1 [R-3] Manual mode
  1.1 [R-4] Cooking temperature
    1.1.1 [R-1] Boundaries 200–500° F / Multiples of 5° F
      1.1.1.1 199 / 200 / 201

This test case specifies that we need to provide a cooking temperature in manual mode that exercises the lower boundary condition consisting of one degree above and below the lower limit of the temperature range. This first test specifies an input temperature value of 199°F. This creates an error, which is the expected behavior for one of two reasons. First, only multiples of 5 are valid, so the value 199°F fails that criterion. Second, the lowest valid value in the temperature range is 200°F, and again the value 199°F fails that criterion. Execution of this test is independent of any prior state, and so the initial oven test environment must be in the idle state.

The next test case, T-2, also uses the test outline path designated 1.1.1.1. This time, the test specifies the use of the legal lower bound value of 200°F. This is also one of the values specified in outline item 1.1.1.2. The expected results contain three components:

1. The oven heats up to the desired temperature within a determined amount of time, which is four minutes according to the oven documentation.

2. The initial requirements indicate that the oven controller maintains the target temperature with ±2°F.

3. The user interface specification calls for displaying the word BAKE in the display field when the heating elements are on. Otherwise, the display is empty.

Test case T-3 uses the same derivation as for T-1, except that the "minimum + 1" value of 201 is the input to the test.

Another test case, T-11, poses an interesting situation, in that three paths from the test outline map to this particular test case. The outline item specified by 1.1.2 shows this path.

Table 3.1 Partial set of test cases derived from the test outline
(full list available in Appendix A5)

Test case ID	Test outline	Prior state	Input	Expected results	Actual results
T-1	1.1.1.1	(idle)	199 Enter key	Display: TEMP ERROR	
T-2	1.1.1.1 1.1.1.2	(idle)	200 Enter key Start key	Oven turns on and heats to 200° within 4 minutes. Temperature in range 198°–202°. Display: BAKE when heating is on	
T-3	1.1.1.1	(idle)	201 Enter key	Display: TEMP ERROR	
. . .					
T-11	1.1.2 1.2.1.1 2.4.1.1	(idle)	Start key	Oven turns on and heats to 350° within 5 minutes. Temperature in range 348°–352°. Display: BAKE when heating is on	
. . .					
T-22	1.3.1.2	run T-2	20 seconds after heating starts in T-2, hit Cancel key	Oven stops heating and shuts off. Display: <empty>	
. . .					

T-35	2.1.2	(idle)
		current
		time must
		be before
		14:05
			Start Time key
			1405
			Enter key
			Start key
				When time reaches 14:05, oven
				  turns on and heats to 350°
				  within 5 minutes.
				Temperature in range 348°–352°.
				Display: BAKE when heating is on	

T-36	2.1.3.1
	2.2.5.1
		(idle)
		current
		time is
		11:20
			310
			Enter key
			Start Time key
			1130
			Enter key
			455
			Enter key
			Start key
				When time reaches 11:30, oven
				  turns on and heats to 455°
				  within 6 minutes.
				Temperature in range 453°–457°.
				Display: BAKE when heating is on	

. . .					

1 [R-3] Manual mode
  1.1 [R-4] Cooking temperature
    1.1.1 [R-1] Boundaries 200–500° F / Multiples of 5° F

         .
         .

    1.1.2 [R-5] Default to 350° F

Interpretation of this outline fragment indicates that the cooking temperature is in manual mode, but that no number is entered, hence the *default* entry. Because this is a valid input sequence, the oven heats up to the temperature of 350° F. Astute readers might note that an unspecified temperature results in a default of 350° F, whereas an out-of-bounds or invalid temperature results in an error message. This is an example of where the refining the outline produces clearer requirements.

Outline item 1.2.1.1 is the second path leading to the test case T-11, and its path is as follows:

1 [R-3] Manual mode
  1.1 [R-4] Cooking temperature

    .
    .

  1.2 [R-8] Start command
    1.2.1 No data / default
      1.2.1.1 oven is idle

This part of the outline also falls under the heading of manual mode. The user interface, as defined, requires that the START key follow entry of the cooking temperature; however, line item 1.2.1 states that no value is entered in conjunction with the START key, and line item 1.2.1.1 specifies that the oven is idle. The oven requirements state that if no cooking temperature is entered, which will happen if the START key is pressed with no associated value, then the temperature defaults to 350° F.

Outline item 2.4.1.1 is the third path leading to the same test condition in T-11. This path calls for issuing the start command with no data specified and the oven in the idle state. Even though the path occurs under the heading of automatic mode, this particular combination can only occur in manual mode. Thus, this test is redundant with the two other paths leading to T-11.

2 [R-3] Automatic mode
    .
    .

  2.4 [R-7] Start command
    2.4.1 No data / default
      2.4.1.1 oven is idle (**Note**: can only have "no data" when in manual mode)
      2.4.1.2 oven is heating
    2.4.2 Enter twice

Is this a problem with the outline? Not necessarily. As we're dealing with less than perfect requirements, our test specifications may have their own inadequacies. Part of the cause is that the outline is created in pieces, in response to information provided by the project authority. The first iteration of the outline uses general oven information. A later revision incorporates user interface information and thus we made additions to the outline to develop tests that exercise the START key as well as the other keys available to the user. It just so happens that the oven controller interprets hitting the START key with no associated number the same way as omitting all numerical input. If the user interface is defined differently, then these three paths will not necessarily result in the same test case.

If having one-to-one correspondence from the test outline to the test cases is important to your organization, then you will need to define three separate test cases, even if their input and expected result descriptions are identical. You could also refer one test case to its clone. For example, the test derived from outline item 1.2.1.1 could contain the instruction "see test case T-11", assuming that test T-11 documents the test resulting from outline item 1.1.2.

By this point, you should have a good understanding of how the test outline in Appendix A4 translates to the test cases in Appendix A5. Creating test cases is a tedious, yet methodical and essential, task. I will not bore you with extensive commentary about each and every test case; however, a few test cases warrant additional explanation.

The test outline item 1.3.1.2, which specifies use of the CANCEL key when the oven is currently heating, serves as the source for test case T-22. Rather than dictate the steps for heating the oven, T-22 simply states to run another test case, such as T-2, to get the oven into a known heating state.

```
1 [R-3] Manual mode
  1.1 [R-4] Cooking temperature
      .
      .
  1.2 [R-8] Start command
      .
      .
  1.3 [R-10] Stop command (CANCEL key)
      1.3.1 No data / default
          1.3.1.1 oven is idle
          1.3.1.2 oven is heating
```

Test cases T-35 and T-36 each depend on the current time. Although the oven state is idle at the start of each test, T-35 requires that the current time is before 14:05, whereas T-36 requires that the current time be set to 11:20. This places some constraints on executing the tests; however, the business at hand is to define the tests. Testers will face this challenge whenever a time element is part of the application.

The actual input sequence, spelled out in the Input column of Table 3.1, depends upon the current user interface. Any subsequent changes in the user interface require corresponding modifications to the test case's input specification. Separating the data values from the interface criteria, as shown in Table 3.2, allows for a generic input description. This new table contains separate columns for each input data value without detailing the actual keystroke sequence. This format is suited for an application where the input order or the keystroke details are not as important. The tester must decide which format best records the necessary information.

Table 3.2 Test cases with input values listed separately

Test ID		Input				Test results	
Test case ID	Test outline	Prior state	Cooking temperature	Start time	Stop time	Expected results	Actual results
T-1	1.1.1.1	(idle)	199	(none)	(none)	Display: TEMP ERROR	
T-2	1.1.1.1 1.1.1.2	(idle)	200	(none)	(none)	Oven turns on and heats to 200° within 4 minutes. Temperature in range 198°–202°. Display: BAKE when heating is on	
T-3	1.1.1.1	(idle)	201	(none)	(none)	Display: TEMP ERROR	
. . .							

In addition to the test outline, which is a valuable source for defining test cases, the user documentation in section 2.3.4 provides more information about the oven controller. This description about automatic and manual modes warrants further testing. We will use Table 2.1 to create tests that assure proper operation of the oven's modes. Of course, creating tests from this source may duplicate some tests created from the outline. Table 3.3 contains a few of these new tests, which ensure that omitting or specifying cooking temperature, start time, and stop time results in proper oven behavior. Test case identifiers in Table 3.3 start from T-100 to distinguish them from other test cases defined in this chapter.

The first test, T-100, originates from the first line of Table 2.1. This test specifies that no values for start time, stop time, or cooking temperature are provided. Once the user tells the oven to "go", by issuing the START command, the oven heats to the default temperature of 350°F and maintains that state until the user hits the CANCEL key. Test case T-101 ensures that the oven shuts off properly.

Test case T-102 traces back to line item f2 in Table 2.1. In this test, the tester provides a cooking temperature of 275°F. This test places the oven into manual mode. Moving on to test T-103, which is a continuation of T-102, the oven shuts off when the user hits the CANCEL key.

The remainder of the test cases follows in a similar manner. Each test case starts from the idle state unless otherwise noted. Whether the test case specifies start time or stop time determines whether the oven operates in manual or automatic mode.

Table 3.3 Test cases derived from the manual/automatic mode description

Test case ID	Test source (from Table 2.1)	Prior state	Input	Expected results	Actual results
T-100	f1	(idle)	Start key	Oven turns on and heats to 350° within 5 minutes. Temperature in range 348°–352°. Display: BAKE when heating is on	
T-101	f1	run T-100	Cancel key	Oven stops heating and shuts off. Display: <empty>	
T-102	f2	(idle)	275 Enter key Start key	Oven turns on and heats to 275° within 4 minutes. Temperature in range 273°–277°. Display: BAKE when heating is on	
T-103	f2	run T-102	Cancel key	Oven stops heating and shuts off. Display: <empty>	
T-104	f3	(idle) current time is 13:10	Stop Time key 1410 Enter key Start key	Oven turns on and heats to 350° within 5 minutes. Temperature in range 348°–352°. Display: timer countdown, starting from 01:00:00 Oven shuts off at 14:10 (when timer = 00:00:00) and sounds buzzer. Display: <empty>	
T-105	f3	run T-104	25 seconds after heating starts in T-104, hit Cancel key	Oven stops heating and shuts off. Display: <empty>	
T-106	f4	(idle) current time is 5:34	455 Enter key Stop Time key 1534 Enter key Start key	Oven turns on and heats to 455° within 6 minutes. Temperature in range 453°–457°. Display: timer countdown, starting from 10:00:00 Oven shuts off at 15:34 (when timer = 00:00:00) and sounds buzzer. Display: <empty>	
. . .					

These tables provide suitable test case documentation, as long as the input and expected results are well defined. The next step is for the tester to prepare the test environment (Chapter 9 covers these details).

3.3   Documentation shortcuts

Creating an outline and test cases from the oven controller example generates a large amount of documentation. It is possible to take many shortcuts to expedite test case creation and documentation. Shortcuts have their drawbacks: an abbreviated paper trail may fail to satisfy stringent test documentation requirements, especially when the shortcuts fail to provide a description of unambiguous input and expected results. However, in an immature organization, such minimal documentation may be a vast improvement over prior efforts, especially when time is of the essence.

Documentation shortcuts only work when those familiar with the project can deduce the omitted steps; however, any information that is *not* documented *will* be lost and forgotten. Whether this approach is suitable depends on the risks that an organization is willing to take. Reasons for avoiding shortcuts include the following:

- to strive for thorough test documentation;
- to bring new employees up to speed;
- to acquire and maintain accreditation by an external standards organization (an external auditor would regard shortcuts as a breach of accreditation).

The shortcut involves using the outline itself to select tests and track test results. Some testers may end up writing all of the test execution notes on a hard copy of the outline. This can get messy very quickly. If possible, it is better to maintain the information via a computer file, using a table, spreadsheet, or dedicated software test tool. The annotated outline provides a checklist of which type of tests to run.

In this example, I'll illustrate the shortcuts using several different spreadsheets. No one format is best; it is up to the tester to decide which format best portrays the necessary information. Although Tables 3.4–3.7 and Appendix A6 portray the same information, they each display the information in different formats. I'll show the first few lines of the resulting sample spreadsheets, whereas Appendix A6 contains a copy of the complete shortcut document.

The shortcut steps are as follows.

Step 1

One column in the spreadsheet contains the original test outline.

Each outline leaf characterizes the input for a test case. Some of the outlines items that are not leaves can also lead to test cases.

Step 2

The tester or the project leader prioritizes the tests by selecting which tests to run.

Two methods exist for identifying which tests to execute. One approach is to use a highlighter pen to color code the outline leaves, where different colors represent different priority levels. Another approach is to provide a separate column for assigning a priority code. Advantages of having a separate column for the priority code include:

- avoid use of color, especially when using black-and-white printouts;
- easier to enter a number on a spreadsheet than to indicate color;
- can reorder the rows of the table based on priority order.

The tester or the project leader determines the meaning for a color or priority code. For example, priority 1 could indicate that the tests must be run prior to delivery, with priority 2 tests reserved for the next incremental release of the product. Different colors can represent different concepts, such as test priority, which system configuration to use, or even which person to run the test. In our example, the lighter and darker highlights in Table 3.4 indicate priorities 1 and 2 respectively.

Step 3

During test execution, the tester writes down the data used to run each test.

If the outline leaf does not specify the actual input value, then the tester will record the data value used to execute that test.

Step 4

The tester records the test result in a separate column.

Often, the tester records the pass/fail outcome rather than the actual generated output. In our example, the tester places a ✓ check mark to indicate a successful test and an ✗ mark for a failed test. Of course, correct execution is a judgment call on the part of the tester. With no expected results identified, the tester judges whether the system behaves appropriately given the specified input.

The abbreviation "n/a" stands for "not applicable". This occurs when a selected test cannot be executed under the current conditions.

Step 5

Organizations that track tests by identifier can add this information to the table.

The spreadsheet contains a column for inserting the test case identifier. Outline nodes that do not translate into a test case have a '-' symbol instead of a test case identifier.

The following tables illustrate different formats for applying the shortcuts. All of the sample spreadsheets contain columns for recording the input data and test result. Table 3.4 shows the use of color-coding. This table also shows a test specified by a node rather than by a leaf. The tester tests outline item 1.1.3 by executing the items 1.1.3.1 and 1.1.3.2 below it. For outline item 1.1.4, the tester tests the valid value 345, as recorded in the data column. In addition, the tester enters the valid value

410 as specified by outline item 1.1.4.1, but does not need to record the value '410' in the data column because the outline item already dictates that data value.

Table 3.4 Test case checklist prioritized by color-coding

Test case outline	Data	Results
1 [R-3] Manual mode		
1.1 [R-4] Cooking temperature		
1.1.1 [R-1] Boundaries 200–500° F / Multiples of 5°F		
1.1.1.1 199 / 200 / 201		
1.1.1.2 195 / 200 / 205	195	✓
1.1.1.3 499 / 500 / 501	499	✗
1.1.1.4 495 / 500 / 505		
1.1.2 [R-5] Default to 350° F		✓
1.1.3 Enter twice	see sublist	✓
1.1.3.1 oven is idle	250, 405	✓
1.1.3.2 oven is heating	205, 450	✓
1.1.4 Valid data	345	✓
1.1.4.1 410		✓
. . .		

Rather than using a color code, Table 3.5 shows the use of a separate column to prioritize test cases. This conveys the same information contained in Table 3.4.

Table 3.5 Test case checklist with a priority code in its own column

Priority	Test case outline	Data	Results
	1 [R-3] Manual mode		
	1.1 [R-4] Cooking temperature		
	1.1.1 [R-1] Boundaries 200–500° F / Multiples of 5°F		
	1.1.1.1 199 / 200 / 201		
2	1.1.1.2 195 / 200 / 205	195	✓
2	1.1.1.3 499 / 500 / 501	499	✗
	1.1.1.4 495 / 500 / 505		
1	1.1.2 [R-5] Default to 350° F		✓
2	1.1.3 Enter twice	see sublist	✓
	1.1.3.1 oven is idle	250, 405	✓
	1.1.3.2 oven is heating	205, 450	✓
1	1.1.4 Valid data	345	✓
1	1.1.4.1 410		✓
	. . .		

Table 3.6 shows the same table entries sorted in priority order. Test cases without a priority code fall to the bottom of the list. The disadvantage is that each outline item no longer appears in context, thus losing the hierarchical outline relation and path information. This prioritized list, however, does provide a quick checklist for testing.

Table 3.6 Test case checklist sorted by priority

Priority	Test case outline	Data	Results
1	1.1.2 [R-5] Default to 350°F		✓
1	1.1.4 Valid data	345	✓
1	1.1.4.1 410		✓
1	1.1.5.2 000		✗
1	2.1.1.2 195 / 200/ 205	195, 205	✓
1	2.1.2 [R-5] Default to 350°F		✓
1	2.2.2.1 oven is idle	0725, 0720	✓
1	2.2.5.1 current time < start time	current=23:58 start=23:59	✓
1	2.2.5.2 current time = start time	current=19:30 start=019:30	✓
1	2.3.2.2 oven is heating		✗
1	2.3.3.2 2359 (upper bound)		✓
1	2.3.5.2 start time = stop time	start=16:47 stop=16:47	✓
1	2.5.1.1 start time specified		✓
2	1.1.1.2 195 / 200 / 205	195	✓
2	1.1.1.3 499 / 500 / 501	499	✗
2	1.1.3 Enter twice	*see sublist*	✓
2	1.1.5.5 negative value	can't be done	n/a
2	2.1.5.6 alphabetical character	can't be done	n/a
2	2.2.1.1.1 Hit Enter key		✓
2	2.2.1.1.2 Hit Stop Time key		✗
2	2.2.1.1.3 Hit Start key		✓
2	2.2.5.3 current time > start time	current=10:57 start=10:56	✓
2	2.3.5.1 start time < stop time	current=19:30 start=23:59	✓
2	2.3.5.3 start time > stop time	start=16:48 stop=16:47	✓
	1 [R-3] Manual mode		
	1.1 [R-4] Cooking temperature		
	1.1.1 [R-1] Boundaries 200–500°F/ Multiples of 5°F		
	1.1.1.1 199 / 200 / 201		
	1.1.1.4 495 / 500 / 505		
	. . .		

Table 3.7 contains both the test case identifier and priority code as separate columns. The corresponding test case lists the details of each test, including the input data. Not every line in the outline has a test case identifier. The drawback is that multiple input conditions may exist for a specific test; however, the goal here is to document what type of test to execute. Since outline item 1.1.3 is a priority test, the associated test case #507 contains the provisions for exercising the conditions in items 1.1.3.1 and 1.1.3.2.

Table 3.7 Test case checklist with test case identifier and priority code

Priority	Test case ID	Test case outline	Results
	501	1 [R-3] Manual mode	
	–	1.1 [R-4] Cooking temperature	
	–	1.1.1 [R-1] Boundaries 200–500° F / Multiples of 5° F	
	502	1.1.1.1 199 / 200 / 201	
2	503	1.1.1.2 195 / 200 / 205	✓
2	504	1.1.1.3 499 / 500 / 501	✗
	505	1.1.1.4 495 / 500 / 505	
1	506	1.1.2 [R-5] Default to 350° F	✓
2	507	1.1.3 Enter twice	✓
	507–a	1.1.3.1 oven is idle	✓
	507–b	1.1.3.2 oven is heating	✓
1	508	1.1.4 Valid data	✓
1	509	1.1.4.1 410	✓
		. . .	

These documentation shortcuts facilitate recording what has been tested. Recall that such documentation makes for incomplete test logs. Chapter 10 discusses how to transform such minimal test logs into more rigorous test documents by providing a much greater degree of traceability and accountability.

3.4   Summary

As we saw in Chapter 2, test outlines help to organize information and highlight the application's input combinations. This information is useful for developing test cases. Each path in the outline translates into a test case. Using a table to record the test case information, the tester lists the input combinations, then assigns a test case identifier and specifies the application's expected behavior. Sometimes, the expected outcome is not readily known and the tester must track down this information.

The tester can circumvent the test case definition table by making notes directly onto the outline. The documentation shortcut requires that the tester knows how the application functions because complete descriptions of input and expected results are lacking. The tester can indicate test priority either by color-coding a test or by assigning a priority code. The tester records the input data used, test execution results, and whether the test passed or failed. Although short-cuts fail to satisfy accepted test documentation practices and may violate accreditation from external standards bodies, they allow the tester to plan ahead, reduce the risk of stabbing in the dark, and provide some documented trail of what was tested.

4 Using Tables and Spreadsheets

4.1 Introduction

For systems with many options at every entry point or for an application with a large input space, a table approach is very effective for defining test cases. A table or its online equivalent, the spreadsheet, in which the columns and rows highlight input combinations, is one of the most commonly used tools for software testing. The term "spreadsheet" often implies a table that is manipulated by a computer tool, so we will use the more generic term "table".

Tables can take on many formats – there is no universal accepted format. The amount of information contained in the tables varies. In addition to describing the test cases, some tables contain additional information pertinent to test execution. If the tester records enough relevant information in a table, a programmer may use the table to fully reproduce a test that failed.

I'll use a simple dialog example to illustrate how to use tables for defining and documenting tests. With today's tools, almost no one would ever test a simple dialog to this level. However, I use this simple example to illustrate the concept of building test tables. Simple here, means that the number of possible input combinations is much smaller than that of a larger and more complex system, thus creating a somewhat smaller test table. I'll also present several shortcuts for documenting the tests, each of which affect the amount of information provided.

Chapter 5 shows how to use tables for other applications such as state transition diagrams, image processing, as well as other aspects of software testing including unit testing, test tracking, and scheduling.

Tables tend to become large and many tools will help the tester automate some tasks. Regardless of whether software tools are used, tables serve a very important role in software testing. The objectives of this chapter are to:

- convey an understanding of how testers use tables;
- convey an understanding of how developers can interpret information in tables;
- help educate development managers and program managers about the magnitude of the testing task;
- help guide a tester working under tight deadlines or when a tool will cost more than just doing the testing;

- illustrate methods for avoiding tedious and repetitive tasks;
- provide guidance on creating tables manually when tools are not available.

I'll discuss some examples.

4.2   Sample application

An application with a graphical user interface (GUI) has a vast number of options that a user can enter at every input field. This quickly translates into a very large number of test cases. With today's technology, many tools automate GUI testing by generating virtually all possible keystrokes and managing the associated attributes. The new tester, however, may not have the luxury of incorporating tools or may not understand the concepts behind testing interfaces. Let us examine one aspect of a GUI, the dialog box.

Consider the following simple dialog box in Figure 4.1. The user types a username and a password, and then hits either the OK button to accept the input or the CANCEL button to abort the dialog. This example is simple for two reasons. First, there are only two input fields and two buttons, and second, we will ignore the attributes associated with each GUI input field.

The goal of this example is to illustrate methods for defining tests involving user input and for tracking related information. With this example, we start by showing the rapid growth in the number of tests and then present methods for managing the sheer volume of tests.

Figure 4.1 Sample dialog box

The focus (current cursor position) can be in one of four locations, each of which must respond correctly to every keystroke based on its context. For example, typing in an alphanumeric key while in the username field results in displaying the newly entered character, whereas typing the same keystroke sequence with the focus on the OK button usually causes the application to ignore the keystroke.

The user can type in a wide range of possible keystrokes, both valid and invalid, at every entry point. The number of possible keystrokes varies according to the type of keyboard in use. Consider a common keyboard with 88 different keys. This allows for more than 600 different keystroke combinations for every input field in the GUI. This value comes from adding up the following combinations:

- 88 different keys – this includes 26 lower case letters, 10 numbers, 12 symbols or punctuation, 12 function keys, and 28 other keys (such as ENTER, INSERT, HOME, PAGE UP, UP ARROW, SHIFT, CONTROL);

- 87 SHIFT combinations – the SHIFT key can be used in conjunction with the remaining 87 keys, some of which result in generating upper case letters and other punctuation;

- 87 CONTROL combinations – the CONTROL key can be used with the 87 other keys;

- 87 ALT combinations – likewise, the ALT key can be used with the 87 other keys;

- 86 CONTROL+SHIFT combinations – there are 86 possible three-key combinations that use the CONTROL, SHIFT, and a third key simultaneously;

- 86 ALT+SHIFT combinations – another common three-key combination is ALT+SHIFT;

- 86 CONTROL+ALT combinations – another common three-key combination is CONTROL+ALT.

Some keystrokes cause different actions depending upon the system's prior state. One example is the space character, in which leading spaces are ignored but spaces after another character are significant. The operating system often determines the behavior of many multi-key combinations, such as the CONTROL+s sequence that saves the current information to a file. This example doesn't even take into account other two-key and three-key combinations nor the context in which the keystroke is entered. To keep this example somewhat manageable, we will limit the two- and three-keystroke options to those most commonly used and exclude operating system considerations. Naturally in a real testing situation, a judgment call must be made as to what types of keystrokes to test. Regardless of the total set of keystroke combinations to be scrutinized, it quickly becomes apparent that all these keystroke options translate into a massive number of test cases.

A table easily maps the input fields to the list of possible keystrokes. A portion of this table is shown in Table 4.1. Limiting the calculation to the more common two- and three-keystroke combinations, a full table has over 600 columns. Even though the two-keystroke combination SHIFT+a is equivalent to uppercase A, the table header lists this as the actual keystroke sequence.

Table 4.1 Listing all possible keystrokes for a dialog box

Next keystroke / Current cursor location	a	b	...	z	0	1	...	9	SHIFT+a	SHIFT+b	...	SHIFT+z	SHIFT+0	...	SHIFT+9	CONTROL+a	CONTROL+a
username field																	
password field																	
OK button																	
CANCEL button																	

Listing all the possible keystrokes generates a huge table. Despite the size factor, there are advantages to this:

1. For novice testers, the exercise of creating a large table illustrates the magnitude of the testing effort.
2. A large table will educate naïve managers – especially those whose short-sighted project planning allocates insufficient time to the testing effort.
3. If a tester is bewildered about where to begin, actually listing all input combinations in a table ignites ideas that then act as a guide down a more productive path.
4. Testers greatly appreciate the benefits acquired by using a test tool.

Fortunately, several methods exist to reduce the table size. Part of the tester's job is to reduce the number of test cases intelligently. The next section presents an approach for identifying redundancies in the test table. Chapter 8 presents even more methods for reducing the number of tests. Since the scope of this book is to help those struggling to get started, let's first examine several methods of documenting tests using tables.

4.3   Documenting test cases

In its raw form, a test table is a matrix that lists the types of possible starting points or initial conditions in the leftmost column and the types of actions to perform across the top. Each cell in the matrix, where a column and row intersect, depicts a separate test case.

Figure 4.2 shows a generic test case table, whose format is that of a state table (see section 5.2 for a description of state tables). Each row represents the various prompts where a user can enter data, and the columns indicate the types of possible user input. Thus, each cell in the table maps a prompt with an input sequence. For example, the highlighted test case, number 34, requires placing the application-

...	CONTROL+z	CONTROL+0	...	CONTROL+9	CONTROL+SHIFT+a	CONTROL+SHIFT+b	...	CONTROL+SHIFT+z	CONTROL+SHIFT+0	...	CONTROL+SHIFT+9	ENTER	TAB	BACKSPACE	DELETE	HOME	Left arrow	Right arrow	Down arrow	Up arrow	...

under-test into the state specified by prompt 3 and then performing the action indicated by input 4. To complete the test case definition, the tester must describe the expected results. The amount of information in each cell varies significantly. The rest of this chapter illustrates different methods for documenting the test cases. When the test is actually performed and the system's behavior is observed, then the tester can evaluate the actual outcome.

Action / Initial state	Input 1	Input 2	Input 3	**Input 4**	Input 5	Input 6
Prompt 1	test case 11	test case 12	test case 13	test case 14	test case 15	test case 16
Prompt 2	test case 21	test case 22	test case 23	test case 24	test case 25	test case 26
Prompt 3	test case 31	test case 32	test case 33	**test case 34**	test case 35	test case 36
Prompt 4	test case 41	test case 42	test case 43	test case 44	test case 45	test case 46
Prompt 5	test case 51	test case 52	test case 53	test case 54	test case 55	test case 56
Prompt 6	test case 61	test case 62	test case 63	test case 64	test case 65	test case 66

Figure 4.2 A table of test cases

Different types of information, such as expected results, actual results, pass/fail status, and even a reference to the problem reporting system, can be recorded in the test tables, as described in the next section. Each method satisfies a particular criterion and can apply to different situations.

4.3.1   Documentation approaches

As stated earlier, a table maps the initial conditions to the different input options. In the dialog box example, the leftmost column of the test table lists the initial conditions, which in this case consists of the two input fields and two buttons. The columns across the top enumerate the various possible keystrokes. Depending on the table's format, the cells in the table represent either an individual test case or a collection of related test cases. To complete the test case, one must define the expected results and provide space to record the actual results and pass/fail status. There are several ways to record this information. All tables shown in this section can be used independently; one format is no better than the other and each has advantages and disadvantages.

The following sample tables illustrate various documentation methods for recording testing of the dialog box. Recall that Table 4.1 contains over 600 columns, so in the name of brevity, the sample tables contain a few columns of interest to illustrate the various methods of recording test case information.

Each table format emphasizes different levels of information. Table formats #2 and #4 introduce concepts specifically related to software testing.

Table format #1	Provide a very brief description of the expected results.
Table format #2	Use boundary value analysis to describe different input conditions.
Table format #3	Document thorough test descriptions in a separate document and reference these in the test table.
Table format #4	Use equivalence class partitioning to combine the inputs that produce similar results.
Table format #5	Define the initial condition, input, and expected results as separate lines in a test case table.

So, which type of table should you use? There is no single right answer. Table format selection depends on which layout is more obvious to the tester and the amount of information that must be present. Some table formats record enough information to enable a tester or programmer to reproduce a failed test. Software test cases are customized for each application-under-test, so it is inevitable that whatever testing approach you use reflects the application's unique peculiarities. In other words, use whatever format best documents and conveys the necessary information both for posterity and for communication with the development team.

Even though a table format is fairly compact, it may be necessary to further condense the amount of information recorded. As with using test outlines, several shortcuts exist for using the test tables. The type of shortcut to employ depends on whether the tester must track input, expected outcome, actual results, or pass/fail status. Section 4.3.2 describes these documentation shortcuts. But first, let's explore different methods for using test tables.

Table format #1

Method: Provide a very brief description of the expected results

One method for test case documentation consists of filling in each cell with the expected results, as shown in Table 4.2. Most of the notation in the table is specific to the application-under-test.

To complete this table, we make some assumptions about the GUI's expected behavior, which must then be confirmed by the developers. The notation in each cell is as follows:

- for brevity, "add b" means that the tester types in the character *b* in the designated field as the rightmost character of the existing input sequence;
- when adding a valid character to the password field, the system responds by echoing an asterisk (*) rather than echoing the input character;
- writing "no change" in a cell indicates that no change takes place – whether visible to the user or internal to the system;
- "error" means that we expect the application to respond with an error message.

Where appropriate, a brief description of other behavior is noted. For example,

- typing the invalid character '#' in the username or password field generates an error;
- hitting the ENTER key results in different actions depending on the position of the active input form;
- the TAB key causes the cursor to move to another region in the dialog box;
- when invoked from the username or password field, the BACKSPACE key erases the previous character.

The latter test is not clearly defined because which character is erased depends on the current cursor placement, and then no indication is given about having an empty field.

Advantages: This provides a checklist for trying out each possible input combination. Each cell maps to a specific test case.

Disadvantages: The specific initial condition is not defined, thus violating the test case criterion of providing unambiguous input. In many situations, the expected results depends upon the GUI's prior state. Consider the test that says to "type the letter k". It is not clear whether k is the first character of an empty field or whether it is appended to the previously entered characters. How will the application react when the tester exceeds the maximum number of characters? By omitting the information describing the initial configuration, different testers will most likely type in different keystrokes for the input fields. Unless the tester records the input state prior to typing in the designated keystroke, the test will not be reproducible.

Table 4.2 Table format #1: recording a brief description

Next keystroke / Input field	a	b	Shift+a	Shift+b	1	#	ENTER	TAB	BACKSPACE	DELETE	HOME	Left arrow	...
username field	add a	add b	add A	add B	add 1	error: invalid char	process username/password	move to password field	erase char at left	erase char at right	move to start of username field	move one char to left	
password field	add *	add *	add *	add *	add *	error: invalid char	process username/password	move to OK button	erase char at left	erase char at right	move to start of password field	move one char to left	
OK button	no change	no change	no change	no change	no change	no change	process username/password	move to CANCEL button	no change	no change	no change	no change	
CANCEL button	no change	no change	no change	no change	no change	no change	exit window	move to username field	no change	no change	no change	no change	

Table format #2

Method: Use boundary value analysis to describe different input conditions

To address some of the limitations found in Table format #1, we can expand the test case table to contain test input conditions that take into account a field's different initial states. Common testing tactics use a concept known as *boundary value analysis*, in which special attention is paid to values at or near a boundary. Boundary value analysis is used extensively when testing numerical ranges, mathematical calculations, buffer sizes, and any feature affected by some type of limit. The typical tests defined at a boundary consist of these three conditions:

- boundary value;
- boundary value − 1;
- boundary value +1.

Applying boundary value analysis to a bounded range (which includes both lower and upper boundaries) results in the following test conditions:

- minimum;
- minimum − 1;
- minimum + 1;
- maximum;
- maximum − 1;
- maximum + 1.

Testers often add another test case:

- a "middle" or "typical" value

for good measure.

This last test is redundant if you account for equivalence class partitioning (as described in Table format #4). In the GUI example, for instance, the application displays the same behavior whether there are 1, 2, 3, or up to maximum−1 number of characters in the username field. However, many programmers and managers inexperienced with testing often mandate that a test case use a "typical" value. It is often easier to create a new test case that pleases the non-testers than it is to waste time arguing that the test is redundant. [Kaner99], [Myers76], and [Myers79] provide more information on boundary value analysis, and [Kit95] provides a detailed example.

Another analysis technique states that many of the seven test conditions listed above are redundant and that as few as three or four test cases are sufficient for verifying boundary correctness. Those interested in such analysis should read up on domain testing in [Beizer90], [Beizer95], and [Binder00]. For now, we are more interested in having a general approach for defining tests, and we proceed with applying boundary value analysis.

In the dialog box example, username and password fields have a minimum and maximum number of allowable characters. Table 4.3 shows how boundary value analysis applies here.

Table 4.3 Applying boundary value analysis to the dialog box example

Boundary value condition	Initial state of username or password field	Expected results after typing in an additional character
minimum	0 characters, an "empty field"	1 character in the field
minimum − 1	It is not possible to specify a field size with −1 characters.	*not possible*
minimum + 1	1 character in the field	2 characters in the field
maximum	"maximum number of characters", even if we do not yet know what that maximum value is.	Application ignores the extra characters. No error message is displayed. Note: This situation actually tests the "max + 1" condition.
maximum − 1	"maximum−1 number of characters"	maximum number of characters in the field
maximum + 1	The dialog box example will not allow us to enter characters that exceed the allowable maximum.	*not possible*
typical value	"min+2 through max−2" characters Not knowing what a "typical" value is, the test will specify the number of characters not included in the prior tests.	Application accepts the new character.

Depending on the application, not every boundary value condition translates into a feasible test case. The tests shown in Table 4.4 (on pp. 84–85) specify five test conditions that exercise the lower and upper field size limits. As a result of applying boundary value analysis, the table has increased in size. Table format #4 presents a technique to further reduce the total number of test cases.

Although Table 4.4 now has provisions for testing behavior on empty, partially filled, and maximum field sizes, it still lacks a complete description of an input field's initial configuration. For example, what are the current characters when the username field is at maximum size? Some of the keystrokes, such as BACKSPACE and DELETE, produce different results based on the cursor's location relative to a non-empty field. For tests that produce errors, the expected results are not clear. How is the error processed? Does the application produce an audible sound, open an error dialog, post an error message, or just ignore the offending keystroke?

These tests focus more on the username and password format. Although not related to boundary value analysis, we define additional tests to account for the validity of username and password pairs, creating four new categories under the OK and CANCEL buttons:

● empty username field;

● empty password field;

- invalid username and password pair (we do not specify which component is invalid);
- valid username and password pair.

Advantages: Separate conditions exist for addressing empty, partial, and full fields, and also valid and invalid username/password pairs. This table serves as a handy checklist of different tests to execute.

Disadvantages: Most of the tests are ambiguous and so cannot be reproduced, due to incomplete descriptions of expected and actual results. For example, when there is already one character in the username field, we do not know what the previous character is. We do not know what username and password pair is being processed. When hitting the BACKSPACE, DELETE, or arrow keys, we do not know the cursor's precise position within a non-empty field.

Most of the tables shown up to now provide general input and output information. A complete test case, by definition, includes an unambiguous input specification and a description of expected behavior. Although the prior examples are remiss on their input descriptions, they nonetheless provide checklists for recording the types of test cases to execute. The next three table formats provide for more complete test case descriptions.

Table format #3

Method: Document thorough test descriptions in a separate document and reference these in the test table

The level of information for expected results can only be precise when unambiguous input conditions are specified. Table 4.5 shows another approach, in which each cell references a thorough test case description that is documented elsewhere. This method has the added advantage that it can be used as an index into separate test case documents. Test case description documents are notorious for being very big, thus having a handy reference to quickly determine where each test fits into the larger scheme is of great value to other readers. The test case identifiers shown in Table 4.5 each contain a prefix that helps group similar tests together.

The amount of information contained in a test case can vary widely. Consider various possibilities for the test tc-402, which, according to the information in Table 4.5, adds the character "a" to the username field that already contains the character "g". Figure 4.3 on p. 87 shows one possible description for this test, which defines the contents of the dialog box prior to typing in the character "a", and it also describes the expected results. The empty portions of the test case will be filled in upon test execution. This test case is not necessarily bad, yet it does not specify *where* to insert the second character "a". This is imprecise and leaves room for interpretation: two different people may execute this test case and achieve different results. One test results in the characters "ga" appearing in the

Table 4.4 Table format #2: more specific input conditions

Current input state		a	b	Shift+a	Shift+b	1	#	ENTER	TAB	BACKSPACE	DELETE	HOME	Left arrow	...
username field	empty field	add a	add b	add A	add B	add 1	error: invalid char	error: missing username	move to password field	no change	no change	no change	no change	
	one character in field	add a	add b	add A	add B	add 1	error: invalid char	process username/ password	move to password field	erase char at left	erase char at right	move to start of username field	move one char to left	
	2 through max–2 characters	add a	add b	add A	add B	add 1	error: invalid char	process username/ password	move to password field	erase char at left	erase char at right	move to start of username field	move one char to left	
	max–1 characters in field	add a	add b	add A	add B	add 1	error: invalid char	process username/ password	move to password field	erase char at left	erase char at right	move to start of username field	move one char to left	
	max characters in field	ignore char: no change	ignore char: no change	ignore char: no change	ignore char: no change	ignore char: no change	error: invalid char	process username/ password	move to password field	erase char at left	erase char at right	move to start of username field	move one char to left	
password field	empty field	add *	add *	add *	add *	add *	error: invalid char	error: missing password	move to OK button	no change	no change	no change	no change	
	one character in field	add *	add *	add *	add *	add *	error: invalid char	process username/ password	move to OK button	erase char at left	erase char at right	move to start of password field	move one char to left	
	2 through max–2 characters	add *	add *	add *	add *	add *	error: invalid char	process username/ password	move to OK button	erase char at left	erase char at right	move to start of password field	move one char to left	
	max–1 characters in field	add *	add *	add *	add *	add *	error: invalid char	process username/ password	move to OK button	erase char at left	erase char at right	move to start of password field	move one char to left	
	max characters in field	ignore char: no change	ignore char: no change	ignore char: no change	ignore char: no change	ignore char: no change	error: invalid char	process username/ password	move to OK button	erase char at left	erase char at right	move to start of password field	move one char to left	

Table 4.4 *continued*

Current input state		a	b	Shift+a	Shift+b	1	#	ENTER	TAB	BACKSPACE	DELETE	HOME	Left arrow	...
OK button	username field is empty	no change	no change	no change	no change	no change	no change	error: missing username	move to CANCEL button	no change	no change	no change	no change	
	password field is empty	no change	no change	no change	no change	no change	no change	error: missing password	move to CANCEL button	no change	no change	no change	no change	
	invalid username/ password pair	no change	no change	no change	no change	no change	no change	error: invalid username/ password	move to CANCEL button	no change	no change	no change	no change	
	valid username/ password pair	no change	no change	no change	no change	no change	no change	process username/ password	move to CANCEL button	no change	no change	no change	no change	
CANCEL button	username field is empty	no change	no change	no change	no change	no change	no change	exit window	move to username field	no change	no change	no change	no change	
	password field is empty	no change	no change	no change	no change	no change	no change	exit window	move to username field	no change	no change	no change	no change	
	invalid username/ password pair	no change	no change	no change	no change	no change	no change	exit window	move to username field	no change	no change	no change	no change	
	valid username/ password pair	no change	no change	no change	no change	no change	no change	exit window	move to username field	no change	no change	no change	no change	

Table 4.5 Table format #3: referencing test cases

Current input state	Next keystroke	a	b	Shift+a	Shift+b	1	#	ENTER	TAB	BACKSPACE	DELETE	HOME	Left arrow	...
username field	empty field	tc-401	tc-419	tc-501	tc-519	n-601	nim-1	tc-200	tc-218	bb-32	sh-82	sh-90	nas-1	
	one character in field	tc-402	tc-420	tc-502	tc-520	n-602	nim-2	tc-201	tc-219	bb-33	sh-83	sh-91	nas-2	
	2 through max-2 characters	tc-403	tc-421	tc-503	tc-521	n-603	nim-3	tc-202	tc-220	bb-34	sh-84	sh-92	nas-3	
	max-1 characters in field	tc-404	tc-422	tc-504	tc-522	n-604	nim-4	tc-203	tc-221	bb-35	sh-85	sh-93	nas-4	
	max characters in field	tc-405	tc-423	tc-505	tc-523	n-605	nim-5	tc-204	tc-222	bb-36	sh-86	sh-94	nas-5	
password field	empty field	tc-406	tc-424	tc-506	tc-524	n-606	nim-6	tc-205	tc-223	bb-37	sh-87	sh-95	nas-6	
	one character in field	tc-407	tc-425	tc-507	tc-525	n-607	nim-7	tc-206	tc-224	bb-38	sh-88	sh-96	nas-7	
	2 through max-2 characters	tc-408	tc-426	tc-508	tc-526	n-608	nim-8	tc-207	tc-225	bb-39	sh-89	sh-97	nas-8	
	max-1 characters in field	tc-409	tc-427	tc-509	tc-527	n-609	nim-9	tc-208	tc-226	bb-40	sh-72	sh-98	nas-9	
	max characters in field	tc-410	tc-428	tc-510	tc-528	n-610	nim-10	tc-209	tc-227	bb-41	sh-73	sh-99	nas-10	
OK button	username field is empty	tc-411	tc-429	tc-511	tc-529	n-611	nim-11	tc-210	tc-228	bb-42	sh-74	sh-100	nas-11	
	password field is empty	tc-412	tc-430	tc-512	tc-530	n-612	nim-12	tc-211	tc-229	bb-43	sh-75	sh-101	nas-12	
	invalid username/ password pair	tc-413	tc-431	tc-513	tc-531	n-613	nim-13	tc-212	tc-230	bb-44	sh-76	sh-102	nas-13	
	valid username/ password pair	tc-414	tc-432	tc-514	tc-532	n-614	nim-14	tc-213	tc-231	bb-45	sh-77	sh-103	nas-14	
CANCEL button	username field is empty	tc-415	tc-433	tc-515	tc-533	n-615	nim-15	tc-214	tc-232	bb-46	sh-78	sh-104	nas-15	
	password field is empty	tc-416	tc-434	tc-516	tc-534	n-616	nim-16	tc-215	tc-233	bb-47	sh-79	Sh-105	nas-16	
	invalid username/ password pair	tc-417	tc-435	tc-517	tc-535	n-617	nim-17	tc-216	tc-234	bb-48	sh-80	sh-106	nas-17	
	valid username/ password pair	tc-418	tc-436	tc-518	tc-536	n-618	nim-18	tc-217	tc-235	bb-49	sh-81	sh-107	nas-18	

username field while another test generates "ag". The revised test case in Figure 4.4 not only specifies where to place the cursor, but it also tests the insertion capability by detailing two methods for executing the test.

Until now, I have not specified the amount of detail contained in a test case. Some traditional testers may argue that a single test case must describe one unique testing scenario and thus take offense at a test case with multiple parts. At this point, our goal is to get the tests defined and produce some kind of "cookbook" for running tests. The fact that someone specifies *what* to test is a feat in itself, provided that the criteria of specifying unambiguous input and expected results are satisfied. How the information is packaged is an individual decision. If this is a major issue with your organization, find out whether any company guidelines exist on the granularity of test case documentation.

Advantages: This table format provides an index into separate test case documents. This intuitive index helps convey how each referenced test case fits into the overall testing scheme. Enough details can be written so that each test case description is complete and unambiguous.

Disadvantages: There is no guarantee that the test cases are thorough. Whether the referenced test cases are unambiguous and repeatable depends on the tester's ability to define complete test cases.

Identification

    Test case ID: *tc-402*   Software version: _____

    Subsystem: *username field tests*   Operating system: _____

    Tester's name: _____   Date of test: _____

Initial setup

    1. *Bring up the Login dialog box*
    2. *Place the character "g" in the username field*
    3. *Make sure that all other input fields are empty*

Input

    1. *Place the cursor in the username field*
    2. *Type the character "a"*

Expected results

    The characters "ga" appear in the username field

Actual results   ☐ Pass ☐ Fail

Figure 4.3 A sample test case

Identification

    Test case ID: _tc-402_   Software version: _____

    Subsystem: _username field tests_   Operating system: _____

    Tester's name: _____   Date of test: _____

Initial setup

1. *Bring up the Login dialog box*
2. *Place the character "g" in the username field*
3. *Make sure that all other input fields are empty*

Input

Part A
1. *Place cursor <u>after</u> the "g" in the username field*
2. *Type the character "a"*

Part B
(Return to initial setup condition)
1. *Place cursor <u>before</u> the "g" in the username field*
2. *Type the character "a"*

Expected results

Part A
The characters "ga" appear in the username field

Part B
The characters "ag" appear in the username field

Actual results   ☐ Pass ☐ Fail

Figure 4.4 A sample test case with several parts

Table format #4

Method: Use equivalence class partitioning to combine the inputs that produce similar results

In the dialog box example, the reader is probably wondering why there are separate test cases for each alphanumeric keystroke when it is obvious that the behavior will be the same. For example, if the username field is empty, does it really matter whether the first character entered is the letter "a", "b" or "w"? The application behaves the same. Likewise, one expects the same response when trying to type an extra character into a field already at its maximum length. This concept, in which different input values yield similar results, is known as *equivalence class partitioning*.

Table 4.6 makes use of equivalence classes by merging columns and rows that exercise similar conditions, thereby reducing the size of the table and the number of

Table 4.6 Using equivalence classes to combine similar columns and rows

Current input state		Next keystroke: Lower case letter	Upper case letter	Number	Valid symbol	Invalid symbol	ENTER	TAB	BACKSPACE	DELETE	HOME	Arrow keys	...
username field	empty field												
	one through max–1 characters												
	max characters in field												
password field	empty field												
	one through max–1 characters												
	max characters in field												
OK button	missing username or password												
	invalid username/ password pair												
	valid username/ password pair												
CANCEL button													

test cases. In this particular example, three different types of equivalence classes apply:

- similar keystrokes;
- current state of username and password fields;
- the CANCEL function.

In the first type of partition, we combine keystrokes producing similar results. One equivalence class contains all the individual lower case letters, while another contains all the upper case letters. One could argue that the input for the sample dialog box application is not case sensitive, thus one equivalence class comprising both lower and upper case letters is sufficient. One could further argue that all alphanumeric input behaves the same and combine all lower case, upper case, and numerals into one large category. Whether alphanumeric input is partitioned into one, two, or three equivalence classes is a decision based upon the application's specific functionality.

Different operating systems and implementations may have different conventions when mapping keys to buttons. In a typical Windows application, for example, typing the characters "c" or "C" when the focus is on the CANCEL button would result in the application closing the window. Likewise, typing "o" or "O" when the focus is on the OK button causes the application to process the username and password. In such a situation, the tester could either define separate equivalence classes for "c" and "C" and for "o" and "O", or combine all alphanumeric characters together but note that these particular characters function the same as the ENTER and SPACE keys when the focus is on the CANCEL or OK button respectively. Since this chapter seeks to illustrate different table formats, all alphanumeric characters are viewed as one equivalence class.

Symbols and other punctuation marks are now grouped into valid and invalid categories, and the contents of each category must be defined. In the dialog box example, the requirements would indicate that valid usernames contain the characters -, _, $, !, &, and ~, which would then make the following characters invalid: @, #, %, *, ^, ", (,), [,], {, }, /, ?, <, >, and other characters appearing on the keyboard. Valid characters for passwords may differ from those for the username. The valid and invalid character set must be defined in the application's requirements.

Some equivalence classes contain only one keystroke, such as the TAB key that causes the focus to jump to a different input field, and the backspace key that erases the previously entered character in the username and password fields.

It may also benefit the tester to create an auxiliary list of null-operator keystrokes, which fall into their own equivalence class. These are the keystrokes that cause no change and are thus ignored or thrown away by the system. This list may vary for each input condition, so that null-operator keystrokes for the username field may differ from those for the CANCEL button.

The second type of equivalence class partition finds that merging some of the rows in the table further reduces the input space for the dialog box example. When adding a new alphanumeric character in the username field, the dialog box application exhibits the same behavior whether there is one, two or three characters in that field. The behavior changes when the maximum number of allowable characters is exceeded. This creates three equivalence classes: one for an empty field, another for the maximum number of characters, and the third that contains any number of characters in between these two extremities. For the OK button category, the rows corresponding to empty usernames and passwords have been combined into one equivalence class called "missing username or password". This is different from the equivalence class "invalid username/password" where the username and password each contain some set of characters, but either the username or the password is incorrect.

The third and last equivalence class partition affects the CANCEL key. The associated tests no longer account for the contents of the username and password fields, because the behavior is to exit the dialog box. When issuing a CANCEL command, the tester must make sure that the username and password values are not updated or used in any way.

Filling in the rest of the table employs the same methods shown in the previous table formats. Table 4.7, in which all alphanumeric input has been combined into one equivalence class, displays various test notation methods by providing a general description of expected results for some tests and by referencing a comprehensive test case for those tests defined elsewhere. Another approach for using this table, which we present in section 4.3.2, is to record information acquired during and pertaining to test execution.

[Kaner99], [Kit95], and [Myers79] provide additional examples on equivalence class partitioning.

Advantages: Using equivalence class partitioning reduces the number of distinct test cases to identify those that truly exercise different features and behavior.

Disadvantages: The tester is still responsible for providing thorough information about the test cases. Simply using equivalence classes does not guarantee the existence of good tests.

Table format #5

Method: Define the initial condition, input, and expected results as separate lines in a test case table

Rather than use a matrix approach in which the rows and columns specify test conditions, we alter the table format so that each separate column describes a different input parameter and associated results. Table 4.8 specifies the initial state for each test case. The contents of the username and password fields are defined, as well as the placement of the cursor. The tester would then type in the keystroke indicated in the *Input* column and then record the actual results in the final column.

Advantages: By providing more detailed information about the contents of the dialog box's input fields, the descriptions are more complete and the tests can be reproduced.

Table 4.7 Table format #4: specifying expected test behavior when using equivalence classes

Current input state	Next keystroke	Alphanumeric key	Valid symbol	Invalid symbol	ENTER	TAB	BACKSPACE	DELETE	HOME	Arrow keys	...
username field	empty field	add char	add char	error: invalid char	tc-1100	move to password field	no change	d-37	no change	tc-567	
	one through max–1 characters	add char	add char	error: invalid char	tc-1101	move to password field	erase char at left	d-36	move to start of username field	tc-568	
	max characters in field	ignore char: no change	ignore char: no change	error: invalid char	tc-1102	move to password field	erase char at left	d-35	move to start of username field	tc-569	
password field	empty field	add char	add char	error: invalid char	tc-1103	move to OK button	no change	d-34	no change	tc-570	
	one through max–1 characters	add char	add char	error: invalid char	tc-1104	move to OK button	erase char at left	d-33	move to start of password field	tc-571	
	max characters in field	ignore char: no change	ignore char: no change	error: invalid char	tc-1105	move to OK button	erase char at left	d-32	move to start of password field	tc-572	
OK button	missing username or password	no change	no change	no change	error: missing username or password	move to CANCEL button	no change	no change	no change	no change	
	invalid username/ password pair	no change	no change	no change	error: invalid username/ password pair	move to CANCEL button	no change	no change	no change	no change	
	valid username/ password pair	no change	no change	no change	tc-1107	move to CANCEL button	no change	no change	no change	no change	
CANCEL button		no change	no change	no change	exit window	move to username field	no change	no change	no change	no change	

Table 4.8 Table format #5: each test case on a separate line

Test case ID	Initial state			Input	Expected results	Actual results
	username	password	cursor location			
tc-401	(empty)	(empty)	place cursor in username field	a	"a" appears in username field	
tc-402	m	(empty)	place cursor after "m" in username field	b	"mb" appears in username field	
tc-403	jasmine	(empty)	place cursor after "j" in username field	a	"jaasmine" appears in username field	
tc-404	joelouis	(empty)	place cursor at end of username field	2	ignore keystroke (maximum number of characters exceeded): no change	
tc-405	Fred	xyz88	place cursor after "d" in username field	#	error: system beeps once and posts "invalid character" in status line	

Disadvantages: The one-line approach makes it more difficult to determine what kind of test conditions are missing. Also, creating a table of this format does not guarantee that the tests will be well defined. By comparison, the matrix format provides the ability to quickly determine what type of condition is being tested. It is the tester's responsibility to provide adequate information to generate thorough test case descriptions.

4.3.2 Test documentation shortcuts

Most of the test tables presented thus far itemize the input options, and for some applications this is enough information to start executing tests. Similar to the test outline, one can get a general idea of what each test will exercise without having any additional information.

These tables assist in tracking vital test information, including test input, expected results, actual results, and test status. Using documentation shortcuts provides the means to include relevant information within the table structure. Shortcuts reduce the amount of information recorded for each test; shortcuts do *not* reduce the total number of test cases to execute.

To illustrate the different documentation approaches, we apply all of the shortcuts described to the tests shown in Table 4.9, which is a table that provides space for 90 test cases. Each shortcut records the test results consistently, so that the same test case in each shortcut method has the same status. Thus of the 90 test cases, four are in failed status and 12 have not been executed. The remaining test cases have passed. When using shortcuts, the test input descriptions are vague, and the expected results are absent. It is important that the tester has enough

Table 4.9 Test case results used to demonstrate the documentation shortcuts

Current cursor location	Next keystroke	Alphanumeric key	Valid symbol	Invalid symbol	ENTER	TAB	BACKSPACE	DELETE	HOME	Arrow keys	...
username field	empty field	passed	passed	passed	passed	passed	passed	not executed	passed	passed	
	one through max–1 characters	passed	passed	passed	passed	passed	passed	not executed	passed	passed	
	max characters in field	passed	passed	passed	passed	passed	passed	not executed	passed	passed	
password field	empty field	passed	passed	passed	passed	failed	passed	not executed	passed	passed	
	one through max–1 characters	passed	passed	passed	passed	passed	passed	not executed	passed	passed	
	max characters in field	passed	passed	passed	passed	passed	passed	not executed	passed	passed	
OK button	missing username or password	passed	passed	passed	passed	passed	passed	not executed	passed	passed	
	invalid username/ password pair	not executed	passed	not executed	passed	failed	failed	not executed	passed	passed	
	valid username/ password pair	passed	not executed	passed	passed	passed	passed	passed	passed	passed	
CANCEL button		passed	passed	passed	passed	passed	failed	not executed	passed	passed	

understanding about the system's behavior to judge whether the test has passed or failed. Selecting which shortcut to apply depends upon what type and how much information to record in each of the table's cells.

Shortcuts are not necessarily bad, when considering that any prior testing effort could have been haphazard, chaotic, undocumented, and non-repeatable. My philosophy is that some documentation is better than none and that this provides a suitable foundation for starting your test efforts and eventually improving your test process.

Each shortcut emphasizes different levels of details.

Shortcut #1	Check each box to indicate whether the test has passed or failed.
Shortcut #2	Record the keystrokes used to run the test.
Shortcut #3	Record the actual results.
Shortcut #4	Check off the tests that have passed and record the problem report number for failed tests.
Shortcut #5	Mix and match the record-keeping methods from the prior shortcuts by writing down whatever information is perceived as relevant.

Shortcut #1

Method: Check each box to indicate whether the test has passed or failed

In Table 4.10, each test that has passed is marked with a ✓ check. Failed tests are marked with a ✗ cross, and empty cells represent tests that have not been executed. Of course, other indicators, such as the words "pass" and "fail" can be used instead of the check and cross marks. This gives a quick glance as to which tests have been run.

If a test is re-executed, then the tester can overwrite the prior mark or color-code the results of subsequent tests.

Advantage: A record exists of what situations and conditions have been exercised. We can easily see which tests have passed and failed.

Disadvantage: No record exists of the actual input value used or of the expected and observed results. We cannot reproduce the test because we do not record the initial state and input keystrokes. There is also no clear specification of the expected results, thus pass/fail status is determined based on the tester's judgment.

Shortcut #2

Method: Record the keystrokes used to run the test

Table 4.11 tracks the keystroke information for every executed test. Some of the tests' input conditions, such as the alphanumeric keystrokes, are also recorded with more detail. For valid and invalid keystrokes, we'll use the list presented in Table format #4. Empty cells indicate tests that have not been executed.

Table 4.10 Shortcut #1: record pass/fail status

Current cursor location	Next keystroke	Alphanumeric key	Valid symbol	Invalid symbol	ENTER	TAB	BACKSPACE	DELETE	HOME	Arrow keys	...
username field	empty field	✓	✓	✓	✓	✓	✓		✓	✓	
	one through max–1 characters	✓	✓	✓	✓	✓	✓		✓	✓	
	max characters in field	✓	✓	✓	✓	✓	✓		✓	✓	
password field	empty field	✓	✓	✓	✓	✗	✓		✓	✓	
	one through max–1 characters	✓	✓	✓	✓	✓	✓		✓	✓	
	max characters in field	✓	✓	✓	✓	✓	✓		✓	✓	
OK button	missing username or password	✓	✓	✓	✓	✓	✓		✓	✓	
	invalid username/password pair		✓	✓	✓	✗	✗		✓	✓	
	valid username/password pair	✓		✓	✓	✓	✓	✓	✓	✓	
CANCEL button		✓	✓	✓	✓	✓	✗		✓	✓	

Table 4.11 Shortcut #2: record input keystrokes

Current cursor location	Next keystroke	Alphanumeric key	Valid symbol	Invalid symbol	ENTER	TAB	BACKSPACE	DELETE	HOME	Arrow keys	...
username field	empty field	a	$	@	ENTER	TAB	BACKSPACE		HOME	right	
	one through max–1 characters	B	-	?	ENTER	TAB	BACKSPACE		HOME	up	
	max–1 characters in field	2	|	%	ENTER	TAB	BACKSPACE		HOME	right	
password field	empty field	F	&	<	ENTER	TAB	BACKSPACE		HOME	up	
	one through max–1 characters	3	!	(	ENTER	TAB	BACKSPACE		HOME	down	
	max characters in field	i	~	@	ENTER	TAB	BACKSPACE		HOME	left	
OK button	missing username or password	n	$	[	ENTER	TAB	BACKSPACE		HOME	up	
	invalid username/ password pair		~		ENTER	TAB	BACKSPACE		HOME	down	
	valid username/ password pair	J		/	ENTER	TAB	BACKSPACE	DELETE	HOME	right	
CANCEL button		g	&	?	ENTER	TAB	BACKSPACE		HOME	down	

Information about failed tests can be recorded in an error log or in a problem reporting system.

Advantage: A record exists of the keystroke used to exercise each condition. If enough information is recorded, especially including the input fields' prior states, then the test can be reproduced.

Disadvantage: Pass/fail status for each test is not recorded in this table. Many tests do not indicate the fields' prior contents. There is no record of the observed results. Some tests cannot be reproduced due to insufficient information. For columns specifying only one keystroke, such as ENTER and BACKSPACE, echoing the keystroke typed does not convey any useful information, other than stating that the test was executed. There is no clear specification of the expected results, thus pass/fail status is determined based on the tester's judgment.

Shortcut #3

Method: Record the actual results

In Table 4.12, the tester records the results in various levels of detail. Each item under the invalid symbol states that an error occurred when entering the specified symbol. For tests in which an error message is expected, the results echo the error message posted by the application. When the application's response does not meet expectations, then the tag FAIL is recorded along with the actual results. There must be a distinction between an expected error message and actual application errors.

Advantage: There is a record of the actual results.

Disadvantage: There is no record of the input used, even though this information can sometimes be deduced from the recorded results. Some tests cannot be reproduced due to insufficient information, especially when the prior state is not specified. For example, hitting the left or right arrow keys will give different results depending upon the cursor's current position. Likewise, the DELETE key will only erase a character if the cursor is to the left of an existing character; no character is erased if the cursor is at the far right of an input field. As failed tests are not indicated, it is not clear whether the actual results match the expected results.

Shortcut #4

Method: Check off the tests that have passed and record the problem report number for failed tests

In Table 4.13, each test that has passed is marked with a check. Failed tests are recorded in the problem tracking system and a reference to the corresponding problem report is recorded in the test table. Empty cells represent tests that have not been executed. This gives the status of test execution at a glance.

Table 4.12 Shortcut #3: record the actual results

Current cursor location	Next keystroke	Alphanumeric key	Valid symbol	Invalid symbol	ENTER	TAB	BACKSPACE	DELETE	HOME	Arrow keys	...
username field	empty field	add a	add $	error @	error: missing username	move to password field	no change		no change	no change: right	
	one through max–1 characters	add B	add -	error ?	process username/ password	move to password field	erase previous char		move to start of field	no change: up	
	max characters in field	add 2	add _	error %	process username/ password	move to password field	erase previous char		move to start of field	move right	
password field	empty field	add F	add &	error ^	error: missing password	FAIL: move to CANCEL button	no change		no change	no change: up	
	one through max–1 characters	add 3	add !	error (	process username/ password	move to OK button	erase previous *		move to start of field	no change: down	
	max characters in field	add i	add ~	error @	process username/ password	move to OK button	erase previous *		move to start of field	move left	
OK button	missing username or password	no change: n	no change: $	no change: [	error: missing username		no change		no change	no change: up	
	invalid username/ password pair		no change: ~		error: invalid password	FAIL: focus does not change	FAIL: get "invalid symbol" message	no change	no change	no change: down	
	valid username/ password pair	no change: J		no change: /	accept username/ password	move to CANCEL button	no change		no change	no change: right	
CANCEL button		no change: g	no change: &	no change: ?	exit window	move to username field	FAIL: exit window		no change	no change: down	

Table 4.13 Shortcut #4: check off passed tests and show problem report for failed tests

Current cursor location	Next keystroke	Alphanumeric key	Valid symbol	Invalid symbol	ENTER	TAB	BACKSPACE	DELETE	HOME	Arrow keys	...
username field	empty field	✓	✓	✓	✓	✓	✓		✓	✓	
	one through max–1 characters	✓	✓	✓	✓	✓	✓		✓	✓	
	max characters in field	✓	✓	✓	✓	✓	✓		✓	✓	
password field	empty field	✓	✓	✓	✓	PR #221	✓		✓	✓	
	one through max–1 characters	✓	✓	✓	✓	✓	✓		✓	✓	
	max characters in field	✓	✓	✓	✓	✓	✓		✓	✓	
OK button	missing username or password	✓	✓	✓	✓	✓	✓		✓	✓	
	invalid username/ password pair		✓		✓	PR #103	PR #65		✓	✓	
	valid username/ password pair	✓		✓	✓	✓	✓	✓	✓	✓	
CANCEL button		✓		✓	✓	✓	PR #47		✓	✓	

Advantage: A record exists of what situations and conditions were exercised. The observed result for each failed test is recorded. It is easy to spot the tests that have not been executed.

Disadvantage: The test case table itself does not describe the input or the observed results. Tests that passed cannot be reproduced because the information pertaining to the initial state and input keystrokes are not tracked. However, information for failed tests is documented in the corresponding problem report, and there is a record of the associated input description – assuming that the problem report description is complete. There is also no clear specification of the expected results, thus pass/fail status is determined based on the tester's judgment.

Shortcut #5

Method: Mix and match the record-keeping methods from the prior shortcuts by writing down whatever information is perceived as relevant

The information captured is recorded in a variety of formats, which can include any of the following methods.

1. Test has not been executed:
   - cell is empty.
2. Test has passed:
   - mark with a ✓;
   - record the keystrokes used;
   - indicate prior condition;
   - record actual results.
3. Test has failed:
   - mark with a ✗;
   - record actual results only;
   - record expected and actual results;
   - reference a problem report number.

The level of information shown in Table 4.14 is not consistent. For some tests that have passed, the tester has placed a ✓ mark, whereas for others the actual results are recorded. Unless some guidelines have been established, the testers will not record test information consistently.

One method for indicating the prior state is to use notation such as "abc+d", which signifies that the field's previous content is "abc" and that the character "d" is added.

Advantage: Depending upon the tester's diligence, it may be possible to achieve thorough test documentation. It is possible to record enough information so that the tests can be reproducible. It is possible to quickly determine which tests have been executed.

Table 4.14 Shortcut #5: record relevant information

Current cursor location	Next keystroke	Alphanumeric key	Valid symbol	Invalid symbol	ENTER	TAB	BACKSPACE	DELETE	HOME	Arrow keys	...
username field	empty field	add a	add $	error :@	error: missing username	✓	✓		no change	no change: right	
	one through max–1 characters	prior name = george, cursor after 'r', type B	KAP + -	error: ?	username = W, password = test2	✓	first char = U, BACKSPACE erases U		move to start of field	no change: up	
	max characters in field	cursor before first char, type 2	add _	error: %	username = test1234, place cursor between 'st' characters	✓	cursor before first char, nothing to erase		move to start of field	move right	
						FAIL: active region moved to username instead of OK button					
password field	empty field	add F	add &	error: ^	error: missing password	✓	✓		no change	no change: up	
	one through max–1 characters	xyz + 3	add !	error: (	process username/ password	✓	first char = U BACKSPACE erases *		move to start of field	no change: down	
	max characters in field	SamSpade + i	add ~	error: @	process username/ password	✓	erase previous *		move to start of field	move left	
OK button	missing username or password	no change: n	no change: $	✓	error: missing username	✓	✓		no change	no change: up	
	invalid username/ password pair		no change: ~		error: invalid password	✗	✗		no change	no change: down	
	valid username/ password pair	no change: J		✓	accept username/ password	✓	✓	✓	no change	no change: right	
CANCEL button		no change: g	no change: &	✓	exit window	✓	✗		no change	no change: down	

Disadvantage: It is possible to short-change the amount of information recorded so that the tests cannot be reproduced. The inconsistent nature of recording information may make it difficult to assess the test status.

Up to this point, the test tables help to reveal most of the input combinations. We stop short of saying *all* input combinations for several reasons. First, it may be physically impossible to enumerate all possible test cases, especially when the combinatorics reveals an astronomical number of potential tests. Second, if a key category has been omitted from the table, whether by oversight or by choice, then the associated tests will not be included. Lastly, testers must never assume that *all* tests will ever be run, because of the sheer volume of tests or due to limited available time. This is as good a time as any to become acquainted with the reality that testers will *never* run each and every potential test case. Recognizing this harsh reality, it becomes more important to write well-defined and targeted tests. One tactic is to provide more detailed test cases so that the input is better defined.

4.3.3   Detailed test descriptions

Using the tables shown previously to document and record test execution circumvents true test case definition because they contain ambiguous input conditions. This creates the risk of being unable to reproduce a test in exactly the same way each time. A good test case must specify the test input, execution condition, and predicted results for an item to be tested [IEEE 610.12]. A complete test case must specify the before and after state of all data, whether this includes buffers, memory contents, data packets, screen dumps, or other entities that contain data. In a GUI environment, a complete test case definition describes the current state including the contents of all fields and any other defined states and variables. Consider all of these possible situations when entering the letter "a" on the username field.

- Is this field empty prior to typing in "a"?
- Does this field need to be purged to try the next test input?
- Is there a leading space?
- Is this test dependent upon data entered in a different dialog box?

Good test cases contain enough detail to alleviate all of this uncertainty. The test tables created earlier in this chapter provide a framework for developing more thorough tests by building a checklist of the input conditions that need to be exercised. Table 4.15 lists testing requirements from which we will build test cases for testing the dialog box example. Since each cell now defines a specific condition to test, let's regard this as a set of testing requirements and label each cell with the notation "TRQ-nn", where "TRQ" is an abbreviation for *test requirement*. As long as this identifier is unique, it doesn't matter what the prefix or value is, nor does it have to follow any particular order.

This type of table helps to implement traceability, by providing a mapping between test requirements and test cases. For example, we know from looking at

Table 4.15 A table of test requirements

Current input state	Next keystroke	Alphanumeric key	Valid symbol	Invalid symbol	ENTER	TAB
username field	empty field	TRQ-1	TRQ-11	TRQ-30	TRQ-45	TRQ-100
	one through max–1 characters	TRQ-2	TRQ-12	TRQ-31	TRQ-46	TRQ-101
	max characters in field	TRQ-3	TRQ-13	TRQ-32	TRQ-47	TRQ-102
password field	empty field	TRQ-4	TRQ-14	TRQ-33	TRQ-48	TRQ-103
	one through max–1 characters	TRQ-5	TRQ-15	TRQ-34	TRQ-49	TRQ-104
	max characters in field	TRQ-6	TRQ-16	TRQ-35	TRQ-50	TRQ-105
OK button	missing username or password	TRQ-7	TRQ-17	TRQ-36	TRQ-51	TRQ-106
	invalid username/password pair	TRQ-8	TRQ-18	TRQ-37	TRQ-52	TRQ-107
	valid username/password pair	TRQ-9	TRQ-19	TRQ-38	TRQ-53	TRQ-108
CANCEL button		TRQ-10	TRQ-20	TRQ-39	TRQ-54	TRQ-109

the table that the test requirement TRQ-200 exercises the event of hitting the BACKSPACE key in an empty username field. Any test case that references TRQ-34 signifies that the test places an invalid symbol in a non-empty password field that does not have the maximum number of characters. Referencing the test requirements becomes an integral part of the test case documentation, and it is the tester's responsibility to ensure that this reference is correct.

The next job is to define detailed tests containing many steps, each of which covers a particular test condition. These comprehensive test descriptions, or test procedures, contain a series of small test cases that must be executed successfully in a pre-determined order.

A test procedure, as defined by IEEE, "specifies the steps for executing a set of test cases or, more generally, the steps used to analyze a software item in order to evaluate a set of features" [IEEE 829]. Another way to think of this is to have a very detailed test scenario with multiple steps and intermediate results. The success of one internal step is necessary to proceed to the next step of the large test scenario. Thus a test case is a combination of specific input and expected results, whereas a test procedure is a list of many input steps each with intermediate expected results.

Usage of the terms *test case* and *test procedure* is inconsistent in current industry. Some people even use these terms interchangeably. If the distinction between these terms seems absurd, focus on the main goal: to provide clear input and expected results descriptions. As long as the tester and the organization are consistent with terminology, it doesn't matter what terms are used. Just as test approaches and documentation formats vary across organizations, so will the local vocabulary. Ideally, it would be helpful if all testers in the software industry could refer to a common definition. To resist offending any purist, I will use the term *test*. This coincides with the IEEE definition, which defines *test* as:

1. a set of one or more test cases;

BACKSPACE	DELETE	SPACE	F1	ALT+a	Null operator keystrokes	HOME	Arrow keys	...
TRQ-200	TRQ-210	TRQ-300	TRQ-310	TRQ-320	TRQ-330	TRQ-400	TRQ-500	
TRQ-201	TRQ-211	TRQ-301	TRQ-311	TRQ-321	TRQ-331	TRQ-401	TRQ-501	
TRQ-202	TRQ-212	TRQ-302	TRQ-312	TRQ-322	TRQ-332	TRQ-402	TRQ-502	
TRQ-203	TRQ-213	TRQ-303	TRQ-313	TRQ-323	TRQ-333	TRQ-403	TRQ-503	
TRQ-204	TRQ-214	TRQ-304	TRQ-314	TRQ-324	TRQ-334	TRQ-404	TRQ-504	
TRQ-205	TRQ-215	TRQ-305	TRQ-315	TRQ-325	TRQ-335	TRQ-405	TRQ-505	
TRQ-206	TRQ-216	TRQ-306	TRQ-316	TRQ-326	TRQ-336	TRQ-406	TRQ-506	
TRQ-207	TRQ-217	TRQ-307	TRQ-317	TRQ-327	TRQ-337	TRQ-407	TRQ-507	
TRQ-208	TRQ-218	TRQ-308	TRQ-318	TRQ-328	TRQ-338	TRQ-408	TRQ-508	
TRQ-209	TRQ-219	TRQ-309	TRQ-319	TRQ-329	TRQ-339	TRQ-409	TRQ-509	

2. a set of one or more test procedures;

3. a set of one or more test cases and procedures [IEEE 829].

The following example, which applies to the sample dialog box, shows the level of detail that some testers may use when specifying tests. For more complex systems, this type of approach may help guide and document a suitable testing approach. Regardless of the type or complexity of the application, the key concepts of specifying the input and intermediary results are the same.

Tables 4.16 to 4.18 each define detailed tests for the dialog box example. The structure of these tests is as follows:

Test procedure	This is a unique identifier. The prefix GT (short for *GUI Test*) is an arbitrary choice to identify this procedure as a dialog box test.
Initial setup	Define the dialog box's initial configuration either by describing the dialog box's contents or by directing the tester to run a special script that populates the dialog box to a known state.
Step	Label each individual part of the test procedure.
Test requirement	For traceability between the test table and the test procedure, state which test requirement is being exercised by this step.
Input	Describe the keystrokes to be entered by the tester.
Expected intermediary result	Describe the expected results from having entered the corresponding input.
Actual results	Having executed that step, indicate whether the test ran successfully. Record whatever unexpected behavior is observed.

These three test procedures vary in their initial setup. Table 4.16 starts with an empty dialog box and directs the user to place the cursor in a designated field. Table 4.17 requires that a script file be run in order to place the application in a known state. Table 4.18 is based upon successful completion of another test procedure. For the sake of defining the tests, we'll make the following assumptions about the dialog box example:

● the maximum number of characters in a field is 8;

● the username and password pair is valid for test procedure GT-410 but invalid for GT-411 and GT-412;

● the application posts an asterisk to echo password characters;

● ALT-a is a keyboard shortcut to move the focus to the password field.

All assumptions about a system must be documented and agreed to by the rest of the development team.

Table 4.16 A test procedure based on test cases for the dialog box example

Test procedure:	GT- 410			
Initial setup:	Start with empty dialog box. Place cursor in the username field.			
Step	Test requirement	Input	Expected intermediary result	Actual results
1	TRQ-1	Type: s	"s" appears in username field	
2	TRQ-2	Type: am	"sam" appears in username field	
3	TRQ-301	Type: space character	"sam " appears in username field	
4	TRQ-101	Hit TAB key	cursor moves to password field	
5	TRQ-4	Type: x	"*" appears in password field	
6	TRQ-5	Type: 5y	"***" appears in password field	
7	TRQ-334	Hit CTRL-A	no change	
8	TRQ-49	Hit ENTER key	username/password pair accepted	

In test procedure GT-411, the file init_user_list.scr is a script that sets up information about the usernames and passwords. The tester must execute this script prior to executing the test procedure.

Table 4.17 Another test procedure based on test cases for the dialog box example

Test procedure:	GT- 411			
Initial setup:	Run setup script `init_user_list.scr`			
Step	*Test requirement*	*Input*	*Expected intermediary result*	*Actual results*
1	TRQ-300	Type: space character	Cursor moves one space to right in username field	
2	TRQ-2	Type: J	" J" appears in username field	
3	TRQ-2	Type: oeq	" Joeq" appears in username field	
4	TRQ-311	Hit F1	Help window pops up	
5	—	Exit help window	Cursor at end of username field	
6	TRQ-501	Hit left arrow	Cursor moves one space left	
7	TRQ-211	Hit DELETE	" Joe" appears in username field	
8	TRQ-2	Type: smith	" Joesmith" appears in username field	
9	TRQ-3	Type: y	Character ignored: cannot exceed maximum number of characters	
10	TRQ-47	Hit ENTER key	Error message: missing password	
11	TRQ-322	Hit ALT-a	Cursor moves to password field	
12	TRQ-4 TRQ-5	Type: qwerty13	"********" appears in password field	
13	TRQ-6	Type: z	Character ignored: cannot exceed maximum number of characters	
14	TRQ-105	Hit TAB key	Focus moves to OK button	
15	TRQ-52	Hit ENTER key	Error message: invalid password	

In test procedure GT-412, the initial setup changes a user password to the value required to successfully run this test procedure. The tester must execute the test procedure GT-307 prior to executing GT-412.

Table 4.18 A third test procedure based on test cases for the dialog box example

Test procedure:	GT- 412			
Initial setup:	Execute test procedure GT-307			
Step	Test requirement	Input	Expected intermediary result	Actual results
1	TRQ-1	Type: 6	"6" appears in username field	
2	TRQ-2	Type: 8	"68" appears in username field	
3	TRQ-401	Hit HOME key	Cursor moves to beginning of username field	
4	TRQ-2	Type: L	"L68" appears in username field	
5	TRQ-101	Hit TAB key	Cursor moves to password field	
6	TRQ-103	Hit TAB key	Focus moves to OK button	
7	TRQ-106	Hit TAB key	Focus moves to CANCEL button	
8	TRQ-109	Hit TAB key	Cursor moves to end of username field	
9	TRQ-2 TRQ-3	Type: MILLER"	"L68MILLE" appears in username field; cannot exceed maximum number of characters	
10	TRQ-322	Hit ALT-a	Cursor moves to password field	
11	TRQ-323	Hit ALT-a	No change	
12	TRQ-4	Type: P	"*" appears in password field	
13	TRQ-5	Type: R	"**" appears in password field	
14	TRQ-104	Hit TAB key	Focus moves to OK button	
15	TRQ-37	Type: @	No change	
16	TRQ-18	Type: $	No change	
17	TRQ-52	Hit ENTER key	Error message: invalid password	

No industry standard format exists for test procedures. A tester may use any appropriate format as long as the necessary information is provided.

As the size of test specifications grows quickly into large sets of test documentation, being able to easily determine which tests execute which conditions becomes important. This is accomplished with a traceability matrix. By mapping the test requirement to the tests that exercise that specific condition, one can quickly determine which test to execute, which test to modify should a requirement change, and which condition has no associated test. Table 4.19, which is truncated, maps the test conditions identified for the dialog box example to the three existing test procedures. Additional examples of requirements mapping matrices can be found in [Hetzel88].

Table 4.19 A traceability matrix for mapping test requirements to test procedures

Test requirement	Test procedure		
	GT-410	GT-411	GT-412
TRQ-1	✓		✓
TRQ-2	✓	✓	✓
TRQ-3		✓	✓
TRQ-4	✓	✓	✓
TRQ-5	✓	✓	✓
TRQ-6		✓	
TRQ-7			
TRQ-8			

We have accomplished much by using test tables, from itemizing the types of input, to grouping similarities into equivalence classes, recording which tests have been executed, recording pass/fail results, and even cross-referencing test conditions to actual tests. These are all notable achievements that give a good start to documenting the testing effort. Although the tests help identify valid and invalid keystrokes to the dialog-under-test, this approach does not concentrate on fully testing the dialog box's syntax and attributes.

The first pass at defining tests for the dialog box example produces different types of tests. Some exercise user input by testing for acceptance of legal characters, others exercise the dialog box's functionality, such as moving from a password field to an OK button. The examples do not cover syntax testing, which focuses on the legal contents of each input field. True syntax testing can only be accomplished when the system's syntax is rigorously defined in strict notation, such as a regular expression. For information on syntax testing, consult [Beizer90] and [Marick95]. This chapter's goal is to provide the novice tester with a place to start, by defining tests that identify valid and invalid keystrokes. Pursuing the rigors of syntax testing will yield additional tests to our preliminary set of tests. Every test design method creates a set of test cases, some of which are unique to that method and others that duplicate tests created by other means. Thus, no one method will generate all possible tests.

4.3.4 Automated test case creation

Most testing groups will use a testing tool to facilitate and automate the tedious task of programming test cases. Understanding the underlying premises of testing software will help us use these tools better. Many commercial testing tools generate the input data, send them to the application-under-test, and automate test execution. Even though many of these tools may often store the test information internally without creating tables as shown in this chapter, be assured that similar information is used to determine the set of test cases. The use of tables and spreadsheets is a very effective tool for listing many of the test cases.

Although Chapter 9 presents more information about testing tools and automation, a few words here apply specifically to GUI testing tools. Many commercially available test tools can automate GUI testing, by generating virtually all keystrokes and checking the state of the corresponding results. Test tools can tell if something happens in response to a keystroke, but they cannot determine whether the right thing happened. The tester often verifies the results log generated by the test tool to ensure that the expected results are achieved. Because these tools execute tests quickly, it may not be worth the time to reduce the large set of tests. These tests typically run overnight and produce a summary report listing the test results. When the tester has access to tools, balance must be maintained between selecting a manageable number of tests that give a good understanding of the system's behavior and executing every possible conceivable test.

4.4   Summary

Tables, or spreadsheets, are vital documentation tools for testing software. Test information recorded in tables can include input combinations, expected outcome, actual outcome, and test status. Comparing the actual results to the expected results determines the test's status.

The test tables and matrices shown in this chapter capture a large amount of information. Similar to the test outline, test tables give an indication of what the test entails without providing all the necessary information to produce a complete test case. The tester, as well as the development team, can get a good idea of which tests to pursue.

A uniform table format does not exist as each organization records information differently. The core criterion is to record the information necessary to perform a good testing job and to document what has been done.

Tables are easy to implement. The use of spreadsheets is an easy way to create and alter test tables. In fact, spreadsheets are one of the best tools for documenting test cases, test results, and test status. Tables can serve multiple purposes depending on how they are used.

Tables emphasize input combinations. A test case matrix lists out most, and sometimes, all possible input combinations. The table lists the tests that need to be defined, created and executed. Testers can then decide the order in which to create the test cases, which can depend upon many factors, including:

● test priority;

● the order in which features are made available to testers;

● available product information necessary to further define tests;

● personal comfort: the tester defines tests for the features he knows the best;

● sample different features: the tester selects a few tests for each feature;

- if all else fails and you can't get to every test, pick random parts of the test table — such as all tests in one column, row, or select alternate cells in the table.

Whether all tests are to be executed is a judgment call. One of the goals of software testing is to reduce the maximal number of test cases to a more manageable number. Test tables can also provide an index of volumes for related test documentation by referencing the corresponding detailed test description. The versatility of tables and ease in which they convey information make them an integral part of testing.

5 Other Types of Tables

5.1 ## Introduction

Tables provide a useful means for documenting many types of information that relate to test case design as well as test execution. In addition to the tables described in Chapter 4 for GUI applications, this chapter explores how tables help to track and document test cases for other types of situations, including:

● applications described using state transition diagrams and state tables;
● applications requiring multiple input combinations;
● applications described using decision tables.

We'll also look at how tables track test-related information such as:

● test planning;
● traceability matrix;
● cross-reference matrix;
● test execution;
● test status.

In addition to examining tables, we'll evaluate test case effectiveness by using coverage analysis to monitor whether the test cases adequately exercise all significant parts of an application.

5.2 ## State machines

A state machine is a behavioral model whose outcome depends upon both previous and current input. A state transition diagram is a pictorial representation of a state machine. Its purpose is to depict the states that a system or component can assume, and it shows the events or circumstances that cause or result from a change from one state to another [IEEE 610.12].

Some state transition diagrams can illustrate complex feature behavior transformations within a system, interactions between objects, flow of logic within a module, and many other situations. A state transition diagram is also useful to model input that must be entered in a defined order, such as a parser, in which each successive keystroke traverses a sequence of states and where each state can be the same as the previous, a new state in the sequence, or an error state. Internal processing can also take place when receiving each new input.

A state transition diagram and its companion table, the state transition table (or state table, for short), contain information that readily converts into test cases. The approach consists of transforming a state transition diagram into a state table, analyzing the state table for completeness, and then creating the corresponding test cases. To demonstrate the use of state transition diagrams as input to testing, we will develop test cases for a stopwatch. The stopwatch can be the entire application or it could be a unit within a larger system. We will treat it as a self-contained feature.

The state transition diagram for the stopwatch consists of three states and the interfaces contains three inputs and one output. Each of the three inputs is an event that affects the system. The interface description is as follows:

Input

START   continue to increment elapsed time from the currently displayed time. The time value increases once every second.

STOP   stop incrementing the elapsed time and display the last time value.

RESET   reset the current time to 0.

Output

Time   current time value.

The state transition diagram in Figure 5.1 depicts the stopwatch's behavior and shows the relations between the inputs and the states. The diagram's circles represent the stopwatch's states, and the arrows represent the transition from one state to another. Each arrow provides two pieces of information. The first value denotes

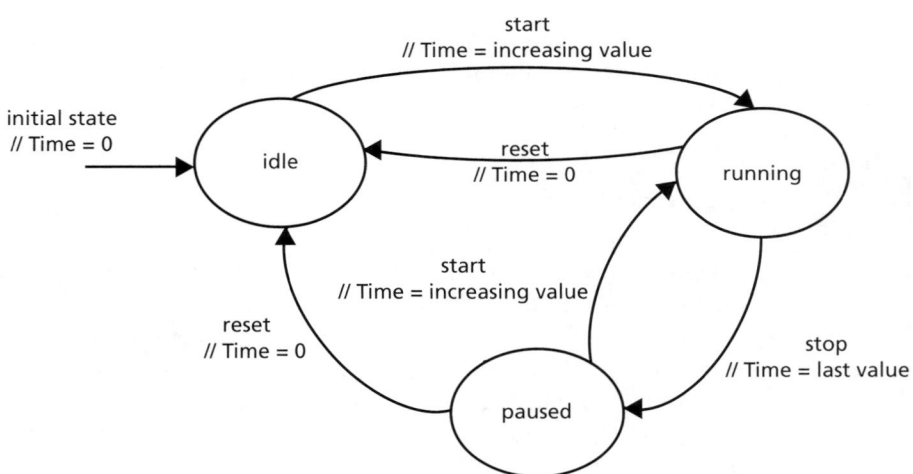

Figure 5.1 State transition diagram illustrating a stopwatch's behavior

the event that causes the transition to occur. The second expression, as denoted by the "//"notation, defines the resulting action that takes place. In this case, certain events affect the time value.

To illustrate a transition in the example, if the stopwatch is currently in the idle state and the user enters the START command, then the stopwatch shifts to the running state and the time variable changes incrementally to reflect elapsed time. The stopwatch remains in the running state until the user triggers another event that causes a change.

The state table in Table 5.1 shows a different representation of the same information contained in Figure 5.1. The first column lists all of the possible events, and the other column headers list all the possible states. A cell represents how each event affects each state. The number in the lower right corner of each cell is a label that identifies the cell. This number will be referenced in upcoming tables to map a test case back to its source.

Table 5.1 State table representation of the state transition diagram

State / Event	Idle	Running	Paused
START	Running // Time = increasing value <div align="right">cell-1</div>	? <div align="right">cell-4</div>	Running // Time = increasing value <div align="right">cell-7</div>
STOP	? <div align="right">cell-2</div>	Paused // Time = last value <div align="right">cell-5</div>	? <div align="right">cell-8</div>
RESET	? <div align="right">cell-3</div>	Idle // Time = 0 <div align="right">cell-6</div>	Idle // Time = 0 <div align="right">cell-9</div>

Ensuring that all transitions in a state transition diagram are defined avoids confusion. This implies that every state and event combination has a defined result. When translating a state transition diagram into its equivalent state table, the information missing from the state transition diagram becomes apparent. In Figure 5.1 four of the events are not defined and are thus missing arcs. One often assumes that missing arcs are actually loops that represent no change in state. Thus if the stopwatch is currently in the running state, issuing the START command would cause no changes and the stopwatch remains in the running state with no changes to the time value. Likewise, if the stopwatch is idle, then hitting the STOP key would cause no change. Some designers may omit loops to prevent cluttering fairly busy diagrams. In these instances, a comment denoting that missing events cause no change is warranted to avoid any further confusion. However, experience tells us that such assumptions often harbor potential problems, so as testers, be sure to define tests that exercise all events from each state. The best recourse is to raise this matter with the developers during a design review.

To define the missing flows in the stopwatch diagram, it makes sense for the RESET key to resort to the idle state, regardless of its prior state. Likewise, the START key transitions the stopwatch to the running state. Cells 3 and 4 of Table 5.2 reflect these points. By following this argument, the STOP key causes all transitions to the paused state, as recorded in cell 8. The state table in Table 5.2 and also the updated state transition diagram in Figure 5.2 contain these added transitions.

Table 5.2 State table with all transitions defined

State Event	Idle	Running	Paused
START	Running // Time = increasing value *cell-1*	Running // Time = increasing value *cell-4*	Running // Time = increasing value *cell-7*
STOP	Idle // Time = 0 *cell-2*	Paused // Time = last value *cell-5*	Paused // Time = last value *cell-8*
RESET	Idle // Time = 0 *cell-3*	Idle // Time = 0 *cell-6*	Idle // Time = 0 *cell-9*

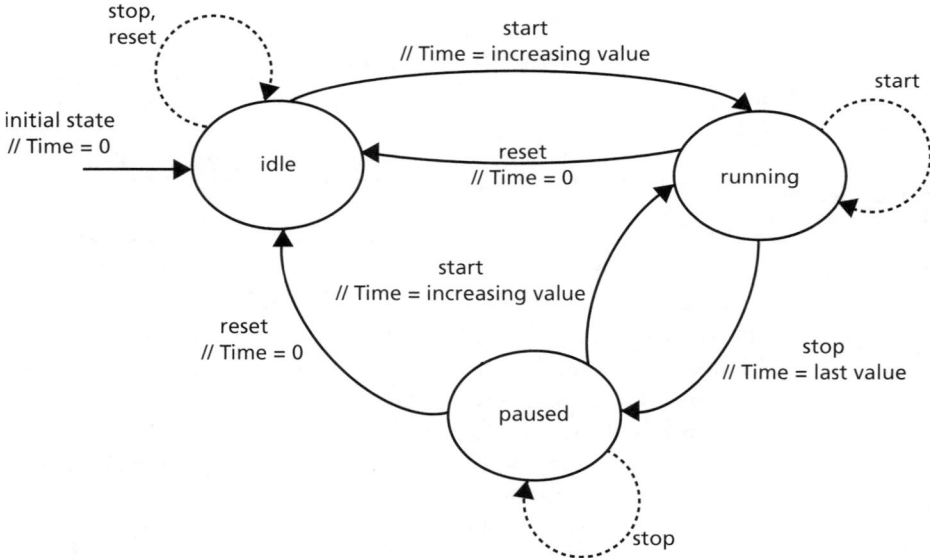

Figure 5.2 State transition diagram with all transactions defined

This stopwatch application presents a simple situation and the completed state table follows rational conclusions. Both options for what action to take upon issuing a STOP command from the idle state are logical. To complete the state table, we made a decision to avoid further ambiguity. Completing a state table for a more convoluted system may not be so obvious. If the development team and reviewers fail to identify such a discrepancy, it is the tester who finds the problem after the code is written.

Our analysis so far has found some missing transactions in the state transition diagram. When testing a state machine, a failed test can indicate any of these conditions:

- a state shown on the state transition diagram is missing from the code;
- a transaction shown on the state transition diagram is missing from the code;
- a transaction results in the wrong state;
- a state performs the wrong function.

Another possible problem can occur when the code contains extra states or transactions not shown in the state transition diagram. Catching this type of error requires a coverage analysis tool (described in section 5.4.3) to pinpoint any code that is not executed. For more information on state machines, refer to [Beizer95], [Binder00], and [Marick95].

5.2.1 Creating test cases from the state table

The information in a state table translates easily into a set of test cases because of its tabular form. Table 5.3 contains a list of test cases produced from the information in Table 5.2. This test case table contains six columns:

Test case ID   a unique identifier for each test case.

Test source   a trace back to the corresponding cell in the state table.

Current state   the initial condition required to run the test.

Event   the input triggered by the user.

Time output   the current time value returned by the stopwatch.

Next state   the new state achieved by the stopwatch.

Test case T-200, which gets its information from cell 1 in Table 5.2, indicates that the stopwatch must start in the idle state and wait for a START event. This transitions the stopwatch into the running state and causes the time value to increment every second. Test case T-201 derives its information from cell 2 and the other test cases are created in a similar manner.

The level of information shown in Table 5.3 is suitable for verifying that the state changes have been correctly implemented in the code. It may be necessary to have more control over the input because this affects the resulting time output. Table 5.4 defines additional test cases that provide more detailed input conditions, by specifying fixed intervals for the input sequence. This updated table contains one input column, labeled "input sequence", for describing the sequence of input commands. In this example, we assume that one second elapses for the

Table 5.3 Test case description

| Test case ID | Test source | Input | | Expected results | |
		Current state	Event	Time output	Next state
T-200	cell 1	Idle	START	Time = increasing value	Running
T-201	cell 2	Idle	STOP	Time = 0	Idle
T-202	cell 3	Idle	RESET	Time = 0	Idle
T-203	cell 4	Running	START	Time = increasing value	Running
T-204	cell 5	Running	STOP	Time = last value	Paused
T-205	cell 6	Running	RESET	Time = 0	Idle
T-206	cell 7	Paused	START	Time = increasing value	Running
T-207	cell 8	Paused	STOP	Time = last value	Paused
T-208	cell 9	Paused	RESET	Time = 0	Idle

first command and then the waiting period is applied. Thus, for test case T-211, the tester invokes the START command and then waits five seconds before issuing the STOP command, for a total elapsed time of six seconds. Whether or not this heuristic is correct must be discussed with the rest of the development team.

Table 5.4 Test case description with more detailed input conditions

| Test case ID | Test source | Input | Expected results | |
		Input sequence	Time output	Next state
T-210	cell 1	Idle START event	Time = 0, 1, 2, 3, …	Running
T-211	cell 1 cell 5	Idle START event Wait 5 seconds STOP event	Time = 0, 1, 2, 3, 4, 5	Paused
T-212	cell 7 cell 5	Run test T-211 START event Wait 3 seconds STOP event	Time = 6, 7, 8, 9	Paused
T-213	cell 9	Run test T-212 RESET event	Time = 0	Idle

We have created test cases from information in state transition diagrams and state tables. Although this is an important step in software testing, there is still more work to do. Establishing an environment in which to execute the tests takes significant effort.

5.2.2   Test execution and testing levels

Many issues affect test execution. They are introduced here to emphasize that more work must be done prior to running the tests. First, some mechanisms must be created to drive the tests. These includes a test driver to invoke the application-under-test and a means by which the tester can enter input to the application and place the stopwatch into a known state. Some means by which to observe the current time and to determine the stopwatch's current state is also needed. For some applications, printing a status variable that confirms the system's current state achieves this purpose. In the stopwatch example, the displayed time gives an indication as to the stopwatch's state:

● Time is 0 when idle;

● Time increases when running;

● Time is constant when paused.

This last case is ambiguous, because it might be possible to change states fast enough for a paused stopwatch to display 0. Thus it is unclear whether a time value of 0 actually signifies an idle or a paused state. The key point here is that the tester must be able to verify the stopwatch's current state in order to determine that the test outcome is correct.

Recording actual results is another component of test execution. We can expand the test case table to provide a column for checking off that the test executed as expected, as shown in Table 5.5. The tester records whether the test case passed or failed. For failed tests, documenting the stopwatch's observable behavior provides valuable information for problem tracking.

Table 5.5 A more complete test case table

		Input		Expected results		Actual results
Test case ID	Test source	Current state	Event	Time output	Next state	Pass/Fail
T-200	cell 1	Idle	START	Time = increasing value	Running	
T-201	cell 2	Idle	STOP	Time = 0	Idle	
T-202	cell 3	Idle	RESET	Time = 0	Idle	
T-203	cell 4	Running	START	Time = increasing value	Running	
T-204	cell 5	Running	STOP	Time = last value	Paused	
T-205	cell 6	Running	RESET	Time = 0	Idle	
T-206	cell 7	Paused	START	Time = increasing value	Running	
T-207	cell 8	Paused	STOP	Time = last value	Paused	
T-208	cell 9	Paused	RESET	Time = 0	Idle	

The test cases in Table 5.5 verify the accuracy of the timing feature in addition to the correctness of the internal states. Exercising such tests requires an external means of confirming the precision of elapsed time, such as using an auxiliary timer to compare expected and actual elapsed time. This becomes a system testing issue because verifying timer accuracy would likely occur if the final product that incorporates the stopwatch unit were to be part of a heavily loaded system, including multi-tasking, interrupts, resource sharing, and other features that might suspend the stopwatch's execution. Performance testing, though vital, is typically evaluated when the entire product has been assembled.

Another question not yet answered is whether we are testing the stopwatch at the system or the unit level. Up until now, this distinction has not mattered. Developing test cases requires a specification about the application-under-test – regardless of the testing level. The use of test tables and outlines applies equally to all levels of testing. The key difference lies in the scope and in the interaction required to execute the tests.

1. Unit level testing concerns the testing of the smallest compilation unit of some application. The goal of unit testing is to demonstrate that each individual unit functions as intended prior to integrating it with other units. The tester typically invokes the unit and enters data via a test driver that sends the test execution information to the unit-under-test.

2. Integration level testing consists of combining the individual units and ensuring that they function together correctly. Several approaches exist for conducting integration testing, as listed on p. 221. These approaches are also well defined in [Beizer90] and [Pressman01].

3. System level testing applies to the entire application as a whole. This is often how the end user views the system. The tester typically interacts with the application by entering data the same way as would the end user.

If the stopwatch were implemented as a self-contained compilation unit, we may be testing at the unit level. In this example, the larger application is structured in such a way that the stopwatch is its own module. Notice that there is no further description about the implementation: it is not known whether the unit is a procedural function, a set of subroutines, or a class. The sample test cases are produced by analyzing the stopwatch's description – not the code used to implement it. Test cases developed from the actual source code run the risk of exercising the code as written – bugs and all – without knowing whether the code is actually correct. Chapter 9 addresses the distinction of creating tests from a behavioral description or from the code's structure, as well as providing more information about unit, integration, and system level testing.

5.3   Test case table with multiple inputs

For applications that take in many input values, using a table to track all the input data to test one situation may be an easy way to define and document the test case. Such a table was first used in Chapter 1, p. 9 where each row corresponds to an individual test case and each column identifies input values and expected results.

To illustrate this approach, consider a loan amortization application that calculates the monthly payment based on constant payments and a constant interest rate. This application takes in three input values. They are:

● interest rate – the yearly interest rate;

● loan length – the total number of months or years for the loan;

● loan amount – the principal amount of the loan.

This application returns three output values:

● monthly payment – the amount of each monthly payment;

● total payments – the total amount paid over the life of the loan;

● total interest – the total interest paid over the life of the loan.

For simplicity, we will not consider prepayment options or other changes in the life of the loan.

Table 5.6 shows a set of test cases for this application. An entire row in this table comprises one individual test case. The first column identifies each unique test case. The next set of columns lists the input values, after which the expected results are included.

Table 5.6 A table of test cases for the loan application

Test case ID	Input			Expected results		
	Interest rate	Loan length	Loan amount	Monthly payment	Total payments	Total interest
a-222	8%	30 years	$80,000	$587.01	$211,324.20	$131,324.20
a-223	8.50%	30 years	$80,000	$615.13	$221,447.08	$141,447.08
a-224	8.50%	15 years	$80,000	$787.79	$141,802.50	$61,802.50
a-225	8%	15 years	$80,000	$764.52	$137,613.90	$57,613.90

Creating the initial table consists of listing the input types as column headers. There are different approaches for defining the input data. Selecting random data values is one approach that will define test cases, taking into account the risk of leaving out some significant input combinations. Another approach is to have the development team define a checklist of critical input combinations that will help identify crucial tests. Working through several iterations of a test case table, as described in section 4.3, may help to highlight the relevant data combinations to test. Risk analysis techniques, presented in Chapter 8, also help to identify pertinent tests. The approach to use depends on the type of application-under-test, the tester's familiarity with the system, and available time.

The input data values in Table 5.6 are selected using intelligent guesswork. The requirements must indicate how to derive the expected results. For the loan example, the tester should obtain the mathematical equations used to create the software algorithm. Another option is to use a loan calculator available commercially or on the web. Using this latter option may yield results that differ slightly

Table 5.7 Tracking test status

Test case ID	Input				Expected results			Actual results			Test statistics		
	Interest rate	Loan length	Loan amount	Monthly payment	Total payments	Total interest	Monthly payments	Total payments	Total interest	Pass/Fail	Date of test	Name of tester	
a-222	8%	30 years	$80,000	$587.01	$211,324.20	$131,324.20							
a-223	8.50%	30 years	$80,000	$615.13	$221,447.08	$141,447.08							
a-224	8.50%	15 years	$80,000	$787.79	$141,802.50	$61,802.50							
a-225	8%	15 years	$80,000	$764.52	$137,613.90	$57,613.90							

from the actual results. The project authority must determine the acceptable threshold. Whatever method is used to determine the expected results, it must follow good testing practices, which includes calculating the expected results by means *other* than executing the code in the application-under-test. The tester must be confident that the expected results are defined correctly.

This table structure lends itself to adding columns for tracking test results, test status, and other pertinent information. Table 5.7 contains additional columns for recording information acquired during test execution.

There is no industry standard format or name for tables that define and track test cases. The only criteria are that the test specifications provide an identifier, clear input descriptions, and clear expected results descriptions. Thus Table 5.7 can also be called a test case table, a test matrix, or whatever other appropriate name makes sense to your organization.

5.4 Decision tables

Decision tables are another useful method to derive test cases. In this section, we discuss how to use decision tables and how to use coverage analysis to measure test effectiveness.

Decision tables provide a means of tracking complex combinations of conditions and the resulting actions that occur based on these conditions in a format that's easy to understand. Decision tables obtain their power from logical expressions. Logical expressions contain the unary operator NOT and the binary operators AND, OR, and XOR (exclusive OR). Each operand, or variable, in a logical expression takes on the value TRUE or FALSE.

Let's first look at a sample decision table. Without much knowledge about the application, one can get a general idea of the functionality by looking at its decision table. Consider the credit card billing system shown in Table 5.8, which shows the different conditions, or states, that a customer account can be in and the resulting actions carried out by the application. A rule defines which combination of conditions produces the resulting action. Each condition takes on one of three values: T (for TRUE), F (for FALSE), or I (for "don't care"). The "don't care" state means that it is immaterial whether that condition is TRUE or FALSE. Thus, the state of a "don't care" condition does not affect the resulting action. The X indicates whether the resulting action takes place.

For example, we read Rule 2 as follows:

IF all of the following conditions are TRUE
- the account shows a non-zero balance
- the customer missed a payment in the last 12 months
- the previous payment was sent on time
- it is irrelevant whether the customer signed up for the bonus rebate plan

THEN the following action takes place

●   calculate finance charge at the high rate

AND the following actions do NOT take place

●   calculate finance charge at the regular rate

●   assess late payment fee

●   calculate cash back rebate.

Table 5.8 A decision table

		Rule 1	Rule 2	Rule 3	Rule 4	Rule 5	Rule 6	Rule 7
condition	account shows credit or 0 balance	T	F	F	F	F	F	F
	customer missed a payment in last 12 months	I	T	T	F	F	F	F
	previous payment was sent late	I	F	T	F	F	T	T
	customer signed up for bonus rebate plan	I	I	I	F	T	F	T
action	calculate finance charge at regular rate				X	X	X	X
	calculate finance charge at high rate		X	X				
	calculate late payment fee			X			X	X
	calculate cash back rebate amount					X		X

Deriving test cases from a decision table is a fairly simple exercise. The seven rules in Table 5.8 each translate into individual test cases. The input for each test consists of selecting data that satisfy the respective condition for each rule. The result consists of the actions that are expected to occur.

Other notation may be used within a decision table. Some may prefer to use the states YES and NO rather than TRUE and FALSE when describing the conditions. Actions may also be labeled with YES and NO to avoid leaving any blank space. In this particular example, two of the actions are mutually exclusive: the finance charge is calculated either at the regular rate or at the high rate. To emphasize this association, the action to calculate the finance charge can take on three states: REGULAR, HIGH, and NONE. The latter applies to Rule 1. Table 5.9 shows such

Table 5.9 A decision table action with three states

		Rule 1	Rule 2	Rule 3	Rule 4	Rule 5	Rule 6	Rule 7
condition	account shows credit or 0 balance	T	F	F	F	F	F	F
	customer missed a payment in last 12 months	I	T	T	F	F	F	F
	previous payment was sent late	I	F	T	F	F	T	T
	customer signed up for bonus rebate plan	I	I	I	F	T	F	T
action	calculate finance charge	none	high	high	regular	regular	regular	regular
	calculate late payment fee			yes			yes	yes
	calculate cash back rebate amount					yes		yes

an approach. Regardless of the notation used, the information content is the same. The driving principle is to provide clear communication.

For more examples and discussions on decision tables, refer to [Beizer90], [Binder00], [Myers76], [Pfleeger01], and [Pressman01].

5.4.1   Reducing the decision table

One goal of testing is to reduce the number of test cases yet still provide the opportunity to find problems.

It is possible to merge rules whose resulting actions are identical and thus simplify the logical expression. The theory behind this comes from hardware logic design, which employs boolean algebra to manipulate and evaluate logical expression. If the logical expression can be written in an equivalent form using fewer variables, then the corresponding hardware circuit will be simpler. Many electrical engineering texts discuss methods of simplifying logical expressions. A good treatise on simplifying logical expression can be found in [Beizer90].

The example in Table 5.8 is already reduced. With four conditions, each of which can take on a TRUE or FALSE state, it is possible to have 2^4 or 16 different combinations. The table shows seven rules, because some of the rules don't care about the state of one or more condition.

5.4.2   Expanding the decision table

Having determined that the decision table in Table 5.8 is already reduced implies that we need only concern ourselves with a smaller number of test cases. But is this a good thing? We will address this shortly. The table is reduced because some rules use "don't care" conditions. Sometimes expanding the decision table to spell out the "don't care" conditions can reveal hidden problems.

Table 5.10 is an expansion of Table 5.8. Rule 1 in Table 5.8, which contains three "don't care" conditions, now expands to eight rules (labeled Rule 1-n) in Table 5.10. Each "don't care" condition now takes on every TRUE/FALSE state. These two tables are logically equivalent, implying that the combinations of conditions result in tests that exercise the same circumstances. For ease of discussion, we'll call the seven test cases derived from Table 5.8 as the *short set of tests*, and the sixteen test cases from Table 5.8 as the *expanded set of tests*. In an ideal world, the expanded set of test cases are redundant with the original short set. However, the same cannot be said of the source code. Without inspecting the actual code, the tester cannot determine whether the short set of tests follow the same paths through the code as the expanded set of tests. One cannot be sure – without actually running the tests – whether the tests derived from Rules 1.2 and 1.3 from the expanded set will provide the same results as Rule 1 from the short set.

Table 5.10 Expanded decision table

		Rule 1								Rule 2		Rule 3		Rule 4	Rule 5	Rule 6	Rule 7
		Rule 1-1	Rule 1-2	Rule 1-3	Rule 1-4	Rule 1-5	Rule 1-6	Rule 1-7	Rule 1-8	Rule 2-1	Rule 2-2	Rule 3-1	Rule 3-2				
condition	account shows credit or 0 balance	T	T	T	T	T	T	T	T	F	F	F	F	-	-	-	-
	customer missed a payment in last 12 months	F	F	F	F	T	T	T	T	T	T	T	T	F	F	F	F
	previous payment was sent late	F	F	T	T	F	F	T	T	F	F	T	T	F	F	F	T
	customer signed up for bonus rebate plan	F	T	F	T	F	T	F	T	F	T	F	T	F	T	T	T
action	calculate finance charge at regular rate													X	X	X	X
	calculate finance charge at high rate									X	X	X	X				
	calculate late payment fee											X	X			X	X
	calculate cash back rebate amount														X	X	X

Let's speculate about the credit card billing system. If this were a newly developed application, executing the short set of test cases may be adequate. In a time crunch, running the short set of test cases ensures the tester of at least hitting the major functionality. If, however, this were a legacy application that had been modified to handle new banking policies, then it is wiser to execute the extended set of test cases. The tester cannot predict whether the internal logic is correct. Without additional information, the tester cannot confidently select which set of test cases to execute.

The question becomes how many test cases must be executed to find bugs and acquire confidence in the application? Here are some possible considerations:

● time pressure;

● project knowledge;

● coverage analysis.

Many projects are the victim of tight schedules. There may not be enough time to adequately test the application. Implementing the test cases in the short decision table provides a basis for exercising key features. If any available time remains, the tester can then select additional tests to execute.

Internal project knowledge helps to shed light on what is most in need of testing. Sometimes tests are selected based on intuition – what one happens to know about the system. When faced with the problem of selecting whether to execute the short or the extended set of test cases, discussing this issue with a knowledgeable developer or the product manager may help identify the best approach. The developers have a better understanding as to the code's structure – how well the code reflects the decision table or whether the code was retrofitted to handle new rules in the decision table. Determining which parts of the application pose risks helps to guide the testing effort towards the areas most in need of test. If the decision table documents risky behavior, then exercising the extended set of tests may raise the confidence in the product. Chapter 8 discusses risk assessment and presents further approaches for selecting relevant tests.

5.4.3 Coverage analysis

Coverage analysis provides the means by which to measure test effectiveness. It consists of using a specialized testing tool to monitor the parts of the code that have been executed. In today's market, many vendors provide commercial coverage analysis tools. We can summarize the use of coverage analysis as follows:

Create test cases.

Install coverage analysis tool in the test environment.

Select type of coverage to monitor.

REPEAT

– Execute more tests.

UNTIL (coverage = 100%).

If executing the short set of tests satisfies the coverage goal, then there is no need to execute additional tests. To illustrate the different types of coverage, consider the following code fragment:

```
.
.
IF (A or B)
      THEN do_something
ENDIF
.
.
```

We will look at three types of coverage, each requiring a different number of test cases.

Statement coverage

requires one test case:

- the IF statement must evaluate to TRUE (in this example).

Branch coverage

requires two test cases:

- the IF statement evaluates to TRUE.
- the IF statement evaluates to FALSE.

Condition coverage

requires four test cases:

- A is TRUE and B is TRUE.
- A is TRUE and B is FALSE.
- A is FALSE and B is TRUE.
- A is FALSE and B is FALSE.

Statement coverage

This monitors whether every line of code has been executed at least once. To achieve 100% statement coverage, not only do you need to execute the IF statement once, but it must evaluate to TRUE in order for the corresponding THEN statement to be executed.

Branch coverage

This monitors whether every branch or decision point has taken on every possible outcome. 100% branch coverage requires two passes through an IF statement, where one pass evaluates the expression to TRUE and the other to FALSE. DO-WHILE and REPEAT-UNTIL loops must also each be executed with both TRUE and FALSE conditions. CASE or SWITCH statements require test cases that take on every possible branch, including default paths.

Condition coverage

This is also known as predicate coverage and monitors whether every operand in a complex logical expression has taken on every TRUE/FALSE value. Complex logical expressions contain the logical operators AND, OR, and XOR. Since the IF statement in the example has a logical expression with two components, there are a total of 2^2, or 4, possible TRUE/FALSE combinations.

Each of these coverage types encompasses the lower level. Achieving 100% branch coverage will, by definition, result in 100% statement coverage. Likewise, achieving 100% condition coverage automatically satisfies 100% branch coverage.

Part of the tester's responsibility is to select the type of coverage measure to monitor. The goal is always to achieve 100% coverage of the target measure. Monitoring coverage helps determine whether any additional tests are necessary. If the goal of 100% branch coverage is achieved by executing the short set of tests, then we can stop testing, being quite confident that all relevant paths through that particular application have been executed. Branch coverage less than 100% requires that the tester execute more tests to eventually achieve complete coverage.

When 100% coverage cannot be achieved, other factors come into play.

1. There is unreachable code. The testers must raise the issue with the developers about removing this unattainable code.

2. The source code provides additional features not documented in the original specification. The tester must consult the project authority who will determine whether the documentation is incomplete or inaccurate and have it corrected.

3. The compiler may also affect condition coverage by ignoring parts of a logical expression that do not affect the outcome. For example, when evaluating the logical expression *X AND Y*, if X is already set to FALSE, then the entire expression evaluates to FALSE regardless of the value of Y. Although this "short circuit" feature saves execution time, the expression's unexecuted portion could be hiding bugs. The tester's recourse is to raise all of these issues with the developers and assess the seriousness of the situation.

Although there are many more types of coverage, the three types described in this section provide ample feedback for evaluating the effectiveness of the tests derived from the decision table. When deciding between the short or extended set of tests, achieving 100% branch coverage is an adequate criterion. This coverage metric determines whether the test cases have exercised every line of code and every branch. For many applications, 100% branch coverage is a suitable goal. Software safety critical systems, however, require a minimum of 100% condition coverage. Further information about coverage – including other types not mentioned here – is available from [Beizer90], [Hamlet01], and [Marick95]. In addition, [Kit95] provides a detailed example on using coverage analysis.

5.5   Applications with complex data

Determining the input to the earlier examples has been relatively easy to do. The keys on a keyboard constructed the input list for the dialog box example. Manipulating the stopwatch's state transition diagram produced a set of tests. Mathematical criteria gave rise to devising input for testing the loan amortization application. Other systems may not package crucial test information as readily, thus knowledge about the system becomes essential in order to develop effective tests. The outline approach in Chapter 2, p. 30, presents one method for drawing out the essential testing information. Tables also help when testing more complex systems.

Image processing is one area that employs complex data. First, there is the image size that can vary from, say, 1×1 to 4096×4096 pixels and all intermediary non-square dimensions resulting in 2^{24} distinct image sizes. Images also vary in pixel depth, such as each pixel having 8- or 24-bits of data. Naturally, the system-under-test must specify the pixel depth and minimum and maximum image size, otherwise, this is another instance of poor system requirements. Not only is there a massive amount of input, considering that a mere 256×256 image contains 2^{16} pixels, but there may be special requirements as to the image content, placement of pictured object, pixel values, and a myriad of other image specific constraints. The outcome can take on many different forms, such as:

- another image with entirely different proprieties than the input;
- a value or set of values based on some calculation of image data;
- a set of coordinates relating to relevant regions within the original image.

As an example, consider an image containing a blue circle on a red background. One algorithm could change the image into a grayscale resulting with a black circle on a dark gray background while another algorithm calculates the coordinates of the circle's center. A third algorithm could move the circle to another location in the image. Yet another algorithm could alter the original circle's dimensions generating an entirely different shape. Many image processing applications generate entirely new images by changing each pixel value based on the values of its neighboring pixels. The possibilities are endless.

Without defining a particular image application, this brief description should give a broad understanding of some of the issues affecting a complex system. In this example, the system-under-test takes in a variety of image types and runs a wide range of image processing algorithms, generating different outcome types. Unfortunately, it is impossible to run every algorithm on every possible image, due to the infinite number of images. The tester's role is to select a suitable number of images and tests that will yield confidence in the image application.

The initial setup to the tests consists of identifying the types of images to use as data input. This in itself yields a very large set of images. The image processing example in Table 5.11 lists a test suite that consists of six image processing operations to run on eight different images. The input condition consists of the image description and the image processing operation to invoke. This produces a result, which can be either a transformed image or a numerical value. The tester must devise a suitable list of input images, often with help from the developers. Since such test cases require a significant amount of detail, Table 5.11 contains references to more comprehensive test case descriptions.

Table 5.11 List of test cases for an image processing application

Image type	Image size	Invert	Rotate _60	Rotate _90	Red_to_ Blue	Calculate _Area	Find_ Centroid
horizontal ramp	1024 × 1024	in-10	r60-20	r90-1	im-100	ca-33	fc-10
horizontal ramp	480 × 768	in-11	r60-21	r90-2	im-103	ca-34	fc-20
horizontal ramp	40 × 40	in-12	r60-22	r90-3	im-24	ca-35	fc-30
blue car on road	1024 × 1024	in-13	r60-23	r90-4	im-31	ca-36	fc-40
black and white squares	480 × 768	in-14	r60-24	r90-5	im-402	ca-37	fc-50
black and white squares	480 × 480	in-15	r60-25	r90-6	im-102	ca-38	fc-60
black and white squares	1024 × 768	in-16	r60-26	r90-7	im-44	ca-39	fc-70
corner highlights	2048 × 2048	in-17	r60-27	r90-8	im-45	ca-40	fc-80

The detailed test case description must provide specific information about the input image, whether this identifies a particular image file or includes instructions on how to create the image. Figure 5.3 shows a typical test case that documents this information.

The test must also state how to evaluate the test results. If the output is another image, then the tester must be able to determine whether the correct image was generated, often by performing a bitwise comparison of the actual and expected images. Acquiring a copy of the expected image poses some problems. Some testers may actually create an image file, whether by programming the value of each pixel or by using image editing software. Other times, the tester executes a test for the first time and captures the resulting image. By examining the generated image to determine correctness, this image then becomes the basis of comparison for future tests.

Another possible format is to list the references to descriptions of the input and expected results. This approach is similar to Table format #5 shown in Table 4.8 in section 4.3.1. In the image processing example shown in Table 5.12, the source image is defined by a specific file and the input is specified as the image operation to be performed. The expected results is either a file, if another image is generated, or one or more numerical values resulting from calculations. When the operation results in another image, it is easier to evaluate the test by performing a bitwise comparison between the actual and expected images. This deterministic method leaves no room for interpretation. In some cases, however, there may be a sketchy description of expected results, in which the tester must interpret whether the actual results are acceptable.

Identification

    Test case ID: *im-563-a*

    Subsystem: *color conversion*

System-under-test

    Build version: *02.13*

    Operating system version: *4.1*

    Platform: *PC Pentium*

    Image hardware revision: *AB-08-x*

Initial setup

    Configure the image acquisition system to process 256 × 1024 images

Input

    1. Load and display image FlipRedGreen_256_1024.bmp

    2. Enter command: Red_to_Blue

    3. Enter command: Green_to_Red

    4. Enter command: Blue_to_Green

Expected results

    1. Image FlipRedGreen_256_1024.bmp is visible on display

    2. All red pixels are now changed to blue

    3. All green pixels are now changed to red

    4. All blue pixels are now changed to green

    5. Final expected image stored in OutputFlipRedGreen_256_1024.bmp

Actual results

Test record

Date of test:	_____	Results:	☐ Pass	☐ Fail
Name of tester:	_____	Problem report filed:	☐ yes	☐ no
Test machine:	_____	Problem report number:	_____	

Figure 5.3 Sample image processing test case

This latter approach leaves room for interpretation, but sometimes that is the only information available to the tester. When using non-deterministic input, such as acquiring a live image, it is difficult, if not impossible, to define expected results precisely. For example, even taking two successive live images of the same subject may result in one image being shifted by one pixel when compared to the second image. Although vague and imprecise descriptions for expected results are less than ideal and sometimes unavoidable, the project team must agree on the acceptable level of rigor.

During test execution, the tester fills in the table's last two columns reserved for recording actual results and pass/fail status. The "actual results" column may not be large enough to record the results from failed tests. The tester may type notes into a file or save the bad image into a separate file.

Table 5.12 Image processing test results

Test case ID	Source image	Image operation	Expected results	Actual results	Pass/Fail status
245	img_245.bmp	Calculate_Area	area = 1024	✓	pass
246	img_245.bmp	Find_Centroid	coord = (200, 768)	✓	pass
247	img_907.bmp	Invert	img_907_inv.bmp	see notes in log_test247.txt	fail
248	img_33.bmp	Rotate_60	img_33_r60.bmp	✓	pass
249	img_33.bmp	Rotate_90	img_33_r90.bmp	✓	pass
250	img_33.bmp	Invert	img_33_inv.bmp	see results in failed_test250.bmp	fail
251	img_33.bmp	Calculate_Area	area = 4042	area = 4000	fail
252	img_906.bmp	Invert	man's face is upside-down	✓ result stored in img_906_out.bmp	pass
253	img_905.bmp	Red_to_Blue	red block is changed to blue	some red pixels appear in upper left corner	fail
. . .					

Table 5.12 provides very condensed information. This shortcut is more of a checklist for tracking which tests are performed and recording their results. Whether these tests are described in enough detail depends on your organization's needs. The tester must balance the trade-off between having a quick reference checklist of which tests to run against providing enough information describing each test in detail.

We have discussed preliminary steps for defining test cases that handle complex input data. Testing a specific image processing algorithm may require many input images each with precise characteristics in order to exercise different functions within the same algorithm. Sometimes the only test is a precise description of the expected results, which requires the tester to make a judgment call. The tables shown above are only a guide for identifying the features that require testing. The key goal is to select what kind of tests to run, rather than randomly picking images and seeing what the results look like.

5.6 Managing tests

Some of the tables shown previously contain more information than just input and expected results. For example, the tester is able to record pass/fail status and problem reporting information. There are, of course, other types of information that blend well with using test tables, such as resource allocation – both for equipment and for staffing.

5.6.1 Test planning

Test planning is an activity that consists of many facets. Although Chapter 9 discusses these topics in further detail, we introduce some of the concepts here. Even with limited understanding of all test planning activities, tables provide information for determining:

● schedule estimation;

● staffing resources;

● equipment needs.

Test tables illustrate the magnitude of the testing effort. This gives some ammunition to fight unreasonable schedules – not that management will necessarily extend the schedule (one can always dream!). It is more effective to substantiate arguments with facts. The statement "There is no way that I can run 12,064 tests in two weeks" – and then waving an enormous test table – has more effect than the lament "There's not enough time for me to test this!"

Calculating the number of cells in the table gives an approximation as to the number of potential test cases. Not all test cases are created equal. Some of the tests originating from the GUI's test tables are fairly trivial, while some tests for the image processing scenario are much more involved, often requiring significant amounts of time just to assemble the input data. Some tests require developer time. Determining the appropriate amount of time to setup and execute the tests is definitely an important component of test planning. Section 2.5 shows a sample schedule estimate.

Staffing is another aspect of test planning. Management can use the test table to assign tasks by inserting the name of the tester responsible for implementing and executing that test case, as shown in Table 5.13.

Table 5.13 A staffing plan showing job assignment

Image type	Image size	Invert	Rotate _60	Rotate _90	Red_to_ Blue	Calculate _Area	Find_ Centroid
horizontal ramp	1024 × 1024						
horizontal ramp	480 × 768	Sam	Lee		Tracy		
horizontal ramp	40 × 40						
blue car on road	1024 × 1024				Lou		
black and white squares	480 × 768						
black and white squares	480 × 480			Chris			
black and white squares	1024 × 768						
corner highlights	2048 × 2048						

Equipment identification consists of listing the hardware, software, peripherals, and other devices needed to execute the tests. While a test table does not directly specify equipment needs, the tester should be able to look at the various test classification and derive a preliminary list of test environment needs.

5.6.2 Test case matrix

We have already seen many examples of matrices in this chapter. In general usage, the term "matrix" implies a table in which the intersection of rows and columns defines the contents of a particular test case. In addition, the software community recognizes the following three special types of matrices: state table, traceability matrix, and cross-reference matrix.

State table matrix

The *state table*, as described in section 5.2, maps events to processing states and it also represents the information from the state transition diagram. This pictorial representation easily conveys a description of the system's behavior.

Traceability matrix

The *traceability matrix* maps test requirements to the test cases and test procedures that implement them, as shown in Table 4.19 on p. 109. The benefit of a traceability matrix is that it helps to identify which test cases result from a specific set of requirements so that the tester can easily determine which test cases are affected by the changes in the requirements. When a test has failed, tracing the test case back to its source requirement may be necessary to determine whether the test case was defined correctly.

Cross-reference matrix

The third type of matrix is a *cross-reference matrix*. We have seen that the general approach to defining tests using tables involves listing the possible inputs and the actions that can be applied to each. Each such input/action pair defines the basis for a test case, or test procedure when more information is necessary to fully define the test. Table 5.14 illustrates a cross-reference matrix, and its cells reference tests documented elsewhere. Some of these tests are test cases labeled *tc number*, some tests are test procedures labeled *tp number*, and other tests are identified by the prefixes *a-* and *st*. The naming scheme for test cases varies across projects. Whatever test naming scheme is used, this test case matrix helps sort the tests into their respective groups. The use of annotations conveys additional information. The asterisk indicates that a test identifier appears more than once within the table. It is perfectly reasonable for a particular test case or test procedure to exercise multiple features as listed in the table. Highlighting can be used to communicate priority, assignment, test status, or other pertinent information. The shaded cells in Table 5.14 identify high priority tests.

The advantage of a cross-reference matrix is that it serves as a condensed guide to a massive set of test suites, by providing a general picture of what the tests entail. Such a table also serves as an index into a set of test case descriptions whose details are recorded elsewhere, whether as a page in a massive test case document or as a separate file on disk. Some large test suites can use this type of matrix instead of a table of contents to function as an online index to test case files, where each test case is stored as a separate file on a network.

The distinction between a traceability matrix and a cross-reference matrix is very subtle. The key difference is that the traceability matrix assigns a unique identifier to each requirement to be tested. Depending on the terminology used in your organization, or if your product specification already labels each requirement with a unique identifier, these two types of matrices may be identical. The point here is to structure the tables in such a way as to maximize the sharing of information.

Table 5.14 A cross-reference matrix

	input 1	input 2	input 3	input 4	input 5	input 6	...
initial state 1	tc 101	tp 21		tc 10	st 55		
initial state 2	tc 102	tp 22		tp 33	st 65*		
initial state 3	tc 103	tp 23	a-899	tp 35	st 65*	tp 432	
initial state 4	tc 104	tp 24	a-898	tc 351	st 72		
initial state 5	tc 105	tp 25	a-897		st 65*	tp 422	
initial state 6	tc 107	tp 26	a-896	tc 4779			
initial state 7	tc 108	tp 27	a-895				
.							

The asterisk (*) denotes that a test case appears more than once within the table.
Shaded cells identify high priority tests.

5.6.3 Tracking test execution and status

Tables easily lend themselves to tracking information pertinent to test execution and their results. Testers can report progress and test status by encoding each cell with status information. This provides a quick summary as to which tests have passed, failed, or have yet to be executed. Section 4.3.2 provides several examples of recording test results in tables. Sometimes the pattern of failures may yield clues to the developers as to which parts of the application are unstable.

Tables can also be used to track information related to test execution, as shown in Table 5.15 which tracks the following information:

- application and hardware versions;
- the machine used to execute the test, assuming that more than one test machine exists;
- date that test was executed;
- name of the tester;
- problem report information for failed tests;
- a note as to whether the test was re-executed.

Additional examples of how to use tables to track test case status can be found in [Black99].

5.7 Summary

Many software testers use tables extensively. Tables apply throughout the entire testing process, from unit testing through system level testing. Not only do tables document the actual test cases, but they also prove useful for recording test execution, test status, and test management information. Using tables during test execution consists of recording such information as the actual results, pass/fail status, application version, date, and the tester's name.

An application described with a state transition diagram can readily be converted into an equivalent state table, which then easily leads to test cases.

For applications that use more complex data combinations, a test table can reference a file that contains the actual input and outcome descriptions.

Decision tables can track complex combinations of conditions and the associated resulting actions. Reducing a decision table consists of merging logically equivalent rules and thus creating a smaller number of rules, which then translate into fewer test cases.

When executing the tests, coverage analysis can evaluate the effectiveness of test cases by monitoring which parts of the code are executed. Many types of coverage measures exist. Statement and branch coverage are two of the most common.

Tables provide a means for managing the testing tasks. Schedule estimates can use the size of the table to determine an approximate number of test cases. Specifying a priority for each test helps identify the more important tests. Further

Table 5.15 Tracking test execution information

| Test case ID | Test environment | | | Test status | | | | | Problem tracking | | | | |
	Application version	Hardware version	Test machine	Pass/Fail	Date of test	Tester's name	Problem report number	Problem resolved	Retest: application version	Retest: date of test	Retest: tester's name	Retest status
d1001	03.04a	1-2.d	#3	Pass	12-Mar	Fred	–					
d1002	03.04a	1-2.d	#3	Pass	12-Mar	Fred	–					
d1003	03.04b	1-2.d	#3	Fail	12-Mar	Joe	#2563	yes	03.05	17-Mar	Fred	Pass
d1004	03.04b	1-2.d	#3	Pass	12-Mar	Joe	–					
d1005	03.04a	1-2.d	#3	Fail	12-Mar	Fred	#2569	yes	03.05	17-Mar	Fred	Fail
d1006	03.05	1-2.g	#2	Fail	15-Mar	Fred	#2571	no				

expansion of tables allows for recording staffing information and resource allocation. By recording which tests have been executed and the associated pass/fail results, management can easily view the current testing status.

Another type of table is a traceability matrix that maps requirements to the corresponding test cases. This helps determine which test cases to execute when validating a requirement and which requirements need test cases.

6 Testing Object-Oriented Software

6.1 Introduction

Testing applications built using object-oriented design employs many of the same techniques presented in earlier chapters. However, unique characteristics of object-oriented systems present some new challenges and require different strategies for testing primarily at the unit test level.

Throughout this chapter we'll explore several examples that illustrate strategies for testing object-oriented software. Other approaches may exist. The testing examples include the following:

- Defining system-level tests from an outline.
- Defining system-level tests from use cases.
- Defining unit tests for a collection of classes.
- Defining unit tests for a hierarchy of classes.

The goal is to provide some test design paradigms to get you started with testing object-oriented software. Limited knowledge of object-oriented software will not prevent you from being an effective tester. Although this chapter is neither a tutorial on object-oriented design nor an all-encompassing guide to object-oriented testing, it does define essential object-oriented concepts. Those wishing to acquire detailed information on object-oriented testing should read [Binder00], [Marick95], and [McGregor01].

6.2 Comparing object-oriented and procedural software

Object-oriented programming provides features not available in procedural software. Object-oriented software centers on a class (the basic unit) and the inheritance and encapsulation that affect a class. Procedural programming, however, controls the flow between software functions. Testing these object-oriented features call for new strategies.

6.2.1   Object-oriented terminology

A *class* is a blueprint that defines the data and behavior (*methods*) common to all objects of a certain kind. An *object* is an instance of a particular class. A common analogy is to envision a cookie cutter. A class is the cookie cutter and it defines what a cookie will look like. The objects are the cookies produced by that one cookie cutter.

Inheritance provides the ability to derive new classes from existing classes. The child class (*derived class*) inherits all the data and behavior (methods) of the parent class (*base class*), and it may also add new features or redefine existing features.

Encapsulation provides the programmers with a well-defined interface to access an object's features in a way that prevents the programmer from directly accessing the object's internal code.

Object-oriented programming also provides the capability to limit the access to class members (data and methods). An object can always access members defined within its own class. Class members tagged as *public* are externally visible, allowing objects of different classes to access these public members. *Private* members, on the other hand, are only available to objects of that class – even a derived class cannot access a parent's private information. Section 6.4.2 illustrates these access rules.

6.2.2   Testing the software

In many cases, we can think of object-oriented software as an application developed using a particular design approach. Modeling is a vital part of object-oriented development. The design approach consists of object-oriented decomposition and specialized diagrams that depict logical and physical models of the system under development. Well-engineered object-oriented design can make it easier to trace from requirements to design to code.

As we have seen in previous chapters and regardless of design methodology, testing concerns several levels, including system testing and unit testing, and we will now consider testing of object-oriented applications within those two categories.

System testing is independent of the process used to create any application. The tester evaluates the application from a user perspective. Internal design details are irrelevant and do not affect how tests are defined. The application's behavior, whether presented as use cases or other forms of requirements, drives the development of test cases. Thus, knowledge about object-oriented software is not necessary for defining system level test cases.

Unit testing of any software application requires programming knowledge and access to implementation details. When dealing with object-oriented code, the meaning of *unit* is different. A class is the smallest unit that can be compiled. The key difference between the two design methodologies is that unit testing of procedural software accesses the units (procedures or functions) directly, whereas access to the class's data and methods may be more restricted. A thorough unit test of object-oriented software consists of ensuring that all the methods within a class and their interfaces function as required. Designing test cases for class inheritance requires additional considerations, as described in section 6.4.2. It is important to note that some object-oriented languages can be implemented in a procedural manner, thus requiring a procedural testing strategy.

Most of the techniques for *defining* test cases apply equally for both procedurally developed applications as well as those developed using object-oriented design. A major difference, however, lies in *executing* the test cases. Executing test cases for object-oriented software undergoing unit testing requires an execution environment that deals with encapsulation, as explained in section 6.4.3.

6.3   System testing example

The Mall Guide system in a local shopping mall has a few select stores that specialize in the following categories:

- women's clothes (3 stores);
- men's clothes (2 stores);
- children's clothes (4 stores);
- women's shoes (2 stores);
- men's shoes (2 stores);
- flowers (1 store);
- gifts (2 stores);
- restaurants (5 stores).

Two types of actors interact with the Mall Guide. The term *actor* represents any person, hardware device, or other system that interacts with the application. In this example, the actors are:

- shoppers who seek to find an appropriate store in the mall;
- administrators who update store names and locations.

The example is shown in Figures 6.1 through 6.5. The user input is described in Figure 6.1. The main menu screen (shown in Figure 6.2) asks the user for the type of store. Figure 6.3 provides a menu with the list of stores. Both the main menu and list of stores screens allow the shopper to request a printed map (shown in Figure 6.4). All the screens allow the shopper to select the help feature (shown in Figure 6.5). The current requirements, up to this point, do not provide any details on the administrator's command interface.

User input information presented in this section serves as the Mall Guide requirements. As seen in previous chapters, incomplete requirements increase the

---

Shopper commands: main menu

1. Shopper touches a store category from a list and is given a list of stores from which to select.
2. Shopper touches map key and a map of the mall is provided on the screen.
3. Shopper touches help key and is provided with a help screen.

Shopper commands: list of stores

4. Shopper touches a particular store name and a map highlighting the store's location is provided on the screen.
5. Shopper touches main menu key and returns to the main menu.
6. Shopper touches help key and is provided with a help screen.

Shopper commands: maps

7. Shopper touches print key and a map is printed out.
8. Shopper touches "return to previous screen" key and the prior screen is displayed.
9. Shopper touches main menu key and returns to the main menu.
10. Shopper touches help key and is provided with a help screen.

Shopper commands: help

11. Shopper touches "return to previous screen" key and the prior screen is displayed.
12. Shopper touches main menu key and returns to the main menu.

Administrator commands

13. Administrator adds a new store name.
14. Administrator removes a store name.
15. Administrator modifies the mall map.

Figure 6.1 Input options for the Mall Guide

burden on the tester to identify missing information and seek resolution from the project authority.

Different strategies exist for developing system level test cases. We'll explore two approaches. The first example uses the outline method described in Chapter 2. An outline is a useful tool to group related information. The second strategy employs uses cases, which focus on actor scenarios. These independent examples yield similar, though not identical, test cases. Whichever approach a tester selects depends on several factors, such as:

● the tester's experience and personal preference;
● the format in which system requirements are presented;
● the availability of tools that can assist in developing test cases.

A tester may sometimes start with one strategy and then switch to another if difficulties arise with applying the initial method.

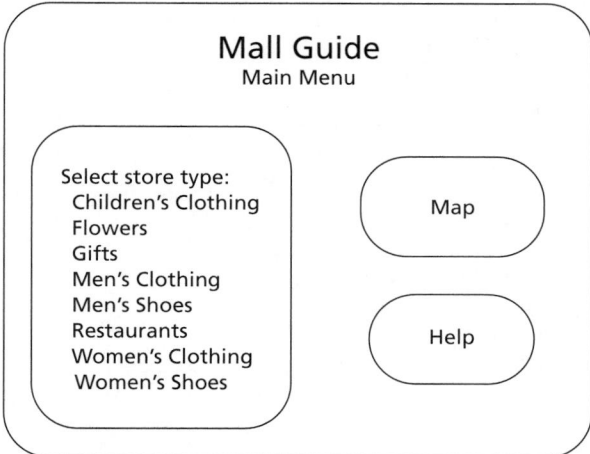

Figure 6.2 Main menu touch screen

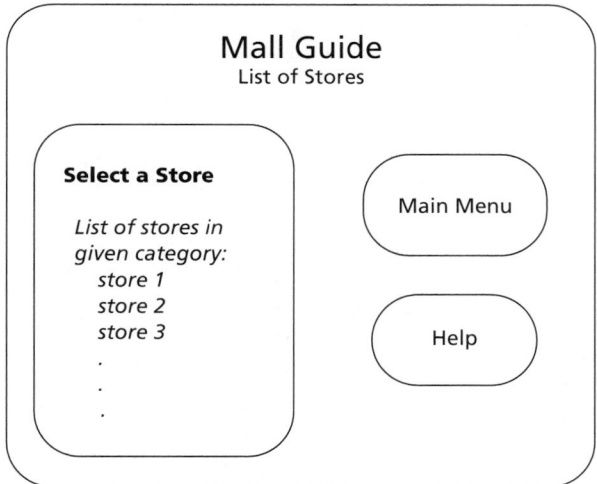

Figure 6.3 Store list touch screen

6.3.1 Test cases from outlines

Since the user input description provided in section 6.3 appears as a list, organizing this information into an outline is a reasonable approach. For other applications, structuring information using tables (per Chapter 4) might be a more suitable approach. For this example and ease of explanation, the shopper and administrator interfaces are handled separately.

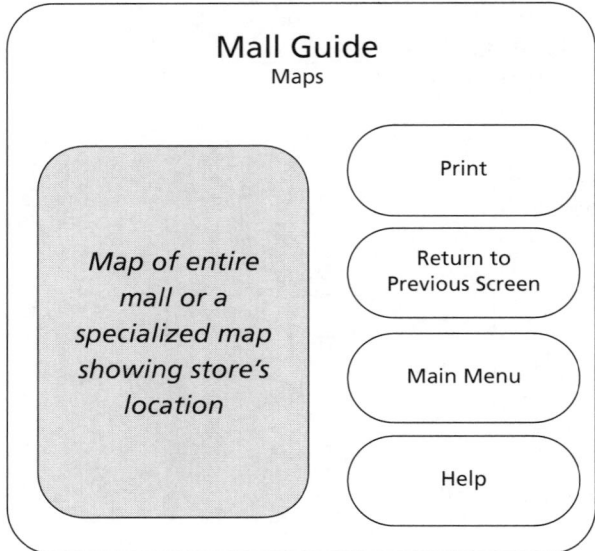

Figure 6.4 Map touch screen

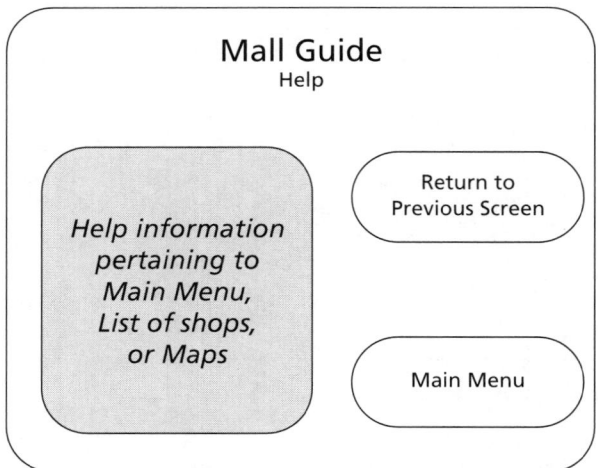

Figure 6.5 Help touch screen

6.3.1.1   *The shopper commands*

An outline can be created by reordering the input options into sequences that a shopper typically performs. The list of store categories also becomes part of the outline. Figure 6.6 shows the resulting outline. The square brackets contain the reference to the original requirement. Brackets with numbers point back to the input

1 Main menu

   1.1 [1] Shopper touches a store category from a list and is given a list of stores from which to select.

      1.1.1 [D] Women's clothes (3 stores).

      1.1.2 [D] Men's clothes (2 stores).

      1.1.3 [D] Children's clothes (4 stores).

      1.1.4 [D] Women's shoes (2 stores).

      1.1.5 [D] Men's shoes (2 stores).

      1.1.6 [D] Flowers (1 store).

      1.1.7 [D] Gifts (2 stores).

      1.1.8 [D] Restaurants (5 stores).

   1.2 [2] Shopper touches map key and a map of the mall is provided on the screen.

      1.2.1 [7] Shopper touches print key and a map is printed out.

      1.2.2 [8] Shopper touches "return to previous screen" key and the prior screen is displayed.

      1.2.3 [9] Shopper touches main menu key and returns to the main menu.

      1.2.4 [10] Shopper touches help key and is provided with a help screen.

         1.2.4.1 [11] Shopper touches "return to previous screen" key and the prior screen is displayed.

         1.2.4.2 [12] Shopper touches main menu key and returns to the main menu.

   1.3 [3] Shopper touches help key and is provided with a help screen.

      1.3.1 [11] Shopper touches "return to previous screen" key and the prior screen is displayed.

      1.3.2 [12] Shopper touches main menu key and returns to the main menu.

2 List of stores

   2.1 [4] Shopper touches a particular store name and a map highlighting the store's location is provided on the screen.

      2.1.1 [7] Shopper touches print key and a map is printed out.

      2.1.2 [8] Shopper touches "return to previous screen" key and the prior screen is displayed.

      2.1.3 [9] Shopper touches main menu key and returns to the main menu.

      2.1.4 [10] Shopper touches help key and is provided with a help screen.

         2.1.4.1 [11] Shopper touches "return to previous screen" key and the prior screen is displayed.

         2.1.4.2 [12] Shopper touches main menu key and returns to the main menu.

   2.2 [5] Shopper touches main menu key and returns to the main menu.

   2.3 [6] Shopper touches help key and is provided with a help screen.

      2.3.1 [11] Shopper touches "return to previous screen" key and the prior screen is displayed.

      2.3.2 [12] Shopper touches main menu key and returns to the main menu.

Figure 6.6 Outline for shopper input sequence

option description in Figure 6.1, whereas items marked with [D] refer to the current mall configuration.

To help identify the various shopper scenarios, the map and help functions each appear multiple times under different items. This highlights the different contexts in which to invoke these features. For example, invoking the help function from the main menu produces a different output than if invoked from the map touch screen. Likewise, hitting the "return to previous screen" key results in the touch screen displaying a different menu depending on the prior state.

This particular outline separates the main menu screen from the list of stores. Another approach may be to insert copies of the list of stores section under each store category, thus copying everything under item number 2 to 1.1.1.1, 1.1.2.1, and so on. This will increase the outline size tremendously and define a test case for every possible shopper input combination. To simplify and reduce the amount of testing, let's decide to use one store category and one associated store name to execute the scenarios under outline item number 2. This, of course, requires discussing the trade-offs and asserting that this approach properly addresses the project risks.

This outline is just one possible interpretation of the user interface description. Different testers may produce different outlines, but the core information remains the same. The intent is to list user actions in order to produce tests that cover all relevant scenarios.

The outline contains 23 leaves, each of which results in a test case. Appendix B1 contains the complete table of 23 test cases, and Table 6.1 shows some of these test cases. The test source column refers to the item in the outline, which traces back to the original user interface requirement.

6.3.1.2   *The administrator commands*

Understanding how the administrator interacts with the system is necessary for producing test cases. The outline in Figure 6.7 helps the tester organize information that pinpoints the missing requirements. Most of the added items come from intelligent assumptions that cover many possible situations, such as whether a category exists or whether the data entered is valid. Incorporating these "what if?" conditions leads to comprehensive test cases.

When information is missing from the requirements, the tester's best approach is to take the problem to the project authority. For our example, the missing information identified is listed below.

1. When adding a store to an existing category, how does the administrator select the category? Pull-down list? Type in category name?

2. How does the administrator create a new category? What if the category name already exists?

3. What is the format for a store name?

4. Can a store name reside under more than one category?

5. When the administrator selects a store name to remove, must he also specify the category?

Table 6.1 Selection of system level test cases for shopper interface
(full list available in Appendix B1)

Test case ID	Test source	Input	Expected results	Actual results
MG-1	1.1.1	From main menu: select "Women's clothes"	The list of stores screen appears and lists 3 women's clothes stores.	
. . .				
MG-5	1.1.5	From main menu: select "Men's shoes"	The list of stores screen appears and lists 2 men's shoes stores.	
. . .				
MG-11	1.2.3	From main menu: (a) hit map key (b) hit "main menu" key	(a) Get a map of the mall posted on the screen. (b) Return to main menu.	
. . .				
MG-17	2.1.2	From main menu: (a) select "Men's clothes" (b) select the second store name from the list (c) hit "return to previous screen" key	(a) The list of stores screen and lists 2 men's clothes stores. (b) Get a map to this store posted on the screen. (c) Return to list of stores screen listing 2 men's clothes stores.	
. . .				

6. When removing a store name, what happens when the updated category is now empty?

7. How does the administrator identify which store name to remove? Point and click on an image of the map? Select store name from a list? Type in store name?

8. How does the administrator identify which store name to add?

9. How does the administrator identify the new location of a store? Type in a number corresponding to a location on the map?

10. Can the administrator move the location of an existing store by clicking and dragging on an image of the mall map?

Once the project authority further defines the requirements, the tester can then finish the outline and eventually define test cases. If the project is under extreme pressure, the tester may take charge of improving the requirements, often replacing missing information with reasonable assumptions. This can be of enormous

1 Administrator commands
    1.1 [13] Administrator adds a new store name.
        1.1.1 Category exists.
            1.1.1.1 Valid store name.
            1.1.1.2 Store name has invalid format.
            1.1.1.3 Store name already exists in this category.
        1.1.2 Category does not exist.
            1.1.2.1 Valid store name.
            1.1.2.2 Store name has invalid format.
            1.1.2.3 Store name already exists and is assigned to another category.
    1.2 [14] Administrator removes a store name.
        1.2.1 Updated category has zero stores.
        1.2.2 Updated category has one or more stores.
    1.3 [15] Administrator modifies the mall map.

Figure 6.7 Initial outline for administrator interface

assistance to the project authority who then merely seeks validation of the improved description rather than schedule resources to complete the product definition, thereby saving unscheduled time and effort.

6.3.2   Test cases from use cases

Use cases are an effective mechanism for documenting requirements. They describe the application's behavior from the actor's perspective. Well-constructed use cases translate easily into test cases. The entire set of use cases rarely presents the entire system requirements, as they often omit information pertinent to performance and load tests.

The use cases in this example contain four sections:

1. Main header. This section contains a unique identifier and a brief description.

2. Success guarantees. This section describes the final state upon successful completion.

3. Main success scenario. This section describes the simplest scenario, in which every step completes normally and no recovery is needed.

4. Extensions. This section lists alternate courses that branch off from a step in the main success scenario. Depending on the resulting action, the extension can either revert back to the main scenario or run to its own completion, such as generating a failure or producing an entirely different outcome.

Use cases can contain additional information, such as preconditions, primary actor, failed end conditions, and triggers, to name just a few. To learn more about use cases, see [Cockburn01].

In the previous example, the outline helped to produce test cases even when the information is incomplete. Here, the use cases serve as vehicle for transforming the user input descriptions into test cases. Three such use cases are shown in Figure 6.8, Figure 6.9, and Figure 6.10. For use case #3 (Figure 6.10), we can assume that an administrator interface exists and speculate as to a common command sequence.

Use case #1 Shopper wants to find a specific store in the mall.

Success guarantees
   Shopper receives a printed map to the desired store.

Main success scenario
   1.   Shopper selects a store category.
   2.   Shopper selects a store name.
   3.   Shopper selects the print function.

Extensions
   1a.   Shopper wants help selecting a store category.
   1b.   Appropriate store category does not exist.
   2a.   Shopper wants help selecting a store name.
   2b.   Desired store does not exist.

Figure 6.8 Use case #1

Each use case generates many test cases. The main success scenario, which is the simplest and most common path through the use case, provides the information for the first use case and serves as the foundation for subsequent tests. At least one test case must exist for each extension to ensure that the system properly handles that event. Table 6.2 lists test cases that come from use case #1. Appendix B2 contains test cases derived from all three use cases. Test case numbering is based on the corresponding use case. For traceability, the table records the extension being validated by the test case.

This set of test cases is obviously different from those produced in section 6.3.1. The main reason is that use cases depict the actor's intent, while the outline lists combinations of user input options. There are no requirements to address what happens if the shopper fails to find the desired store in the mall, as in test case u1-3.

Different testers can suggest different test cases that emanate from the same use case. The question then becomes whether this new set of test cases exercises every

Use case #2 Shopper wants to find all gift stores and map the best route to each store.

Success guarantees

Shopper receives a printed map for each gift store.

Main success scenario

1. Shopper selects a store category.
2. Shopper selects the first store name.
3. Shopper selects the print function.
4. Shopper returns to the list of stores.
5. Shopper selects the second store name.
6. Shopper selects the print function.

Extensions

(none)

Figure 6.9 Use case #2

Use case #3 Administrator wants to add a new store to the Mall Guide.

Success guarantees

New store name appears under List of stores.

New store location appears on the mall map.

Main success scenario

1. Administrator selects the store category.
2. Administrator adds the store name.
3. Administrator updates the map.

Extensions

1a. Appropriate category does not exist.
2a. Store name already exists.
3a. Location selected already assigned to another store.

Figure 6.10 Use case #3

Table 6.2 Test cases for use case #1

Test case ID	Test source	Initial system state	Input	Expected results	Actual results
u1-1	use case #1	Start test from the main menu.	(a) select "Men's clothes" (b) select the first store name (c) hit print key	(a) The list of stores screen appears and lists 2 men's clothes stores. (b) Get a map to this store posted on the screen. (c) Get a printed copy of the map.	
u1-2	use case #1 extension 1a	Start test from the main menu.	(a) hit help key (b) hit "return to previous screen" key	(a) Get the help screen providing information about the main menu. (b) Return to main menu.	
u1-3	use case #1 extension 1b	Start test from the main menu.	[No input: Shopper wants to find a book store].	Main menu does not list books as a store category.	
u1-4	use case #1 extension 2a	Start test from the main menu.	(a) select "Restaurants" (b) hit help key	(a) The list of stores screen appears and lists 5 restaurants. (b) Get the help screen providing information about the list of stores menu.	
u1-5	use case #1 extension 2b	"Lorna's Shoes" is not a valid store name. Start test from the main menu.	Select "Women's shoes"	The list of stores screen appears and lists 2 women's shoes stores, but "Lorna's Shoes" is not included.	

user input option. The cross-reference matrix Table 6.3 tracks which input options (from the list in Figure 6.1) have a corresponding test case. The matrix cannot adequately map administrator commands due to incomplete requirements. Even though the matrix shows that four use cases execute input option 13 (add a new store name), no distinction exists between successful addition, missing store category, or invalid store name – all separate situations addressed by the use case. Despite these deficiencies, the matrix detects the need for additional test cases.

Many applications – not just object-oriented software – employ use cases to fully document system requirements. Use cases help transform the user interface descriptions into test cases (as shown in this example).

6.4 Unit testing of classes

Although classes are unique to object-oriented programming, the approaches to defining test cases are often the same as for procedural applications. One instance involves classes that implement state machines. State transition diagrams and state tables, as discussed in section 5.2, lead readily into a set of test cases. The use of

Table 6.3 Mapping user input to test cases

Test case / Input option	u1-1	u1-2	u1-3	u1-4	u1-5	u2-1	u3-1	u3-2	u3-3	u3-4
1	✓			✓	✓	✓	✓	✓		
2										
3		✓								
4	✓					✓	✓	✓		
5										
6				✓						
7	✓					✓	✓			
8						✓				
9										
10										
11		✓								
12										
13							✓	✓	✓	✓
14										
15							✓	✓		✓

another test design technique, called orthogonal array testing, is effective when the permutations of a small input domain generate an enormous number of test cases.

We'll also look at two areas specific to object-oriented software: inheritance and the environment for test execution. Creating a test execution environment for testing classes at the unit level requires special considerations due to the effect of using encapsulation to hide complexity.

6.4.1 Testing using orthogonal arrays

Some applications have a small and finite number of input values, but listing all the possible permutations of values generates a massive number of tests. One approach to reducing the number of test cases is to apply a combinatorial method known as orthogonal array testing. This method is suitable for testing all software applications – not just object-oriented software.

Orthogonal array testing is based on a statistical technique borrowed from manufacturing. To apply the technique, the software must have independent sets of states. The goal is to pair each state (from one set) with every other state (from another set) at least once. Applying the combinatory method to reduce the number of test consists of identifying unique pairs of states. An example will clarify this.

A bookstore application processes the information shown in Figure 6.11. In an object-oriented application, the three classes book, purchase, and shipping each have a finite number of possible states. In a procedural application, three procedures (most likely named order_book, purchase_book, and ship_book) each have arguments with a finite set of values. To facilitate the discussion, the terms class and state are used.

Book	Purchase	Shipping
in_stock	cash	overnight
special_order	check	economy
out_of_print	charge	ground
		pick-up

Figure 6.11 Classes and states in the bookstore example

Two classes have three states each and one class has four states, so testing every combination of states requires $3^2 \times 4^1$ or 36 test cases. Selecting a state from each of two classes (known as pair-wise combinations) only requires the 12 test cases shown in Table 6.4, thereby reducing the number of possible test cases.

Looking at just the book and shipping columns (ignoring the purchase column) in the array shows every possible combination of these two classes. Likewise, ignoring the book class shows every combination of the purchase and shipping states. Because the shipping class has more states than the other two classes, inspecting the pairings of the book and purchase columns shows every possible combination with some duplication. Test cases 1 and 4 present one instance of duplication, where the book and purchase classes have the states "in_stock" and "cash", respectively. These two tests are still unique because of the different shipping states.

For other applications in which the classes each contain the same number of states, no duplication appears in the array. For example, three classes each with three states would have an array specifying nine test cases with no two pairs of values appearing more than once in the array.

Table 6.4 Applying orthogonal arrays

Test case	Book	Purchase	Shipping
1	in_stock	cash	overnight
2	in_stock	check	economy
3	in_stock	charge	ground
4	in_stock	cash	pick-up
5	special_order	check	overnight
6	special_order	charge	economy
7	special_order	cash	ground
8	special_order	check	pick-up
9	out_of_print	charge	overnight
10	out_of_print	cash	economy
11	out_of_print	check	ground
12	out_of_print	charge	pick-up

Test case 1 in Table 6.4 says to test the combination which has book set to "in_stock", purchase set to "cash", and shipping set to "overnight". How to implement this test case depends upon the development environment. In object-oriented programming, this test consists of having an object of class book in state "in_stock" send a message that passes an object of class purchase in state "cash" to an object of class shipping in state "overnight". In a procedural language, the test consists of passing the parameters "in_stock", "cash", and "overnight" to the procedures order_book, purchase_book, and ship_book, respectively.

Some combinations may seem improbable. For example, can a user actually purchase a book that's out of print? The tester may view this as a non-feasible combination and remove it from the set of test cases. On the other hand, executing such a test ensures that the application traps this condition and returns the proper error message.

When reducing the number of test cases, the possibility of missing crucial combinations always exists. Using risk analysis (see Chapter 8) helps identify pertinent tests. If the reduced set of tests omits a vital combination, it may be easier to simply create additional tests rather than modify the combinatorial scheme to incorporate the required test condition.

Orthogonal array testing is a powerful technique to use any time a system presents a small input domain with a large number of permutations. [McGregor01], [Nguyen01], and [Pressman01] present additional examples. For a formal discussion, [Cohen97] describes the theory supporting orthogonal array testing, provides detailed examples and analysis from case histories, and explains how to use other combinations (such as triple and n-way combinations).

6.4.2 Testing inheritance

Inheritance creates new classes that reuse and extend previously created classes. This allows for expanding the features of existing code without actually modifying the original code. This powerful programming concept raises some issues with software testing. A derived class, or a child of a parent class, inherits the same capabilities as the original parent class yet also adds its own characteristics. The central idea is that after having written and debugged the parent class, you don't want to alter the code for fear of introducing new bugs. Another reason for using inheritance is that you may not have access to the source code. This frequently occurs when code is distributed as part of a class library. A developer may also define class hierarchies as part of the original design. Knowing when to use inheritance is one aspect of good object-oriented design. Improper use of inheritance – or any other coding technique, for that matter – can make testing and debugging more difficult.

Let's consider a generic example. Figure 6.12 shows the inheritance structure for three classes.

● Class A.

- Class B, child of Class A.
- Class C, child of Class B and grandchild of Class A.

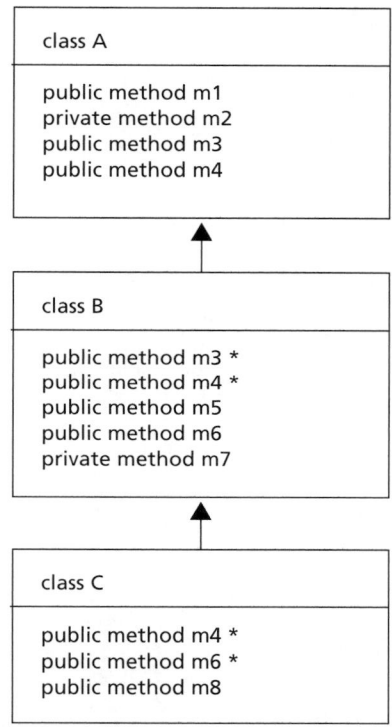

* denotes a new method that overrides the previous method

Figure 6.12 Inheritance example

Even though prior testing confirms that the parent class works correctly by itself, the question is whether the methods defined by the parent work when called by the child. Each class can define specific methods, and, depending on the programming language, inheritance allows a child to redefine (override) some of the methods. In addition, specifying whether the method is public or private affects whether it is accessible to the child. Public methods are visible to all derived classes, whereas private methods are not. Because of inheritance, one cannot assume that the methods of class A will work when called from an object of class B. Thus, we need to test the interactions of A in the context of B. Likewise, we need to test the interactions of A in the context of C and the interactions of B in the context of C. Bugs typically exist in the interactions as you move up or down a class level in the hierarchy.

A design with a shallow inheritance structure is less complicated to test. Flattening a class creates a diagram that highlights all inherited features. This

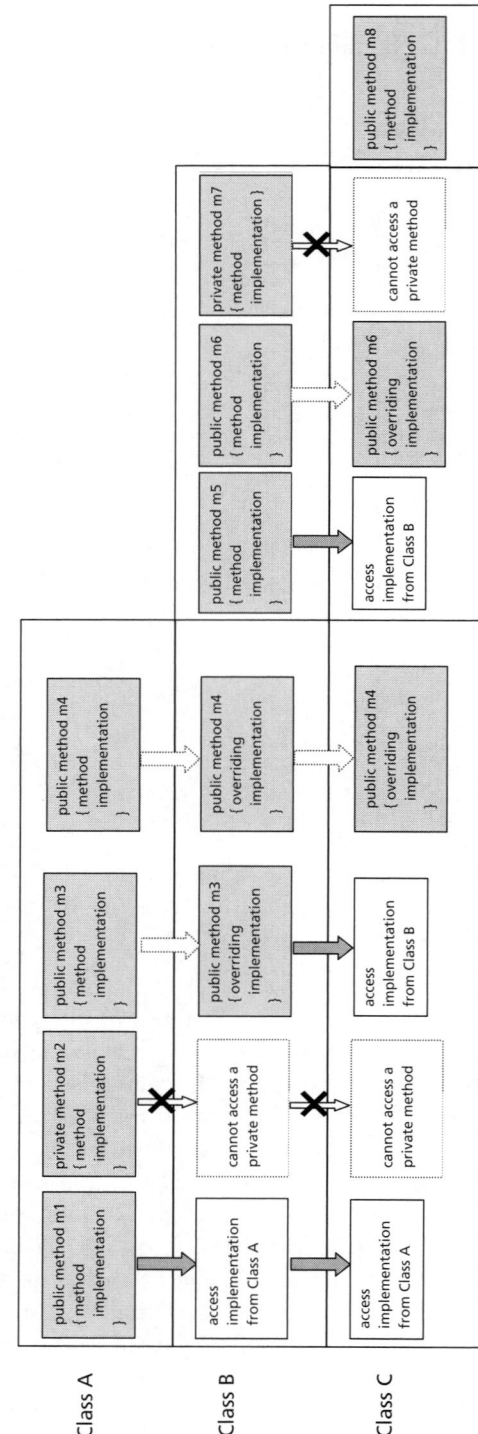
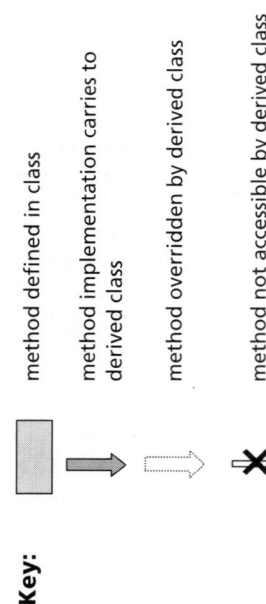

Figure 6.13 Flattening a class hierarchy

diagram, shown in Figure 6.13, lists all methods in both the parent class and derived classes as well as specifying which method is visible to each class.

The goal is to test each method in the context of every class that can access it. Using the diagram in Figure 6.13 helps identify the test conditions shown in Table 6.5. The "class.method" notation is shorthand to associate the method with the class that defines it. The first test condition says to test the method m1 (defined by class A) in the context of class A, class B, and class C.

Table 6.5 Conditions for testing methods

Method	Test from this class
A.m1	class A, B, C
A.m2	class A
A.m3	class A
B.m3	class B, C
A.m4	class A
B.m4	class B
C.m4	class C
B.m5	class B, C
B.m6	class B
C.m6	class C
B.m7	class B
C.m8	class C

The strategy presented here allows the tester to identify which methods are visible to derived classes. For more information and extensive examples on inheritance, see [Binder00], [Marick95], and [McGregor01]. The next step is to create an environment in which to execute these tests.

6.4.3   Test execution issues

After defining the test cases, the next step is to formulate an environment in which to execute the tests. This requires special test software, known as a driver, to invoke the software-under-test. The typical driver consists of the following features:

● packaging input and data;

● invoking the software-under-test;

● capturing the resulting outcome.

Creating a driver to test a class calls for additional considerations. The very nature of object-oriented design uses encapsulation to hide complexity, thereby limiting which data and methods are visible outside of the class. Thus, other classes cannot invoke this data and methods without creating some special access.

The driver must get around encapsulation to control and observe a class's internal data and methods. There are several ways to achieve this, such as:

● providing a test case method for each class;

● creating a parallel class, which appears identical to the original except for the addition of code needed for testing;

● creating a child class that inherits the methods to be tested.

All of these approaches alter the class and thus modify the actual application. Consequently, the tested implementation may not be identical to the released code. It is important that the testing environment be as close as possible to the deployment environment, otherwise, you are not fully testing the end product.

Sometimes the programmer will provide a special interface – hidden from other users – that the tester can use to access internal features. These trap doors may sometimes remain in the final production code. The danger is that this allows a malicious user to sabotage the system.

Drivers for testing classes can take on many forms. The testers must analyze the tradeoffs when deciding on a driver scheme. Creating effective and reusable test drivers takes significant planning and effort, even if commercial tools are used. For further details and examples on drivers for testing object-oriented software, refer to [Binder00] and [McGregor01].

6.5 Summary

Many of the techniques presented in earlier chapters apply readily to defining test cases for object-oriented software. This is especially true at the system test level, where defining test cases is independent of how the software is designed. The outline approach helps to organize the requirements. Use cases are an effective means of documenting requirements that translate readily into test cases.

Although classes are a unique component in object-oriented software, defining test cases uses some of the same approaches as in procedural software.

Inheritance, an integral part of object-oriented software, defines a hierarchy of classes. Flattening a class lists all the inherited features and specifies which methods are visible to the child class.

Some small input domains lead to a set of permutations that is too large for exhaustive testing. Orthogonal array testing is a powerful technique that reduces the number of test cases by ensuring the existence of a test case for every pair-wise combination.

Creating a test execution environment in which to test object-oriented software requires added consideration. Classes, due to encapsulation, restrict access to methods and internal states. Drivers must therefore be able to access, control, and observe internal data and methods.

7   Testing Web Applications

7.1   Introduction

Web-based applications present new challenges, both for developers and for testers. These challenges include:

- short release cycles;
- constantly changing technology;
- possible huge number of users during initial website launch;
- inability to control the user's running environment;
- 24-hour availability of the website.

The quality of a website must be evident from the onset. Any difficulty – whether in response time, accuracy of information, or ease of use – will compel the user to click to a competitor's site. Such problems translate into lost users, lost sales, and poor company image. Testing priorities differ based on the type of website being tested. For content-only sites, availability is the main concern, whereas interactive sites are concerned with the speed and reliability of interaction.

Using the test design techniques presented in earlier chapters helps define tests based on functionality, but this is just a subset of what web testing requires. Many strategies used to test web-based systems originate from client-server applications, such as a company's private intranet. This chapter presents an overview of the approaches needed to test web-based applications – as well as any application for which usability, security, databases, and other such testing tasks are relevant – and provides test cases for a sample application. For detailed discussion on testing web applications, refer to [Nguyen01] and [Splaine01].

7.2   Sample application

A storefront is a common web application. The generic pages that a company may portray are the presentation of the products, company information (such as history, locations, contact information, etc.), and company policies (such as refunds). The application may also include company philosophy, careers with the company, promotional items or banners that are used to help bring in investment dollars to run the business. This common practice is intended to support the variety of users who stumble across the website or have it bookmarked. This disparity of users, not just in experience, but for the purpose of visiting the website poses a critical challenge for designing test cases.

This sample storefront application sells books. For each book it lists the title, author, genre, price, and a brief description. It may display an image of a book. The customer may browse through the books, similar to a library, based upon title, author, genre, price, or keywords found in the description.

The customer selects various items by placing them in the shopping cart, a common tool found on many storefronts. When the customer is ready to purchase the items, they can display the selected items before actually making the purchase. The customer subsequently purchases the actual books.

As the inventory and focus of the store change with seasons and sales, the storefront needs to change easily and quickly without affecting the security or integrity of the site. To accomplish this, the GUI, in most cases, is and should be kept separate from the business rules of the application.

The environment in which a web application runs contains many components. The network administrator determines the actual configuration. The tester may need to understand a particular network setup in order to define some of the tests. Figure 7.1 shows a simple configuration that contains the following components:

1. The user views the website through a browser connected to the internet.

2. The website software can execute on the user's browser, at the host web server connected elsewhere on the internet, or on an application server. Where the software executes depends on how the developer designs the system.

3. A firewall, which is a combination of hardware and software, exists to keep a network secure from intruders. The user can also install a firewall to protect his computer from external attacks.

4. A proxy server is software whose purpose is to be the sole connection between a private network and the internet. A proxy server performs many functions that include preventing certain files from entering or leaving the network as well as improving performance by caching data.

5. Many web applications use a database to store the data necessary to run the website.

By comparison, a client-server configuration consists of one or more user computers connected to a server via a local area network (LAN) or wide area network (WAN).

Placement of the storefront on the web causes the site to have the same issues as a bricks-and-mortar store except it is visited from the patron's computer. These issues include:

● handling customer traffic;

● customer volume;

● payment for products;

Users
Web Browers

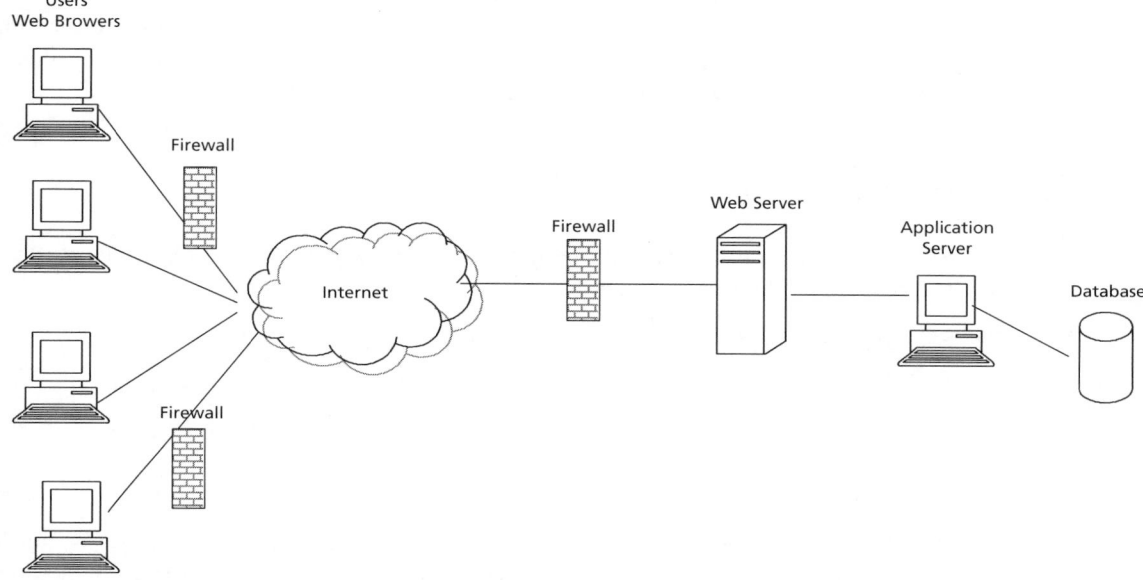

Figure 7.1 A sample web environment

- delivery of products;
- security of customer information;
- customer service during the visit;
- retention of the customer base.

Customer expectation of a site includes navigation that is easy to use and intuitive, quick response times, 24-hour availability of the site, reliability, no crashes or long delays, and indication of progress when using the site. A customer who is quickly annoyed by these types of issues while using the website may not return – resulting in lost revenue.

 **7.3**   **Functional and usability issues**

The first tests for a website should focus on the site's intended behavior by assessing the following issues:

- functionality;
- usability;
- navigation;
- forms;
- page content.

Executing these tests in an isolated and controlled test environment helps ensure that the core features of the website are correct, prior to accessing the site via the internet. After executing controlled environment tests, any new problems are most likely to be due to interactions from the live environment.

7.3.1   Functional testing

Functional testing involves making sure the features that most affect user interactions work properly. These include:

- forms (discussed in section 7.3.4);
- searches (referenced in section 7.9);
- pop-up windows;
- shopping carts;
- online payments.

Defining test cases for functionality testing involves various techniques, such as tables and outlines, presented in prior chapters. With regard to the bookstore example, Table 7.1 provides some sample test cases without benefit of an outline showing the derivation. Since the shopping cart is an essential part of the customer interaction, the tests combine access to the shopping cart while continuing to interact with the website.

The test case table format differs slightly from prior chapters, yet it specifies the same type of information. Two columns indicate the test input. The "input description" column provides a generic narrative of the test, while the tester records the actual data used under the "input data" column. This allows the tester to use the same test cases with different input data. This also allows the tester to define tests prior to knowing the actual information posted by the website.

Functional testing also evaluates the content of dynamically generated pages. These pages are created as users request them, often posting information that results from searching the database. Section 7.3.5 discusses dynamic code in more detail, while section 7.9 covers issues that pertain to testing databases.

Another aspect of functionality testing is to verify many behind-the-scenes features not readily apparent to the user, such as connections to legacy systems, connections to databases, connection to third-party applications (e-commerce, license servers, encryption engines, etc.), and business scenarios.

7.3.2   Usability testing

Many users have low tolerance for anything that is difficult to use or that does not work. A user's first impression of the site is important, and many websites have become cluttered with an increasing number of features. For general-use websites, frustrated users can easily click over to a competitor's site. For subscription-based

Table 7.1 Sample functional test cases

Test case ID	Input description	Input data	Expected results	Actual results
W-1	1. Go to page with a listing of some books. 2. Select and add book(s) to shopping cart. 3. View shopping cart.	web page = books added =	Shopping cart lists book(s) selected.	
W-2	1. Add book(s) to shopping cart by going to various pages, or with searches. 2. View shopping cart.	books added = web page(s) = search criteria =	Shopping cart lists all book(s) selected – even after conducting searches or changing page(s).	
W-3	1. Select but do *not* add book to shopping cart. 2. View shopping cart.	book selected =	Shopping cart does not list book last selected.	
W-4	1. Select some books and add to shopping cart. 2. Do *not* view shopping cart. 3. Go to checkout.	books added =	Books placed in shopping cart are listed at checkout.	
W-5	1. Select some books and add to shopping cart. 2. Remove a book from shopping cart.	books added = book removed =	Shopping cart is up-dated to reflect the book that was removed.	

websites, irritated users can become increasingly disgruntled as they wait for upgrades that solve problems encountered with the existing site. Failure to address these issues will result in the loss of a subscription. To address these concerns, usability testing assesses the website's user friendliness and suitability by gathering information about how users interact with the site. The idea is to give product teams targeted user feedback about the "look and feel", structure, navigation and features, because different communities of users have different requirements for assimilating and managing information.

The key to usability testing is to study what a user actually does. An observer records the user's actions and reactions to determine what types of problems the user encounters and how he overcomes them. The main steps to usability testing are to:

- identify the website's purpose;
- identify the intended users;
- define tests and conduct the usability testing;
- analyze the acquired information.

Successful usability testing does not present only positives, it also shows the weaknesses in the design. These weaknesses can be as subtle as the amount of time it takes the user to complete the desired actions in a test case or as profound as the user being completely lost in the paradigm used to design the pages. Addressing these weaknesses early in the development process allows for more efficient product development by eliminating or reducing the amount of re-work.

Identify the website's purpose

The designers must understand why people come to this website and what type of tasks they might perform. Depending on the application, the user might:

- get product information;
- purchase a product;
- get travel information, such as finding a flight and reserving a ticket;
- get user-specific information, such as that found in a bank account;
- play games;
- listen to music.

This information helps the designer keep the website focused and simple. Understanding the website's goals facilitates in identifying the target audience and devising typical scenarios for the intended users to try out.

Identify the intended users

What is an ordinary user? You will need to identify the profiles of typical users by specifying such characteristics as gender, age, education level, experience, skills, and demographics. What type of customer does the site attract? If this were a travel site, for example, is it intended for business travelers, recreational travelers or travel agents? Also, identifying keywords in the site's home page helps it be found by more users. Chosen keywords target the intended users.

This user profile is important in developing the test design and in choosing the sample subjects. The next step is to obtain participants who are as close as possible to the intended users. One inexpensive approach is for company employees to play the role of test participants and work through a task list.

Define tests and conduct the usability testing

This step consists of preparing and executing usability testing. Usability test cases are a defined set of tasks for the participants to follow. They must be clearly defined and easy to follow. Defining the test cases should take into consideration the knowledge of the participants. In the bookstore example, the instructions may include search for a particular book on specific topic and then place an order.

Execution of the usability test cases consists of observing participants' reactions and emotions as they try to perform the requested tasks. The observer must not provide any background information or initial help. The participants give feedback on what they like and dislike about the site and what frustrations they have while using the site. The observer records such information as:

- whether the user completes a task successfully;
- how much time a user needs to complete a task;
- the number of pages accessed for completing each task;
- where the user encounters difficulties or makes mistakes;
- how the user seeks assistance when lost;
- whether the online help provides enough information;
- what users say out loud and where in the task they say it;
- non-verbal cues such as gestures and facial expressions;
- whether users click through pages or use the search capability;
- how users react to the download time for specific pages;
- point at which users get confused and even fail to complete a task;
- number of clicks between tasks, number of seconds between clicks, as well as number of pages browsed and which pages browsed.

Usability testing can employ other data collection methods such as videotaping and recording keystrokes. Usability tests can occur at the development site or at a specialized usability lab. A usability lab provides a controlled environment with full observation, recording, and reporting facilities. Although this approach is costly, both in terms of equipment and personnel, it provides a more thorough evaluation.

Another facet of usability testing is to provide a questionnaire to explore the participants' opinions about a site or site prototype, thus providing qualitative and quantitative information. The user answers questions on a rating scale where applicable. Other questions are open ended. The questionnaire should probe for:

- whether the user felt successful in using the site;
- feedback on navigation and other features of the sites;
- whether the user would recommend this product to friends;
- whether the user understood the terminology;
- ideas for improvement;
- what the user liked or disliked about the website, and why.

No matter what the approach taken for usability testing, all results should be documented. Documentation is key to successfully completing this step.

Analyze the acquired information

The usability test report contains a summary of the observed results, list of usability problems, identification of any trends, an analysis of the videotapes, selected quotes from the participants, and a statistical analysis of the questionnaire. The findings and recommendations normally focus on ease of use and suggestions for a specific redesign of an application component. The goal is to improve the website based on the usability evaluation.

For more information on usability testing, refer to the many publications currently available such as [Dumas99] and [Rubin94].

7.3.3   Navigation testing

Good navigation is an essential part of a website, especially those that are complex and provide a lot of information. Assessing navigation is a major part of usability testing. Most users expect the following:

- easy and quick access to the information they want;
- logical hierarchy of pages;
- confirmation of where they are at any point;
- facility to return to previous states or the home page;
- consistent look and layout of every page;
- uncluttered pages.

Key issues with navigation testing include:

- moving to and from pages;
- scrolling through pages;
- clicking on all images and their thumbnails to ensure they work;
- testing all links (both within and outside the website) for validity and correctness;
- ensuring no broken links exist;
- viewing tables and forms to verify proper layout, which can vary under different browsers;
- verifying that windows with multiple frames are processed as if each were a single-page frame;
- measuring load time of every web page;
- ensuring compatibility and consistent usage of buttons, keyboard shortcuts, and mouse actions.

Table 7.2 displays some sample navigation test cases relating to the bookstore example.

Link testing

As part of navigation testing, the tester must ensure that all links work as expected. This means:

- following all links presented on a website, including hyperlinked text, linked graphics, or JavaScript-enabled controls (code written in JavaScript that is downloaded to the user's browser for execution);

Table 7.2 Sample navigation test cases

Test case ID	Input description	Input data	Expected results	Actual results
W-6	1. Search for query that generates at least 3 pages of output. 2. Scroll down by one book.	query =	1. Search results in 3 or more pages of output. 2. Top-most book entry scrolls off top of screen and next book entry appears at the bottom of screen, except when near bottom of list.	
W-7	1. Search for query that generates at least 3 pages of output. 2. Scroll down by one page.	query =	1. Search results in 3 or more pages of output. 2. Current screen contents scrolls up and next page appears, except when at top of list or at bottom of list.	

● verifying that the pages retrieved are the ones expected;

● ensuring that all errors are user friendly; for example making sure that no '404 – Not found' errors exist.

Testing links manually can be very time consuming and leaves room for human error if a link is missed. Automation of this task is recommended, and is easily accomplished with automated link checking tools. These automated link checking tools, commonly referred to as "site spiders", traverse the links in the website. Several types of site spiders are available which will check links on a per-page basis, or check dynamic links, i.e. follow the links on referenced pages. Link testing capabilities vary from tool to tool. Although a site spider can dramatically reduce the test time, a disadvantage to using automation for link testing is that the content returned from the link is not necessarily verified for validity.

Another common feature of a website application is "mouse over" text. This appears on the screen when the mouse is over the object. Because content can change frequently, the simplest approach is to prepare a checklist of "mouse over" attributes for testers to keep handy while performing functional or page content tests. The tester then tests the "mouse over" features as they are encountered and records the results accordingly. This also helps ensure that the developer did not miss a "mouse over" caption.

7.3.4   Forms testing

Websites that use forms need tests to ensure that each field works properly and that the form posts all data as intended by the designers. Testing of forms includes the following actions:

- using the tab key to verify that the form traverses fields in the proper order, both forwards and backwards;

- testing boundary values;

- checking that the forms traps invalid data correctly, especially date and numeric formats;

- verifying that the form updates information correctly.

In the bookstore example, the user enters data on a form to pay for the purchases. Figure 7.2 displays the web page and Table 7.3 provides some sample test cases. Using an outline or table, as presented in prior chapters, produces a more thorough set of test cases. Equivalence class partitioning and boundary value analysis are some techniques that help define tests for verifying the operation of most fields. Refer to Chapter 4 for examples on applying these techniques.

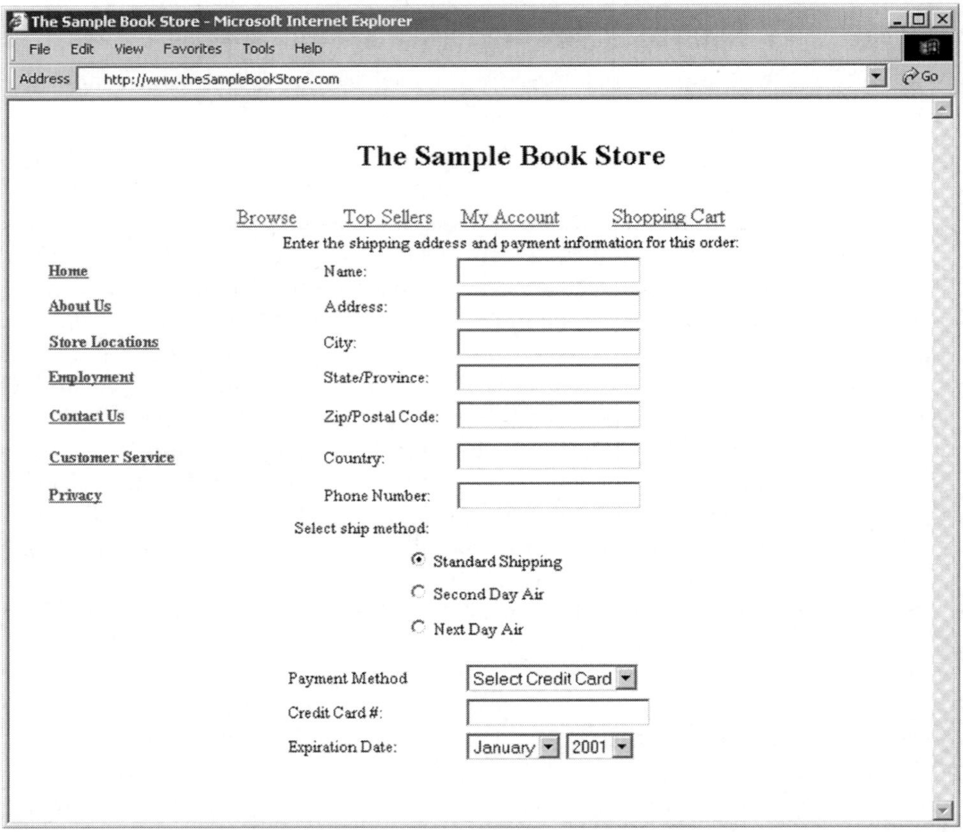

Figure 7.2 Sample form for purchasing books

Table 7.3 Sample test cases for testing forms

Test case ID	Input description	Input data	Expected results	Actual results
W-8	Tab from field to field.	starting field =	Fields traversed in proper order.	
W-9	Enter the maximum number of characters that the field accepts.	field name = characters typed =	Field accepts the input.	
W-10	Exceed the maximum number of characters that the field accepts.	field name = characters typed =	Field rejects the characters.	
W-11	Omit information in an optional field.	field name =	Application accepts the form (provided that the user completes the rest of the form correctly).	
W-12	Omit information in a required field.	field name =	Form requires user to provide information in a required field.	

7.3.5   Page content testing

Each web page must be tested for correct content from the user perspective. These tests fall into two categories: ensuring that each component functions correctly and ensuring that the content of each is correct. The first category of tests checks that:

- all images and graphics display correctly across various browsers;
- all content is present per the requirements;
- page structures are consistent across browsers;
- critical pages maintain same content from version to version;
- all parts of table or form are present and in the right place;
- links to relevant content inside and out of the site are accurate;
- "mouse over" text objects are correct;
- web pages are visually appealing.

Reviewing the content is one way to ensure correctness. This includes checking content for accuracy as well as proofreading for proper spelling, grammar, and terminology.

Dynamic pages are automatically created as users request them; these full pages do not reside on any server. For example, when conducting a search for a particular subject, the database may have been updated, thus listing completely different results each time the same search is conducted. The web page needs to have an appropriate message displayed when no data is presented, as well as when the amount of data presented is greater than the determined page size.

A typical use for dynamically generated HTML pages is the presentation of search results. With regard to the bookstore example, the customer can search for books related to a category (e.g. software testing), by author, or by title. Section 7.9 provides sample tests for viewing different search results.

Since most websites undergo continual changes in content, the tester must make sure that these changes have no adverse effect on the whole site. Regression testing consists of running existing tests to verify that the site still works as expected. Such tests can include:

● determining whether the new pages download the same as the prior pages;

● checking whether the new pages are identical with prior versions;

● checking whether vital information is the same or different;

● verifying whether links are still correct.

Table 7.4 shows a few sample test cases for the bookstore example. These particular tests are loosely worded and function more as a generic checklist for testing page content. The tester can define tests that specify the precise image, table, or other object to test.

Table 7.4 Sample test cases for testing page content

Test case ID	Input description	Input data	Expected results	Actual results
W-13	View images and graphics.	page viewed = browsers =	Images and graphics display correctly on selected browsers.	
W-14	View table.	table viewed = browsers =	Table displays correctly on selected browsers.	
W-15	Place mouse over every object.	objects tested =	The proper text appears over every object.	
W-16	Search for a book category (such as "software testing").	search category =	Search result lists all books in that category.	

7.4 Configuration and compatibility testing

A key challenge for web applications is ensuring that the user sees a web page as the designer intended. The user can select different browser software and browser options, use different network software and online service, and run other concurrent applications. The web application may incorporate servers, databases, and various connectivity devices.

For both user and web application, hardware settings and configuration also affect the environment. These include CPU types, RAM, graphic display cards, video capture cards, sound cards, monitors, network cards, and connection types (e.g. T1, DSL, modem) may all affect the appearance of the web page. While the web application environment usually remains static, the user's environment can be expected to run the gamut and include several variations depending on the given user. Thus, the goal of configuration and compatibility testing is to ensure the application functions correctly across the internet.

When writing test cases for configuration testing, different environment and configuration setup issues can affect the user's experience. Good requirements provide answers to the following questions. The tester can then use this information to develop appropriate test cases.

1. Is the user behind a firewall or proxy server?

2. Does the user connect through a load-balancing server (a machine that maintains an equal load on all the available web servers, see section 7.5)?

3. Does the browser accept cookies? (A cookie is a packet of data sent by a web server and then stored on the user's hard disk. It keeps track of the user's information and preferences.)

4. Are high-security settings enabled?

5. What technologies are the developers of the web page using? For example, if the web page uses ActiveX controls or Java scripting, the tester must know which versions of the browser support these implementations.

6. Are secure server tools (childproof blocking mechanisms) being used?

Compatibility testing ensures product functionality and reliability on the supported browsers and platforms that exist on the customer's computer. The proliferation of browsers and browser versions, each running on different operating systems and on different platforms, and each with different graphics capabilities and plug-ins, has created hundreds of different user environments. The user's browser connects to a server and other communication devices that must interact correctly to execute the web application.

Since the test cycle may not allow time for all environmental flavors to be tested, the following guidelines may help to prioritize tests.

1. Ask the developers about particularly vulnerable configuration or incompatible scenarios and target these troublesome areas.

2. Focus on more commonly used browser versions on the market. Ideally, the tester must know the current browser market share.

3. Focus on the most likely platforms used by the customers.

4. Focus on major releases of the software application, including features and key changes.

Table 7.5 serves as a guideline for testing web applications by listing the platform and browser environments to be tested. The intent is to execute the same test cases on different platform and browser combinations, and then check off the appropriate box after having executed the test cases.

Table 7.5 Browser compatibility table

Browser / Platform	Netscape Communicator 4.5	Netscape Communicator 4.7	America Online 4.0	Internet Explorer 4.01	Internet Explorer 5.0	...
Windows 95						
Windows 98						
Windows NT						
Windows 2000						
Windows ME						
Mac OS X						
iMac						
Macintosh 8.1						
Linux				*not applicable*	*not applicable*	
...						

The ideal, of course, is to execute every test suite on every browser/platform combination. In reality, time and people resources limit the number of tests that can be executed. Dividing the testing of the browser/platform combinations across the test team can help expedite test execution. Each team member is responsible for testing a specific set of test cases in a particular browser/platform environment. Use risk analysis (see Chapter 8) to determine which tests to execute on all required browser/platform combinations and which tests to execute in some of the selected environments. This ensures complete coverage of the prioritized platforms.

In addition to testing minimal functionality of the website in each browser/platform combination, the test cases in Table 7.6 apply while performing compatibility testing. The tester must repeat these tests for every browser/platform combination.

7.5   Reliability and availability

A key requirement of a website is that it be available whenever the user requests it, often 24 hours a day, every day. The number of users accessing a website simultaneously may also affect the site's availability. To assess availability, the tester must build tests around anticipated usage spikes, which can include:

- for store applications: promotional campaigns and sales;
- for business cycles: month-end and quarter-end dates;
- for banking applications: direct deposit dates;
- during maintenance: required downtime for backups, upgrades, and other operations.

Testers must also check for resource issues (such as memory leaks and database limitations) that can degrade performance or even bring the web application to a halt, resulting in loss of future business. Memory leaks occur when memory that is no longer being used has not been returned to the pool of free memory. Memory

Table 7.6 Sample compatibility test cases

Test case ID	Input description	Input data	Browser version and platform	Expected results	Actual results
W-17	Add the website to list of favorites and try to recall once the session is closed.	web page =		The website should appear and function properly.	
W-18	Create a shortcut to the web page and try to access the shortcut after closing the session.	web page =		The website should appear and function properly.	
W-19	Use the BACK button after submitting the credit card information or logging out.	web page displayed prior to using BACK button =		The credit card information must not appear, and a default screen or main page is presented to the user.	
W-20	Open multiple sessions of the website.	web page accessed =		Each session is usable.	
W-21	Test with cookies set on and off.	web page =		The functionality of the website performs as designed.	
W-22	Use the print option of the browser.	web page =		The print output is representative of the page where the print was requested.	

leaks can be slow, hard to determine, and eventually, if undetected, bring the computer system to a halt. Database limitations include keeping the database running efficiently (optimization), ensuring that the input agrees with the defined variable, performing regular database backups, and ensuring that the logs do not use all remaining hard disk space.

It is important for the tester to be aware of the architecture of the system in order to conduct adequate availability and reliability testing. For example, if the system contains two web servers for load balancing, the tester must be able to report the performance of the system with one web server. Load balancing maintains an equal load on all the available web servers. If for some reason one of the web servers is removed from the production, i.e. for maintenance, the website should continue to perform at a reduced but acceptable level.

Unique problems come into play for a system with 24-hour access. When do you run a load test on the system? Or, does a system with 24-hour access require a duplicate test system for load type testing? Some key areas to explore include:

● testing in production during off-peak usage;
● need for similar or duplicate test/production hardware;
● performance scaling;
● user authentication.

Table 7.7 sites a few example test cases for reliability and availability testing of the storefront example.

Table 7.7 Sample reliability and availability test cases

Test case ID	Input description	Input data	Expected results	Actual results
W-23	Four users login and purchase the same book at the same time.	user 1 = user 2 = user 3 = user 4 = book =	All four users can add the same book to their respective shopping cart at the same time.	
W-24	During a database upgrade, repeat test W-23.		The database upgrade is successful, and users can purchase the books successfully, with no degraded performance noted in the system.	
W-25	While printing month-end reports, use the website to purchase a book.	book =	Month-end reports are printed and the book is purchased successfully, with no degraded performance noted in the system.	
W-26	Create and execute an automated test script to continually purchase a book every 3 minutes.	book 1 = book 2 = book 3 = book n =	Each book is successfully purchased, with no degraded performance noted in the system.	
W-27	Conduct a volume test, which initiates 10 new users every 20 minutes. Run this test for one hour.		All users can access the system and can perform various functions of the website, with no degraded performance noted in the system.	
W-28	Repeat test W-27, with fewer resources, i.e. one less web server.	resource removed =	All users can access the system and can perform various functions of the website, with no degraded performance noted in the system.	

7.6 Performance

Performance testing, which evaluates system performance under normal and heavy usage, is crucial to the success of any web application. A system that takes too long to respond may frustrate the user who can then quickly move to a competitor's site. Given enough time, every page request will eventually be delivered; however, this may not satisfy the user's needs. The question then becomes: what is "too slow"?

Performance testing seeks to ensure that the website server responds to browser requests within defined parameters.

The very nature of the web and the fact that different users interact differently with the application greatly affect performance. Several aspects that can affect performance include the following:

- high activity and volume at launch;
- time of day;
- activity spikes due to marketing promotions;
- bottlenecks due to hundreds of users on a network;
- download time;
- usage patterns;
- think time;
- user arrival rates;
- client platforms;
- internet access speeds;
- abandonment rates.

Testing from the local system is good for checking quality, but one cannot measure response time due to internet-related delays. Testing from remote geographic location brings in the effect of all the related delays. The size of each page and the number of images used on the website can also affect the performance of the application. Implementing browser caching test scenarios to ensure adequate response time is a key area of observation during performance testing.

Performance testing should begin early in the test cycle. Many organizations plan performance tests in the last round of testing. This may not be the most effective method of planning, especially if the result of the performance test identifies major design flaws. Performance tests should begin once the test team has determined that the functionality of the application is stable.

Table 7.8 provides examples of test cases to consider during performance testing. Timing, which is a primary concern, must be defined in the requirements.

7.6.1   Scalability testing

Scalability concerns the website's ability to handle the volumes and types of activities that can occur after launch. The organization needs to ensure the delivery of acceptable performance under many situations and that it can support transaction levels after the site's launch. The following types of scenarios affect scalability:

- how closely the test environment matches the production environment;
- millions of users accessing the site during launch;
- activity spikes due to marketing promotions.

Table 7.8 Sample performance test cases

Test case ID	Input description	Input data	Expected results	Actual results
W-29	1. Search for a book. 2. Record the response time to the query. 3. Repeat this test up to 4 times.	query =	Record the Min, Max and Average response times, and ensure they satisfy the requirements.	
W-30	1. Select the NEXT page from a set of browsing options. 2. Record the response time to display the next page. 3. Repeat this test up to 4 times.	current page = next page =	Record the Min, Max and Average response times, and ensure they satisfy the requirements.	
W-31	1. Submit a completed purchase form. 2. Record the response time to receive purchase confirmation. 3. Repeat this test up to 4 times.	book(s) purchased =	Record the Min, Max andAverage response times, and ensure they satisfy the requirements.	
W-32	1. Turn browser caching on. 2. Complete a form. 3. Submit the form. 4. Record the response time measuring end-to-end response time (i.e. Browser–Web–Website–Web–Browser). 5. Repeat this test up to 4 times.	form submitted =	Record the Min, Max and Average response times, and ensure they satisfy the requirements.	
W-33	1. Turn browser caching off. 2. Complete a form. 3. Submit the form. 4. Record the response time measuring end-to-end response time (i.e. Browser–Web–Website–Web–Browser). 5. Repeat this test up to 4 times.	form submitted =	Record the Min, Max and Average response times, and ensure they satisfy the requirements.	
W-34	1. Login from a remote location or use a dial-up connection to access the website. 2. Complete a form. 3. Submit the form. 4. Record the response time measuring end-to-end response time. 5. Repeat this test up to 4 times.	remote location = form submitted =	Record the Min, Max and Average response times, and ensure they satisfy the requirements.	
W-35	1. Initiate a browser request. 2. Record the response time of the website server response. 3. Repeat this test up to 4 times.	request submitted =	Record the Min, Max and Average response times, and ensure they satisfy the requirements.	

The key goals to ensure scalability of the system include:

● determine which types of scenarios to anticipate;
● identify business cycles;

- plan for capacity by modeling the users expected to access the site;
- identify the levels and types of activity that can degrade performance;
- produce performance measures such as requests per second and transactions per second.

Another aspect of scalability testing is to identify the different types of visitors and their expected interactions. Casual users are curious and browse around the website. Other visitors seek to conduct business, such as requesting information, invoking bank transactions, or purchasing products from a retailer. These type of tests reflect the different types of users:

- simple navigation around site;
- basic operations on site;
- deep operation of key features.

The next step is to estimate the number of each type of visitors during different times.

Refer to the publication [Segue00] for a detailed discussion on scalability issues and for examples of scalability test scenarios.

7.6.2   Load testing

The purpose of load testing is to model real world experiences, typically by generating many simultaneous users accessing the website. Automation increases the ability to conduct a valid load test, because you can emulate thousands of users by sending simultaneous requests to the application or the server. In order to create adequate load scripts, the tester uses information from daily usage logs to mimic a realistic user load. In some cases usage logs are not readily available, and the tester must rely on the requirements specifications to understand the system's performance requirements.

Since it may not be feasible for an organization to mirror the test environment to match the production environment, the tester must provide solid test results to the project team to be able to extrapolate the measurements from the test environment. This may prove to be a difficult task since the comparison may not be a one-to-one ratio. In this case, it will be important for the project team to understand and agree upon the final results.

Preparing for a load test

Load testing must be carefully planned to successfully complete the load test the first time, thus shortening the amount of test time. In reality, even with the best planning, load testing may need to be repeated at least once, and uses more time than initially thought due to the time necessary to setup the load test.

For successful completion of a load test, the following guideline includes several good points for preparing the load test.

1. Understand the load requirements of the system. Investigate the total and concurrent number of users the website may need to support. Newly released applications will not have history statistics available. The test team may have to rely on the requirement specification to collect specific targets, such as:
   - number of users in either unique hits per day, per week, or per month;
   - total concurrent users: worst-case scenario at peak time;
   - peak request rate: number of pages to be served per second;
2. Identify the tools, such as test tools and monitoring tools, to be used to conduct the load test.
3. Generate enough users and transactions to assess capacity and performance that will hold up to a live environment.
4. Establish a baseline: Create scripts to simulate a single user with a single browser.
5. Create test scripts to simulate multiple sessions played on multiple browsers.
6. Identify any other applications that are running on the application server to capture the correct system activity. (Multiple applications running concurrently on one system will affect performance.)
7. Execute the test(s) multiple times.
8. Identify the players who will be monitoring the system performance during the test.
9. Conduct formal inspections on test scripts.
10. Prepare test results that capture the minimum, maximum and average response time of the system.

Executing the load test

Executing the load test requires taking time and care in setting up the actual load test. Refer to section 7.10 for information on planning and conducting load tests in a production environment.

7.6.3   Stress testing

Stress testing consists of subjecting the system to varying and maximum loads to evaluate the resulting performance. Automated test tools exist that simulate loads on any website and execute the tests continuously for several hours or days. These tools can report the following type of information:

- number of requests, transactions, and kilobytes per second;
- round-trip time (elapsed time from when a user makes a request to when the user receives the resulting information);
- number of concurrent connections;

- degradation of performance;
- types of visitors to the site;
- number of each type of visitor during a period of time;
- CPU and memory usage of the application servers.

Another type of stress testing is to verify that the application is reliable when available memory or processors are nearing a known limit. For example, if the system can handle 50 concurrent users, create a test script that runs for several hours, sustaining 50 users. Using monitoring tools during this test can help to identify potential system bottlenecks. With this information, the developers can predict additional hardware or design changes needed to accommodate future increases in user access. This type of testing, however, requires a high degree of randomness in the execution of each simulated user. Otherwise, you might see performance peaks and troughs that are regular and totally artificial. One way to alleviate this problem is to insert randomness into the time between one action and the next for each user, as well as vary the time between ending one test and starting the next.

Stress testing is not limited to the user's view of the web applications. The backend database must also undergo stress testing to help identify potential bottlenecks. The tester must decide whether to execute such tests in an isolated environment or through a web environment. Specific test scenarios may include the following:

1. Supposing the database can handle an inventory of 100,000 books, compare the time it takes to enter the 100th record vs the 99,999th record into the database.

2. Executing tests with 100 users accessing the same record from the database, while comparing the response time to having one user request the record.

Several factors, listed below, can affect the test team's ability to prepare and execute stress tests.

1. Is the test environment comparable to the production environment, in memory and processors? If not, a test may need to run in the production environments. Refer to section 7.10 for details on conducting a test in the production environment.

2. Is the test environment free of other traffic, as to not skew the results of the stress test?

3. What are the worst-case scenarios? Create the test cases that execute these conditions.

Once stress testing is completed, the project team must decide if the degradations noted in the system are acceptable under the stress conditions applied. Degradation can occur for any scenarios listed above. Performance is expected to slow down when an extreme number of users hit the site simultaneously. Risk management as discussed in Chapter 8 can help assess the degradations.

 **7.7**

Security testing

Security is a primary concern when communicating and conducting business – especially sensitive and business-critical transactions – over the internet. The user wants assurance that personal and financial information is secure. Finding the vulnerabilities in an application that would grant an unauthorized user access to the system is important.

Regardless of whether the application requires the user to enter a password to access the website, the tester must check for the internet threats known today. Finding answers to the following questions helps identify additional security related tests.

1. What precautions exist to prevent or limit attacks from hackers?
2. Are the browser settings set to ensure maximum-security protection?
3. How does the website handle access rights?
4. Does the application have a virus detection program for users logging in through a telnet or third-party intranet provider?
5. Does the application handle transaction tampering, i.e. changing the original ship-to address?
6. Does the e-commerce vendor provide a mechanism to prevent credit card fraud?
7. Are log files in place and are they audited periodically to automatically detect suspicious behavior?
8. How does the website encrypt data?
9. How does the website authenticate users?
10. Does viewing the source code disclose any vital information?
11. Can the system be accessed and tampered with by direct modem dial-up into the database?
12. How safe is credit card or user information? And what is considered safe enough?
13. Does the application allow for a file to be digitally signed? (This uses public key encryption technology to ensure that a third party has not tampered with the file.)

The hardware and software that comprise the firewall are a key component in keeping a network secure from intruders. The goal of testing the firewall is to defeat and bypass security mechanisms in order to determine their effectiveness. Logging and examining network traffic – both incoming and outgoing – is a primary firewall testing activity. Another aspect is performing penetration tests, in which an authorized individual actually attempts to break into the network. Firewall testing ensures that:

● packet filtering works as designed;

- the firewall correctly implements the company's security policy. For example, if the policy states that the firewall must forward all incoming mail traffic to the mail server, then the tester must verify that this does happen;

- the firewall triggers an alarm when necessary;

- no leakages exist in the security perimeter created by a firewall. A leakage occurs when access routes into a network other than through a protected gate exist, thus allowing someone to bypass firewall defenses to reach the network;

- the firewall hides information and addresses from the internal network it protects;

- adequate logging of events helps track down an intruder and finds security holes caused by an incident.

Thoroughly verifying a website's security requires special knowledge about information technology. Often, security experts from outside the organization will assess security matters that pertain to browser settings, security protocols, firewalls, cryptography, as well as malicious use of cookies, viruses, and ActiveX controls. Although the average tester may lack expertise in these areas, the tester can effectively evaluate certain situations such as logins and online payments.

Security testing requires extra caution. Careless testing procedures can cause unintentional damage or disruption by overloading a network with service requests and tying up ports on host machines. In addition, the organization must safeguard test results to prevent unauthorized persons from finding out about the system's vulnerabilities.

7.8 End-to-end transaction testing

End-to-end transactions follow the workflow of the customer from beginning of the visit until the customer leaves the site. This tests all parts that make up a particular transaction, which could include web browsers, web servers, application servers, databases, and middleware. Conducting business in such a manner is the basis of e-commerce. The test cases for end-to-end transaction testing complement usability testing by following the workflow logic and combining a number of user actions in the actual test. For the storefront example, the workflow is as follows:

1. Customer visits the site.
2. Customer browses through the books.
3. Customer selects books and adds them to the shopping cart.
4. Customer provides a shipping address.
5. Customer pays for the purchases.
6. Store sends the customer receipt via e-mail.

End-to-end transactions include processing any adverse conditions that result from customer requests. For the bookstore example, this includes the following:

1. The selected book is not in stock.

2. The book needs to be specially ordered.

3. The customer wants to remove one or more selected books from the shopping cart.

4. The customer wants to cancel the order (before or after purchase).

5. The customer wants a refund.

6. The credit card used for purchase was rejected (i.e. is no longer valid).

Because of the various combinations of user actions used, the focus of test cases needs to resemble the flow through the website. However, the test cases need not be overly detailed. For example, the tester can decide whether to use only mouse actions, only keyboard actions, or what combination of mouse and keyboard actions. Specifying such details falls under functional testing. Here, the result of test execution is to look at a combination of actions. Table 7.9 lists sample test cases for end-to-end transaction testing.

7.9 Database testing

Database testing is often an essential part of web testing, since many websites typically provide some sort of search capability. The website usually stores products or information in a database that simplifies and expedites searches for the selected items. Some applications have users enter data that becomes part of the database.

Database testing involves some in-depth knowledge of the given application and requires a more defined plan of approach to test the data. At a minimum, the tester must have the ability to query the database consistently at specified points in the workflow. It is important for the tester to be aware of the database design concepts and implementation rules. Key issues for database testing include:

● data integrity;

● data validity (input into database in proper form);

● data manipulation and updates (updating the number of books sold, books available, etc.).

Data integrity is a major component for implementing a successful website. The organization must put controls in place to detect data corruption. Data corruption is often noticed only in its advanced stages, since corruption takes place in a "building block" approach. It starts out small and the problem worsens as time passes or as the number of transactions increase. Providing appropriate checkpoints can help mitigate data corruption. For example, keeping and reviewing a daily transaction log can facilitate tracking database changes.

Database testing must also account for data validity. Data validity ensures that accurate information is provided to the patrons and that accurate information is passed back to the database. Generally, the defect rate is much higher in the data than the application itself. One approach is to look at the workflow and check the

Table 7.9 Sample end-to-end transaction test cases

Test case ID	Input description	Input data	Expected results	Actual results
W-36	1. Browse through the site and add some book(s) to the shopping cart. 2. View the shopping cart. 3. Remove a book from the shopping cart.	books added = book removed =	Shopping cart lists book(s) added, but not the book that was removed.	
W-37	1. Browse through the site and add some book(s) to the shopping cart. 2. Purchase books. 3. Before entering credit card number, cancel the order.	books added =	Exit purchase menu and return to shopping cart page.	
W-38	1. Browse through the site and add some book(s) to the shopping cart, including some special order items. 2. Purchase books. 3. Submit the form.	books added = purchase information provided =	Transaction is processed and confirming e-mail message is sent.	
W-39	1. Browse through the site and add some book(s) to the shopping cart. 2. Purchase books via credit card. 3. Submit transaction. 4. Ask for refund.	books selected =	1. Transaction is processed and confirming e-mail message sent. 2. Separate e-mail message sent to confirm order cancellation.	
W-40	1. Browse through the site and add some book(s) to the shopping cart. 2. Purchase books. 3. Provide an invalid credit card.	books added = credit card =	Purchase is refused, and user is linked back to another page.	
W-41	1. Browse through the site and add some book(s) to the shopping cart. 2. Purchase books but do not fill in all required fields. 3. Submit the form.	books added = fields omitted =	Error message posted, highlighting missing information.	

database at the points of change. This consists of isolating the actions that modify the database and inspecting the altered content for correctness. It is important for the tester to understand the risk areas and prioritize the testing accordingly. Conducting a risk assessment as described in Chapter 8 will reveal the higher priority test cases that help mitigate the risks.

Testing a database operates at two levels: administrative functions and user features. The database administrator can perform restricted actions not available to the website patron. For the bookstore example, the most common administrative action includes:

● adding new books to the inventory;
● deleting existing books from the inventory;
● updating specific fields, such as pricing changes.

The following checklist helps to formulate many additional administrative test cases:

1. Understand the database design.
2. Identify the major risks.
3. Understand the security controls of the design; understand which user IDs have read/write access to the database controls.
4. Understand the procedures of the database maintenance updates and upgrades.
5. Ensure the performance requirements are being met.
6. Ensure operationability and performance when several users conduct the same task or query simultaneously (and include maximum simultaneous or concurrent users per specifications).
7. Ensure that backup and recovery procedures work as designed and don't impact availability requirements.
8. Ensure that the database allows the maximum number of connections that the system is designed to handle.
9. Ensure that database operations have enough space and memory for the amount of data. Include expansion of the system when these physical limitations of space and memory are exceeded.

In the bookstore example, the web application and user web interface remains stable over time. The only changes occur when adding books and tracking customer lists (if the application actually tracks customer usage for the possibility of sending future sales promotions). User access to this database consists primarily of searching for information. For other websites, in which the database changes continually, optimization and speed of results from searches and inputs remain critical. Table 7.10 provides some generic test case examples for testing the bookstore application. The information in the expected results column will vary depending on the database requirements. For example, specifying a non-existent author name can result in one of several possible outcomes. The application can post an error message, suggest an alternate spelling, or provide a list of books written by authors with a similar name.

 ## 7.10 Post-implementation testing

The main reason for conducting a post-implementation test is to verify the behavior of the application in the production environment. In most cases, it is not feasible to duplicate the test environment to match the production environment, thus the product team must plan for a final test in the production environment. In addition, the organization will value ensuring that the website can be found through search engines, site spiders, and meta tags.

Table 7.10 Sample database test cases

Test case ID	Input description	Input data	Expected results	Actual results
W-42	Search for a book by specifying a valid author name.	author =	Post a list of books written by this author.	
W-43	Search for a book by specifying a valid, but not unique, author name.	author =	Post a list of books written by all authors with this name.	
W-44	Search for a book by specifying a valid author name and title combination.	author = title =	Post information about this book.	
W-45	Search for a book by specifying a non-existent author name.	author =	Author name not found. Post a suggestion of alternate spellings.	
W-46	Search for a book by specifying a valid author name but non-existent title.	author = title =	Title not found. List all books written by this author.	
W-47	1. Search for a valid book by title. 2. Administrator changes the book's price. 3. Search for same book by title.	title = new price =	1. Post book information. 2. Update database. 3. Post book information, with new price listed.	
W-48	Execute these steps concurrently: • Administrator adds a new book. • Customer searches for this new book.	author = title =	Search result can post incomplete information, such as blank fields.	
W-49	Have multiple users conduct the same query simultaneously.*	search criteria = number of users =	Accurate results are presented to all users, with an acceptable response time.	

* Each query is conducted on separate computers on the network/internet setup using appropriate individual browser.

Since most web-based organizations strive to be online 24 hours a day, post-implementation testing commonly takes place in a "production maintenance window". The most likely timeframe for this window is when customer usage is low, which could occur at 1:00 on a Sunday morning, unless that time coincides with peak usage on the other side of the world.

7.10.1 Post-implementation strategy

Establishing a well-orchestrated set of tasks prior to the actual test or maintenance window increases confidence in the quality of software releases. By executing these tests prior to product delivery, the tester has a better chance to uncover problems that were not seen during the test cycle, and thus assess the actual performance of the new system in the production environment.

Conducting post-implementations tests requires the following information:

- timeline of events;
- post-implementation team identification;
- acceptance test checklist;
- load test checklist with load scripts available;
- rollback plan in case of failure.

Preparation is a key factor to successful and efficient completion and response for the post-implementation strategy. The more planning done ahead of time, the more time saved in the long run.

7.10.2   Timeline

A timeline lists the important events that must take place. This timeline, shown in Table 7.11, includes the time, the task, and the person responsible for each task.

The term *smoke test* describes an initial set of tests that determine if a new version of the application performs well enough for further testing. Once the application has passed this first checkpoint, testers perform tests to determine whether the application can be released. Often these tests are the user acceptance tests that validate the system against the user's requirements and ensure that the application is ready for operational use. Other times, these could be regression tests (with some new tests to verify new features) that assess the application's suitability for release. In this context, the term *acceptance test* refers to the tests selected by the tester – with concurrence from the product manager – that determine the product's readiness. The *go/no go decision* is the point at which the product manager determines whether to release the new product in its current form.

Table 7.11 Timeline of events

Time	Task	Person assigned	Task complete (Pass/Fail)
1:00 a.m.	Roll out new components: *List components and version number identified in Release Notes*	Developer	
1:45 a.m.	Bring system online and run smoke test.	Developer	
2:00 a.m.	Acceptance test begins.	Tester #1	
2:45 a.m.	Load test begins.	Tester #2	
3:30 a.m.	Load test ends.	Tester #2	
4:00 a.m.	Acceptance test ends.	Tester #1	
4:15 a.m.	Go/no go decision.	Product Manager	
4:15 a.m.	Proceed to rollback plan if needed.	All	

7.10.3   Post-implementation team

A chart of the team members involved in the post-implementation maintenance window, as shown in Table 7.12, lists the key participants who need to be on-site or on-call during the test. Modify this table according to the specific title, role, name, contact information, and number of individuals within each organization.

Table 7.12 Post-implementation team

Role	Function	Person responsible	On-site / On-call	Contact information
Lead Developer	On-site support		On-site	
Tester #1	Acceptance test – suite 1		On-site	
Tester #2	Acceptance test – suite 2		On-site	
Tester #n	Acceptance test – suite n		On-site	
Tester #m	Load test		On-site	
Developer	Monitor productions system		On-site	
Product Manager	Authority to make go/ no go decision		On-call	

7.10.4   Acceptance test checklist

Table 7.13 provides a checklist for the testers to use during the maintenance window for performing the acceptance test.

Table 7.13 Acceptance test checklist

Responsible tester	Component test	Test complete (Pass/Fail)
Tester #1	*List browser/platform to be used.*	
	End-to-end transaction.	
	Verify billing.	
	Verify log files on server.	
	Etc.	
Tester #2	*List browser/platform to be used.*	
	End-to-end transaction.	
	Help file.	
	Remove a book from the shopping cart.	
	Verify that high priority problems found during prior testing have been properly fixed, etc.	
Tester #n	*List browser/platform to be used.*	
	Etc.	

7.10.5   Load test checklist

Table 7.14 helps the tester track the steps in conducting the load tests. Since time is limited during the maintenance window, the load test scripts must be ready in advance of the post-implementation testing.

Table 7.14 Load test checklist

Responsible tester	Component test	Test complete (Pass/Fail)
Tester #1	Execute load test scripts.	
	Work with systems engineering to monitor performance of the system.	
	Re-execute load test scripts.	
	Provide results to manager.	

7.10.6   Rollback plan

In case the release must be rolled back, a contingency strategy outlining a full rollback plan is needed. This plan orchestrates a clean procedure to return the production environment to the original state, followed by a repeat of the acceptance tests to verify that the restored state is functional. Table 7.15 shows a possible timeline for a product rollback.

Table 7.15 Rollback plan timeline

Time	Task	Person assigned	Task complete (Pass/Fail)
4:30 a.m.	Roll back new components: *List components and version number: (Before the actual testing begins, this list must be approved.)*	Developer	
5:30 a.m.	Bring system online and run smoke test.	Developer	
5:45 a.m.	Acceptance test begins.	Tester #1	
6:00 a.m.	Load test begins.	Tester #2	
7:00 a.m.	Load test ends.	Tester #2	
7:30 a.m.	Acceptance test ends.	Tester #1	

7.11   Summary

Testing web applications presents new challenges that emanate from continually changing technology, the proliferation of browsers, the inability to control the user's environment, the unpredictable number of users, and the site's availability 24 hours a day.

Several aspects and appropriate approaches are discussed in this chapter. The key is to prepare for the tests, execute them, and document the results according to the approaches taken.

Functional testing asserts whether the main features function correctly, but this evaluates only one aspect of a web application. Other types of testing address issues specific to the web environment, many of which apply equally well to the client-server environment.

Usability testing evaluates whether a site is user friendly by observing users as they interact with the site.

Navigation testing ensures that the user can accomplish the desired tasks by verifying access to pages, images, links, and other page components.

Testing a form ensures that each field works properly.

Testing page content ensures that the information provided by the website is correct.

Configuration and compatibility testing make sure that the application functions correctly across the various hardware and software environments.

Reliability and availability testing assesses whether the website is accessible whenever the users request it by testing around anticipated peak usage such as marketing promotions and high-activity cycles.

Performance testing ensures that the website server responds to browser requests within defined parameters. As part of performance testing, scalability testing assesses the website's ability to meet the load requirements. Load testing evaluates how the system functions when processing many simultaneous requests from a multitude of users. Stress testing subjects the system to varying loads.

Security testing attempts to find an application's vulnerabilities in order to evaluate the safeguarding of vital and confidential information.

End-to-end transaction testing tests all parts that make up a particular transaction by following a customer's workflow from entering to leaving the site.

Database testing verifies the integrity of stored data, often product information that is used by the website.

Post-implementation testing verifies an application's behavior in the production environment. This includes providing a rollback plan, if necessary, to roll back a release and restore the production environment to the original state in a methodical and controlled fashion.

8 Reducing the Number of Test Cases

8.1 Introduction

The test design methods presented in this book tend to create a large number of test cases. For most projects it is nearly impossible to execute all of these tests. Although many project schedules are strapped due to tight time constraints, many other reasons exist that necessitate reducing the number of test cases, for example:

- imminent ship date;
- impossibly large number of test cases;
- limited staffing resources;
- limited access to test equipment.

This chapter presents several techniques that reduce the number of test cases. Although no one method will identify the best test cases, the intent is to categorize the tests on a scale from most important down to least important. The methods described help identify and prioritize key testing areas, which then guides the tester to create and execute the most crucial test cases first. Any remaining available time can then be used to focus on the next tier of tests.

The true art of testing is to select a *meaningful* subset of test cases that are most likely to uncover problems, thereby reducing the total number of tests while maintaining confidence in the product's operation. Failure to assess the application's potential problems often results in testing the least critical features. Without proper risk assessment, neophyte testers often select inappropriate tests resulting in some undesirable consequences such as:

- a tendency to implement and execute the easiest tests;
- focus on one feature, while ignoring others;
- focus on the features that the tester knows well;
- failure to test an entire feature.

Two methods presented in earlier chapters are effective at reducing the number of test cases and thus warrant mention here. A tester can apply either or both of these methods during the design phase to identify unique characteristics, and thus avoid creating redundant test cases. These test design methods are:

1. Equivalence class partitioning consists of dividing the input domain into groups, such that each member of a group evokes similar responses from the application. The tester then creates test cases by selecting representative data from each group. The example in Chapter 4, p. 88, uses equivalence classes to combine keystrokes that produce similar results.

2. Orthogonal array testing provides good test coverage when an input domain is small but too large to accommodate testing every possible permutation of the input values. The input domain must have parameters that take on a finite set of possible values, such as enumerated types, a bounded set of numbers, or states in a state machine. The example in Chapter 6, p. 154, shows how to select test cases that test interactions between independent parameters.

This chapter presents four schemes that focus on prioritizing the existing set of test cases. These reduction schemes are as follows:

● priority category scheme;
● risk analysis;
● interviewing to identify problem areas;
● combination schemes.

All of these reduction methods are independent, and no one method is better than the other. Different test case prioritization schemes may generate different lists of prioritized features to test. However, using several of these methods in conjunction with one another results in a more thorough evaluation of product risks. It also raises confidence when different prioritization schemes yield similar conclusions.

8.2   Prioritization guidelines

Test case prioritization is a compromise: the tester selects the situations to execute at the expense of those to omit. The risk is that some application features will not be tested. The goal of prioritization is to reduce the set of test cases based on some rational, non-arbitrary, criteria, while aiming to select the most appropriate tests.

The prioritization schemes basically address these key concepts:

1. What features *must* be tested?
2. What are the consequences if some features are not tested?

The main guide for selecting tests is to assess risk: What price is the project authority – and the company – willing to pay if a test is *not* executed? If the excluded test had been executed, it might have found a problem prior to product delivery. There is no perfect answer. However, initiating a dialog, early in the project life cycle, about the consequences of potential application failures is a vital part of a project.

At the end of the test case prioritization exercise, the tester and the project authority must feel confident with the tests that have been selected for execution.

If someone is distressed about the omitted tests, then re-evaluate the list and apply another prioritization scheme to analyze the application from another point of view. Ideally, the project authority, and possibly other project members, must buy in – and sign off – to the prioritized set of tests.

8.3 Priority category scheme

The easiest scheme for categorizing tests is to assign a priority code directly to each test description. Although this approach may appear to be arbitrary, it is based on the comparison "is test X more important than test Y?"

The test descriptions can vary in form, such as a test outline, a spreadsheet, a list of tests, a test document's table of contents, or actual test case descriptions. The tester can conduct this exercise himself or as a group exercise with input from the developers, managers, and customer representative. To illustrate, let's consider the following three-level priority categorization scheme.

Priority 1   This test must be executed.

Priority 2   If time permits, execute this test.

Priority 3   If this test is not executed, the team won't be upset.

Assigning priority codes is as simple as writing a number adjacent to each test description. Once the priority codes have been assigned, the tester estimates the amount of time required to execute the tests selected in each category. If the time estimate falls within the allotted schedule, then the partitioning exercise is completed and you have identified the tests to use. Otherwise, further partitioning is required.

The second round of partitioning can either reuse the same scale or use a new priority scheme. This example uses a new five-level scale to further classify the tests.

Priority 1a   This test must pass, otherwise, the delivery is in jeopardy.

Priority 2a   This test must be executed prior to delivery.

Priority 3a   If time permits, execute this test.

Priority 4a   This test can wait until the next release or shortly after the delivery date.

Priority 5a   We'll probably never execute this test.

Priority 1a calls attention to the application's most critical features: not only must the test be executed, but the test must also execute successfully. The tests in the original Priority 3 are now moved to Priority 5a. The tests from Priority 2 are now divided between Priorities 3a, 4a, and 5a, whereas the tests from Priority 1 are now partitioned into the new 5-level scheme. Chances are that none of the tests from Priorities 1 and 2 will be reassigned to Priority 5a, but do try to evaluate the validity of tests and determine whether any tests can be downgraded to a lower classification.

The tester proceeds to prioritize each test by assigning codes until the number of tests in Priorities 1a and 2a results in an acceptable time estimate. If the time estimate continues to exceed the allotted schedule, the project authority must reassess the selected tests and try to further downgrade tests into lower priority. If, after several rounds, the time estimate to execute tests in the top priorities still exceeds the schedule restrictions, the project authority must make some difficult decisions. For many projects, especially those custom-built for a particular client, the project authority may have the option of incremental delivery. In this case, the most important customer-driven features are tested first and released to the customer. This is soon followed by another release, with the rest of the features having been tested. Many customers can wait a few weeks for some new features provided that their immediate needs are met. On the other hand, organizations producing shrink-wrap or other such mass-commercial applications have a tight market window with no possibility of incremental releases. A project authority facing such pressures must resort to changing project scope, recruiting more testers, foregoing adequate testing, or other painful business decisions.

The priority classifications illustrated above represent sample partitioning schemes. Priorities can be defined differently based on the organization's needs. For example, other possible priority categories might include features:

● required by a customer;
● necessary to increase market share;
● that use new technology.

8.4　Risk analysis

All software projects benefit from risk analysis. Standards governing safety critical applications require risk analysis as an integral part of planning and developing software. An application is safety critical if a failure causes catastrophic results, such as financial ruin or loss of human life.

Even for non-critical software, using risk analysis at the beginning of a project highlights the potential problem areas, whose failures have more serious adverse consequences. This allows developers and product managers to pay special attention when designing the application and consequently to mitigate the risks. The tester uses the results of risk analysis to select the most crucial tests.

8.4.1　Components of risk

Risk analysis is a well-defined process that prioritizes modules for testing. Risk contains two components:

1. Probability of occurrence (or fault likelihood) – The likelihood of a problem occurring.

2. Severity of impact (or failure impact) – The impact this problem would have if it were to occur.

Risk analysis consists of first listing the potential problems, and then assigning a probability and severity value for each identified problem. By ranking the results, the tester can identify the potential problems most in need of immediate attention and select test cases to address those needs.

Table 8.1 documents risk analysis for a sample system. The table is structured as follows:

Problem ID – A unique identifier to facilitate referring to a risk factor.

Potential problem – Brief description of the problem.

Probability of occurrence – Probability value, on a scale of 1 (low) to 10 (high).

Severity of impact – Severity value on a scale of 1 (low) to 10 (high).

Risk exposure – Product of probability of occurrence and severity of impact.

Table 8.1 Risk analysis table

Problem ID	Potential problem	Probability of occurrence	Severity of impact	Risk exposure
A	Loss of power	1	10	10
B	Corrupted file header	2	1	2
C	Unauthorized user gains access	6	8	48
D	Databases not synchronized	3	5	15
E	Unclear user documentation	9	1	9
F	Lost sales	1	8	8
G	Slow throughput	5	3	15
. . .				

The probability and severity values in Table 8.1 range from 1 to 10. Some organizations may prefer to use the 3-level high, medium, low scale. Still others may use a scale ranging from 1 to 100 or decimal values between 0 and 1. Whichever scale is used is immaterial provided that the values are used consistently throughout the analysis.

Some projects keep track of historical information that allow the tester to calculate probability values mathematically and assign severity values based on established data. If the organization has no guidelines – or experience – for selecting these values, the easiest approach is to first select the problems that rate lowest and highest, respectively, and then rank the other problems relative to these extremes. The numbers may be far from perfect, but they put the potential problems in some relative order and thus identify important tests.

Multiplying the probability and severity values yields the *risk exposure*. This result ranks the risks by order of exposure: the higher the risk exposure, the more important it is to test for that condition. According to the calculations in Table

8.1, the potential problems ranked by risk exposure are C, D, G, A, E, F, and B. Although problems D and G have the same risk exposure, they differ by their probability and severity values.

For some organizations, the risk exposure produces enough information to determine the high priority tests. Thus, if you use just risk exposure as your criterion, you are done with severity and probability. Others may wish to further analyze the risk components by weighing the probability and severity values separately. The next section describes this analysis.

8.4.2   Risk matrix

A risk matrix allows the tester to evaluate and rank potential problems by giving more weight to the probability or severity value as necessary. Use of a risk matrix disregards the risk exposure. The tester uses the risk matrix to assign thresholds that classify the potential problems into priority categories.

Typically, the risk matrix contains four quadrants, as shown in Figure 8.1, with each quadrant representing a priority class defined as follows:

Priority 1   high severity and high probability.

Priority 2   high severity and low probability.

Priority 3   low severity and high probability.

Priority 4   low severity and low probability.

In this particular example, a risk with high severity is deemed more important than a problem with high probability. Thus, all risks mapped in the upper left quadrant fall into Priority 2. For an entirely different application, the consensus may be to swap the definitions of Priorities 2 and 3, as shown in Figure 8.2. An organization favoring Figure 8.2 seeks to minimize the total number of defects by focusing on problems with a high probability of occurrence.

Although dividing a risk matrix into quadrants is most common, testers can determine thresholds using different types of boundaries based on application-specific needs. Sometimes the best threshold limits are those that appease management fears and address customer needs.

If severity and probability tend to be of equal weight, then a diagonal band prioritization scheme, as shown in Figure 8.3, may be more appropriate. This threshold pattern is a compromise for those who have difficulty selecting between Priority 2 and Priority 3 in the quadrant scheme.

Some managers fear that ignoring any problem with high severity, regardless of probability, may make the organization liable for negligence. The prioritization scheme shown in Figure 8.4 addresses this concern by assigning top priority to all high severity problems. The remainder of the risk matrix is partitioned into several lower priorities, whether as quadrants (shown in figure) or diagonal bands.

If the threshold limits are all horizontal on the risk matrix, then prioritization is based solely on severity, without any regard to the probability component. This is equivalent to the priority categorization scheme described in section 8.3.

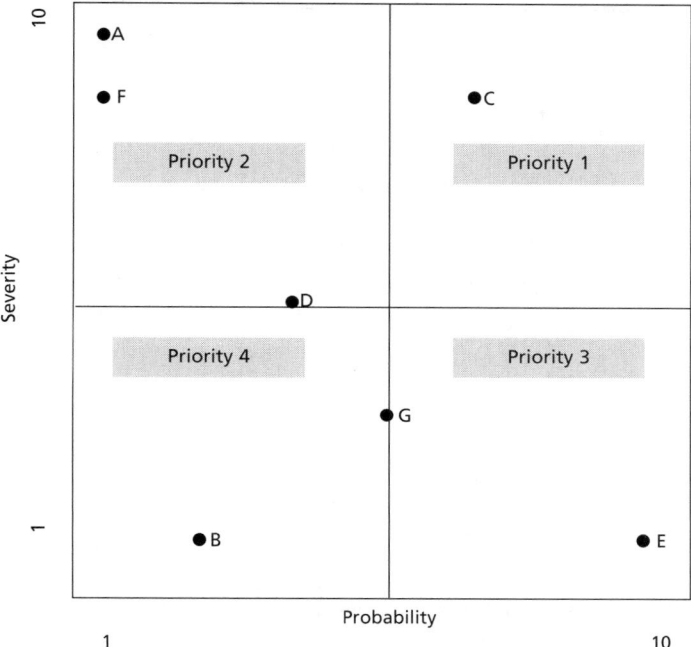

Figure 8.1 Threshold by quadrant

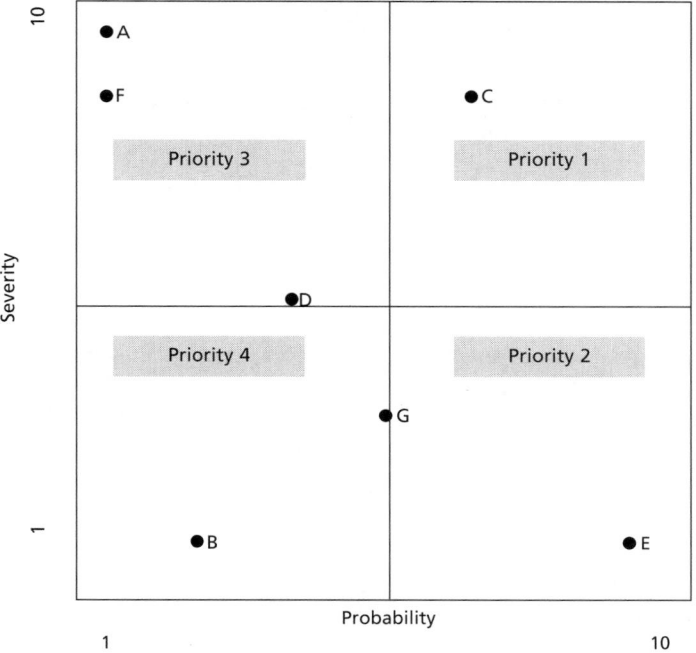

Figure 8.2 Alternate threshold by quadrant

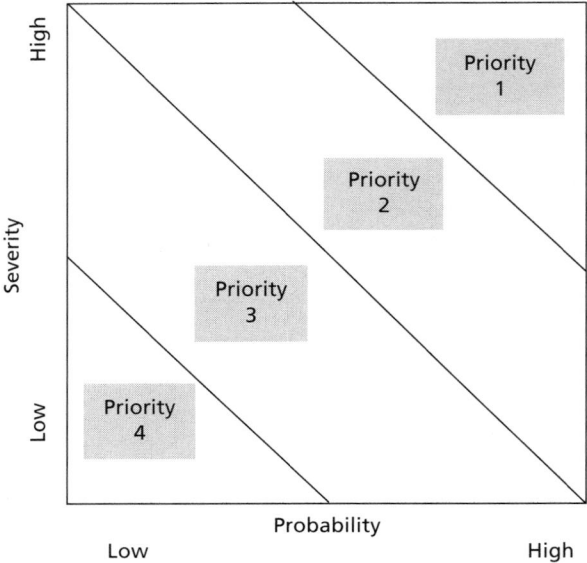

Figure 8.3 Threshold by diagonal bands

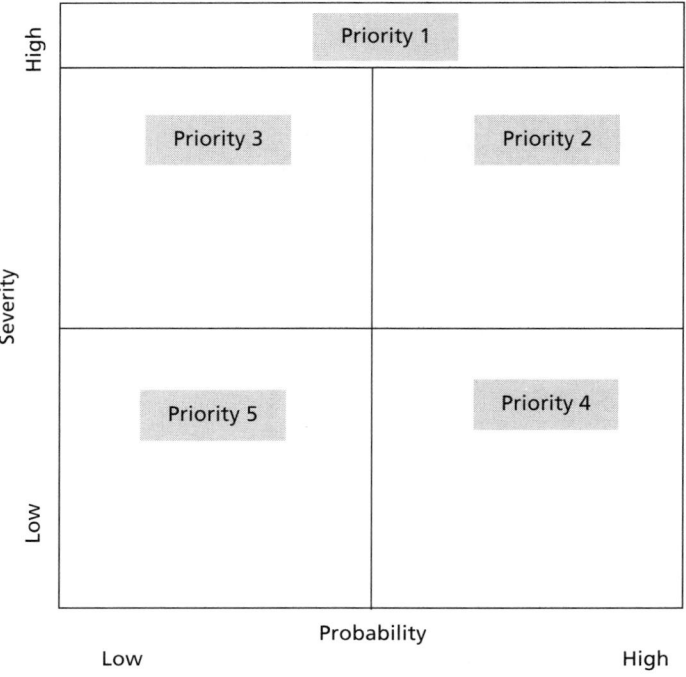

Figure 8.4 Threshold based on high severity

8.4.3   Risk analysis in the real world

Many types of development environments benefit from using risk analysis. Software safety critical applications developed under a mature software development process have well-defined risk thresholds based on historical data, statistical information, and are subject to industry standards and government regulations. For the less structured environment, the tester may want to consider past projects and see whether serious problems were discovered, and then adjust the new thresholds accordingly. For organizations new to risk analysis and those with little information about past projects, the objective is to draw a line in the sand and establish some criteria for selecting tests – even if that threshold is purely arbitrary. Whether an accurate threshold was chosen will only be known over time, as post-release feedback and problem reporting information becomes available.

A very thorough discussion on risk analysis, as well as other methods for addressing the needs of safety critical applications, can be found in [Leveson95].

Many software engineering texts describe a complete process for risk analysis. In addition to identifying, assessing, and prioritizing risk as described above, a formal risk analysis process includes strategies for managing, resolving, and monitoring risk. [Pressman01] and [McConnell98] provide more information on risk management.

8.5   Interviewing to identify problem areas

While the focus of the previous sections center on risk analysis, sometimes people issues contribute significantly to product quality. To select a set of tests intelligently, it is sometimes more important to know about the people and environment that have affected the project, than to simply be familiar with application features. A tester who joins a project late in its development not only faces a steep learning curve relative to the application itself, but also lacks the vital behind-the-scenes knowledge that permeates every project. The tester lacks internal knowledge related to design decisions, failed experiments, developers' skills, and lessons learned – all significant information to help isolate problematic areas.

One way to acquire this information is to probe the very people closest to the project. Many enlightened developers take pride in producing good work, and they will provide insight in differentiating between mandatory and optional test cases. Often, intuition and gut reaction are fair indicators of problematic areas. This is a polite way of saying that some criteria cannot be easily calculated or quantified. Nonetheless, innate knowledge of the product provides valuable insight into uncovering problems.

Politics and group dynamics may affect the outcome of an interview. Gathering a large group may foster brainstorming and get the participants into heavy discussion. On the other hand, some people may be reluctant to provide frank and honest answers in front of an audience, thus, calling for one-on-one conversations. The number of meetings held and the number of people interviewed will vary depending on the number of participants or the complexity of the project.

This section contains a list of questions that delve into vital internal details. The goals of this exercise are to:

- discover what makes each team member worry;
- identify potential problems;
- focus the test effort on the areas most likely to be unstable.

Scope and terminology vary among different projects. Some questions are more suitable to projects customized for a specific end user while others can apply to mass-produced software. Since the underlying intent is to identify the parts of the application most in need of testing, the questions use the generic term *module*. Depending on your application, a module could refer to a component, function, object, class, subsystem, or other type of unit. Modify the questions to accurately reflect your organization's specific needs.

In most instances, one or more modules seem to be the common answer to many of the questions. Count the number of times that each feature is given as an answer. Once the potential problematic features have been identified, the tester must then prioritize these areas for testing, based on which features should be evaluated first. This approach helps in handling tight deadlines. If the tester runs out of time, at least the most likely troublesome areas will have been tested first.

8.5.1   Development issues

The developers themselves are often the best judge of what product components are potential problem areas. Gather members of the development team and pose each of the following questions. (While using this approach is no guarantee that testing will find all the problems, team members usually concur that the most likely problem areas are being evaluated at the expense of less problematic features.)

D-1.   Is there application or usage of new technology? Are different technologies being combined? If so, in what areas?

Application of any new technology requires a learning curve. Sometimes, the technology may be so new that it is unproven or severely buggy.

D-2.   Are you adding to code that's already buggy? If so, which modules?

Bugs tend to cluster. Changes made to buggy code will most likely create new problems or amplify existing problems.

D-3.   Are you modifying code that's been changed many times before? If so, which modules?

When modifying code written by someone else, the developer may not fully understand the nuances created by the original author. Some modules generate side effects that are not well known. The new developer could make assumptions about the old code that are not correct.

D-4.   What has failed in the past?

The tester should assure that past problems have been corrected and that they do not manifest themselves in other ways.

D-5.   Which code modules have high complexity?

If a module's code looks convoluted, it is probably hiding bugs. The more branches in a module – referring to the number of IF statements and WHILE loops – the more tests are required in order to execute every statement and branch. *Cyclomatic complexity* is a measure of the number of such branches. Many test tools report the cyclomatic complexity for each module. Some organizations limit the amount of complexity that a function can have, because functions with high complexity tend to have many problems. More information on cyclomatic complexity is available in [Beizer90], [McCabe82], and [Pressman01].

D-6.   Which features had incomplete or no requirements?

How can the developer conclude whether the module behaves properly if the intended functionality is not well understood? This leaves the door open for interpretation and unintended effects.

D-7.   What was really difficult to design and implement?

Chances are that the developer spent a lot of time in this area. Focus some testing here because the developer will have blind spots and may have omitted certain features. The developer may have made some error-prone assumptions.

Also, the developer may have received a lot of help, so any existing problems will most likely be difficult to find.

D-8.   What was really easy to design and implement?

Some developers may consider certain tasks so obvious and intuitive that they blast through this work without adequate design or testing. As a tester, do not dismiss an area simply because it was easy to implement.

D-9.   What components have been reused?

Not all components are "one size fits all". A reused component may not exhibit all the necessary functionality required in the new environment. Ensure that the reused component does not provide unwanted side effects.

D-10. Has the architecture changed? If so, which modules are affected?

Any change in high-level design can affect the scope of lower-level modules.

D-11. What are candidates for memory leaks?

Many applications lock up due to running out of memory. Determine whether any modules need to be evaluated for eating up memory.

D-12. Have there been inadequate resources, such as inadequate speed or memory capacity?

Throughput may be a serious factor. Determine what type of timing tests and data size tests are appropriate.

D-13. Has there been a change in development hardware?

Some development platforms dictate such requirements as special data formats, specific addresses, device interfaces, or packaging of files. If SCSI devices are listed in a different order, for example, this may cause trouble with existing features.

D-14. Has there been a change in the development environment?

Using different operating systems may affect library calls. Different file versions may be required for software builds.

D-15. What areas affect data integrity?

For example, a database upgrade can create data mismatches or cause loss of all data.

D-16. Are there any tests that the developers feel *must* be executed?

Give the developers an open-ended question, in case their main concerns have not been expressed in any of the previous questions.

8.5.2   Customer issues

For some companies, dissatisfied customers and lost sales are the main threat. What's important to the customer may not always be what the project team values. Many developers would rather focus their energies on state-of-the-art technology and intriguing problems at the exclusion of customer priorities. The testing priorities must focus on the issues that would most adversely affect the end user. Be sure to obtain input from those in Sales, Marketing, Help Desk, and Technical Support. Find out what the users expect when they first use the product.

C-1. What does the customer complain about?

Even if some complaints seem cosmetic or trivial, they are important to the end user. A customer, who loses confidence due to small irritations, may be skeptical about the rest of the product. In this situation, the user's perception carries significant weight.

C-2. What features are important to the customer?

Make sure that the customer's most desired features work as expected.

C-3. What are the customer's priorities?

Understand how the customer plans to use the application. Special requirements may be based on such customized issues as porting to a specific platform, interfacing with a certain application, satisfying a throughput goal, or handling special data formats.

C-4.   What are the showstoppers? Will any failed feature void a sale or delay shipping?

There may be some un-documented features promised to the customer.

If sales are lost, the company could potentially go out of business (then there would be no product to test, but that's not the point!). Address business critical issues first by assuring that the deal-breaker features work as expected.

C-5.   What promises have marketing and sales made to the customer?

There may be some un-documented features promised to the customer. Find out whether such promises were made and determine whether you need to verify these application features. If you encounter any severe re-direction in the project's goals, escalate the issue to the project authority.

8.5.3   Management issues

Test managers try to provide team members with well-communicated requirements to be performed with suitable schedules. These questions probe whether management issues have affected the project.

M-1.   Where has excessive schedule pressure been felt?

Tight deadlines and overtime hours are notorious for making people cut corners. Evidence of rushed work often includes poor designs, lack of reviews, and inadequate testing. Furthermore, an overworked developer can make some poor decisions due to burnout. Find out if any product features were developed under duress.

M-2.   Has there been major management disagreement? If so, where?

Are there any turf battles? Have the developers received conflicting information? The tester must consult the project authority and find out what the *real* project goals are.

M-3.   Has the project been redirected? For which features have requirements changed frequently?

Changing the requirements can seriously alter the architecture, user interface, and other design considerations. There may not always be enough time to scrap existing work and start over. Modules that have been retrofitted to implement changes may not always correctly execute the new requirements.

M-4.   For which features have requirements not been understood?

It is almost impossible to design a module that works correctly if its correct behavior is not known. The developer may make false assumptions about intended behavior.

8.5.4   Personnel issues

The skills and caliber of the people producing the work can have a significant effect on product quality. The vast majority of developers strive to do exceptional work, though there's the occasional instance when someone's work has caused an excessive amount of re-work. The questions pursue this issue. Some of these questions are quite sensitive, so it is important to provide opportunity for people to answer honestly. This may require interviewing people individually, or even submitting written answers to provide anonymity.

P-1.   Where has personnel changed? Did a developer take over the work of another developer?

A developer carries vital information in his head; not all design information is documented. If a developer is taking over someone else's tasks, whether due to change in personnel or due to an unexpected medical emergency, the replacing developer may not know the original intent of certain approaches and decisions. Find out whether the new developer received enough information and guidance about the existing work.

P-2.   Is there a developer who's new to the product?

Even if a well-respected developer joins a project, it takes time to acquire application-specific information. If the developer joined when the project is in panic mode, there is very little time to come up to speed. There is the risk that the developer made some incorrect assumptions about the application.

On the other hand, some developers are extremely thorough and persistent in understanding all aspects of a project. Such a person will have invested significant effort in ensuring that the code functions as required.

Thus, this question may not always identify a problematic area.

P-3.   Is there a developer whose work is not thorough or of high caliber? If so, which modules are affected?

Some developers have acquired a reputation of not producing the best quality work. Some require more supervision than others. Whether these developers are simply inexperienced or dealing with new technical challenges, their work requires extra attention. Find out whether these modules were properly reviewed. If so, then the reviewers would have mitigated the potential problems. Otherwise, these modules may require more scrutiny.

P-4.   Is there a developer who has a negative attitude? If so, which modules are affected?

Every now and then, a person exists who, for whatever reason, is not at all invested in the project's success. This person may do the minimum work to get by, maybe to the point of sabotage. Ideally, such a person would be removed from a project before doing serious harm. Needless to say, this is a project risk.

P-5.   What parts of the system do many team members not understand?

This question may seem redundant with M-4. Asking a similar question will either solidify the previous answer or identify new issues that need attention.

P-6.   Which developers are instrumental in the project's success?

While this question will not identify problems areas, it never hurts to bring the discussion back to a positive point. When interviewing a group of people, this gives an opportunity for key contributors to receive recognition in front of peers. This also identifies the people most knowledgeable about the project, should the tester need to acquire more information.

8.6   Combination schemes

Enumerating all combinations of input results in a large number of tests. For example, testing a drawing application could consist of specifying every possible graphical shape with every available color annotated with every font invoked from every user prompt with every... the list goes on. This becomes an exercise in calculating each and every possible combination. From a testing point of view, testing *every* one thing with *every* other possibility does not always increase confidence in the product. When time is tight, we cannot execute every permutation. Thus, the tester has to draw the line somewhere.

For truly modular systems, where features are implemented as independent units, testing representative values from each set often provides adequate confidence in the total product. Ideally, each piece is tested in isolation to make sure that it works properly within its small part of the world. The next step is to gradually combine the individual pieces and make sure that they work together properly. This concept is not new: it is the foundation of unit testing and integration testing, as described in Chapter 9.

When evaluating the entire application, use these questions to start thinking about simplifying the set of tests.

1. What can be kept constant?
2. What combinations are least likely?
3. What combinations are most likely?
4. Must every situation be tested in every mode?
5. Is it possible to test some features using only one configuration?

Making assumptions about an application is an exercise in analyzing trade-offs: what aspect to test at the expense of not testing another state.

Checklists, or inventories as introduced in Chapter 1, provide a means for tracking whether the application's features have been tested. This consists of listing every type of state and then ensuring that every occurrence is executed at least once during test execution. If testing every item on the checklist is impossible, use risk analysis or the interviewing technique to assure that the crucial features are tested.

Provide a rational reason for every assumption made. Most importantly — explain which conditions will *not* be tested and DOCUMENT YOUR REASONS. This serves two very important purposes: (1) It announces to the project authority and the development team which features will NOT be tested, and (2) you have written proof in case someone accuses you of neglecting a specific feature. Regardless of which features will be omitted from test execution, get concurrence from the project authority.

Here is an example of a test simplification scheme, along with its justification, for a fictitious image processing application. Let's revisit the sample image processing example from section 5.5. The project authority defines the capabilities of the system and Figure 8.5 lists a summary of these requirements.

Requirements for the Image Processing Application

Image sizes processed: [256..4096] × [256..4096]

    256 × 256 is the smallest image size. Anything smaller loses key features.

    4096 × 4096 is the largest image size.

    All non-square images sizes in between these limits are also processed

Image input modes:

    Capture from camera: Ability to transfer images from ACME-12, FotoXP, and PictureThis camera models.

    Read from memory: Ability to load image data into memory and transfer image file to the image processing application.

Image processing algorithms provided in this release:

    Algorithms that generate output images:

        Invert

        Rotate_60

        Rotate_90

        Flip_Horizontal

        Flip_Vertical

        Red_to_Blue

    Algorithms that generate data values:

        Calculate_Area

        Find_Centroid

Image output modes: for algorithms that generate an output image

    Send to display: Image shows up on a XYZ monitor with resolution of 1280 × 1024.

    Store in memory: Image data sent to memory for transfer to an image file.

Data output mode: for algorithms that generate data values

    Output data appears in popup window and is also written to a log file.

Figure 8.5 Summary of sample image processing application

This simple example has the potential for a massive number of test cases. Consider the following combinations:

- There are a total of 14,753,281 different image sizes supported by the application. That's $(4,096-256+1)^2$.

- Trying each of the 8 image algorithm with each image size just once requires $(8 \times 14,753,281)$ or 118,026,248 tests.

Naturally, applying equivalence class partitioning and other risk-based assessments will help reduce the number of tests to execute. In this case, we'll work with the project authority and identify what the customer will most likely use. The real issue is to clarify which features are system requirements versus which features are user requirements. It may be that one user's particular needs contain just a subset of the entire system capabilities. Even if this is not the case, the project authority can still make some assumptions about the typical user. We'll consider that Figure 8.6 describes the main user interactions.

Main user interactions

Even though the application is designed to handle all image sizes from 256 × 256 to 4096 × 4096, we will focus testing on the three video formats and the FotoXP camera used by the customer. Thus, the majority of image acquisition, processing, and display tests will use these image sizes: 640 × 480, 800 × 600, and 1024 × 768.

Other reasons for limiting image sizes include:

1. Reconfiguring the system to handle a different image size is time consuming. The tester must edit a configuration file and then reinitialize the system.

2. In the two years that the customer has been using this system, the user has never used any other image sizes than the three listed above.

The next release of the application must support a new customer whose environment requires support of 256 × 512 and 512 × 512 images. We will test the acquisition, processing, and display of those image sizes at a later date.

Figure 8.6 Test strategy simplification scheme

By analyzing one client's typical usage we have reduced the number of image sizes to test from 14,753,281 down to 3. Though we still have to exercise all of the image processing algorithms, we have drastically reduced the number of tests. The output monitor's 1280 × 1024 resolution also limits the image size that can be displayed.

This approach centers on making sure that the system handles typical user scenarios, rather than exercising devious tests that attempt to uncover system problems. As with all reduction schemes described in this chapter, the project authority must approve the selected set of tests.

8.7   Tracking selected test cases

As seen from the previous chapters, many formats exist for tracking test cases. One method can be as informal as annotating an existing list of tests, while other methods use spreadsheets for tracking tests. Regardless of the method used, the tester must be able to identify which tests to execute and the status of the results.

8.7.1   Requirements traceability matrix

The prioritization schemes presented in this chapter often list the features to be tested and not the test cases. The tester must determine which test cases correspond to the targeted features. A requirements traceability matrix, which maps requirements to test cases, achieves this goal and provides the following information:

● which test cases exercise a specific feature;
● which requirements have no corresponding test case;
● which features still need to be tested;
● which test cases are affected by changes in the requirements.

Table 8.2 shows a portion of a traceability matrix, which lists the application features as rows and the test cases as column headers. For every feature that must be tested, there must be at least one check mark corresponding to a test case. This implies that at least one test exists to exercise that condition. In this example, the two highlighted rows indicate that features 3 and 8 have top priority. According to the traceability matrix below, running test case TC 8 would test feature 3. However, no test case exists for exercising feature 8, so you would need to create a new test case.

Table 8.2 Traceability matrix

	TC 1	TC 2	TC 3	TC 4	TC 5	TC 6	TC 7	TC 8	TC 9
feature 1			✓			✓			
feature 2		✓							
feature 3								✓	
feature 4							✓		
feature 5				✓					
feature 6				✓			✓		
feature 7	✓								
feature 8									
feature 9									
feature 10				✓					

8.7.2 Risk and test case matrix

Modifying the risk table by including a test case identification column helps to map each identified risk to an associated test case. Table 8.3 is an expansion of Table 8.1. The added column contains a reference to the test case that the tester must execute.

Another approach for mapping risks to test cases is to use a traceability table similar to Table 8.2 except that risks replace the list of features.

Table 8.3 Risk and test case map

Problem ID	Potential problem	Probability of occurrence	Severity of impact	Risk exposure	Test case
A	Loss of power	1	10	10	TC-77
B	Corrupted file header	2	1	2	TC-81
					TC-83
C	Unauthorized user gains access	6	8	48	TC-102
					TC-119
D	Databases not synchronized	3	5	15	TC-30
E	Unclear user documentation	9	1	9	TC-31
F	Lost sales	1	8	8	TC-41
G	Slow throughput	5	3	15	TC-110

8.7.3 Documentation shortcuts

Many document shortcuts help track which tests to execute. The simplest method is to annotate existing test documents – whether these are an outline, matrix, test table, or a table of contents – using either a highlight pen or writing in a priority code. Chapter 3, p. 66, contains an example of identifying high priority tests in an outline. Another method is to add columns in existing test tables for indicating test priority and the results of the executed tests.

8.8 Summary

One of the tester's responsibilities is to narrow down a large set of test cases and select those that are most important to execute. A tester can first limit the number of tests created by applying equivalence class partitioning or orthogonal array testing to identify tests that exercise the same set of features. After having defined, and even created, the test cases, using a prioritization scheme helps limit the number of tests to execute. Selection criteria vary according to projects, though most can be based on factors relating to:

● customer needs;
● severity of failure;

- probability of failure;
- developer's skills;
- development environment;
- management issues.

Assigning a priority code to each test partitions the tests into high, medium, and low priority categories. This separates the more immediate tests from those that can be postponed.

Risk analysis as a formal approach for software safety critical systems, ranks problems based on statistical data. However, the concepts of risk analysis readily apply to new projects by assigning severity and probability values. These values can determine a risk exposure value that identifies the riskiest problems. The probability and severity values are also the data used in a risk matrix. Partitioning this matrix categorizes the problems into priority classes.

Interviewing various project team members highlights modules that could contain problems. Evaluation criteria focus on the development environment, customer priorities, management issues, and personnel issues.

The tester will often have to make assumptions about which configurations or combinations of data are most likely to be used, thus executing tests for more common scenarios while avoiding the least likely situations.

While all of these approaches may result in a different, but overlapping, set of test cases, the main intent is to generate communication between the project team members and identify the most important factors, while discussing the trade-offs of postponing some tests.

Creating Quality Software

9.1 Introduction

The emphasis of this book is on defining test cases, which is just one aspect of software testing. In this chapter, we'll look briefly at the remaining software testing tasks and at other software engineering topics that contribute to product quality. Software engineering encompasses many facets, each of which is its own discipline and requires its own processes. Other authors, such as [Pfleeger01] and [Pressman01], provide thorough discussions on all software engineering concepts.

9.2 Development environment infrastructure

The software engineering disciplines presented in this section are vital components of successful software development and testing. They permeate through the entire project. This section addresses why each of these disciplines is important for effective software testing.

9.2.1 Requirements

Good requirements establish a common understanding between the customer (or the customer representative) and the software developers. Requirements describe the capabilities of the system from the user's perspective, and they drive the design, which describes how the capabilities are satisfied by the system. System requirements address internal interfaces, design constraints (the bounds within which the design must fit), and performance issues such as accuracy and timing.

A successful project is one that meets its requirements. Good requirements are verifiable and unambiguous, which implies that we can write one or more test cases for every requirement.

Relevance to software testing

Requirements are the basis against which to evaluate the final product. Testing validates the software against the requirements to assure that we are building the right product. We use requirements to define test cases by specifying the input and output conditions and by creating "what if?" scenarios. In the project's early phase, reviewing the requirements determines if they are adequate and correctly reflect what the customer needs. When requirements are poor or not present, the burden falls on the tester to uncover enough information about the application in order to produce test cases.

For more information

The IEEE standards [IEEE 830] and [IEEE 1233] describe how to write requirements and provide examples. Other references on requirements include [Gause89], [Hamlet01], and [Wiegers99]. In addition, [Robertson99] discusses methods for testing requirements.

9.2.2   Project management

Project management is the discipline that manages schedules and resources. Successful projects need organization and the ability to continually assess and communicate status. Software project management consists of two areas: project planning and project tracking.

Software project planning establishes reasonable plans for performing the software engineering and for managing the software project. A good project plan will:

- define the project objective;
- define the development strategy;
- define the work to be done;
- identify risks and mitigation plans;
- identify the necessary resources,
- assign resources;
- define product deliverables;
- break down the project into small, definable tasks;
- define the schedule;
- identify critical paths;
- identify which standards to adhere to.

Software project tracking provides adequate visibility into actual progress so that management can take effective actions when project performance deviates significantly from the planned activities. Key project tracking activities consist of:

- using major and minor milestones to track progress;
- identifying potential problems before they happen;
- invoking recovery plans (how to recover from a problem) when things go wrong.

Upon project completion, comparing actual versus planned task durations provides feedback on estimation accuracy. Historical information from prior plans and lessons learned improve future planning abilities.

Relevance to software testing

Software testing consists of many phases and is a parallel activity to other software development tasks. Good project plans recognize that software testing involves many tasks and that the total effort (including test planning, test design, building the test environment, test execution, and other testing tasks) can take up to half of the overall schedule. In many hectic projects, test execution time is squeezed due to slippages in the development schedule. Good project management looks for these bottlenecks and alters the schedule accordingly.

For more information

For more references on project management, look at [IEEE 1058], [Humphrey89], [McConnell98], and [Boehm81] which provides examples of project planning charts.

9.2.3 Software configuration management

Software Configuration Management (SCM) controls the complex software development environment and maintains the integrity of components as they change throughout the development lifecycle. SCM tracks source code, requirements documents, design documents, test cases, user manuals, and any other artifacts produced as part of the project.

Many commercial tools support SCM activities. They:

- co-ordinate the work of many different people;
- provide the means to determine product status;
- support multiple and parallel development streams;
- provide an audit trail of changes.

SCM entails the following activities:

Version control maintains each component's history as it changes over time. One can always access a component's prior state. The main mechanism is to control the checkin and checkout of each component.

Configuration control consists of tracking all the components needed to construct a particular version of the system, including documents and test specifications. This part of SCM also tracks dependencies between source code files. Some organizations must also track all tools such as compilers, linkers, flash tools, and other binary files, that are necessary for creating each system version.

Change control is the process that initiates, approves, and monitors the progress of change, whether these changes are bug fixes or enhancements.

Build control is what generates each application. This is an automated build process, such as a make utility, that knows exactly what each level of the system contains. To reduce build time, an effective build process will only rebuild those components that need rebuilding. The build control process produces: (1) the resulting executable application and (2) the associated bill of materials. The bill of materials lists every component and corresponding version used to generate the executable application.

Process management assesses software development activities by tracking the progress of components through the development lifecycle phases. For example, the process can require that a component go through testing prior to release. Process management also ensures that appropriate change requests exist – and are approved – prior to modifying code, design, and other documents.

Relevance to software testing

By placing every artifact under configuration control, the tester can easily create the environment for any version of the product. Many problems occur when the wrong versions of objects are inadvertently used, a common occurrence when configuration management is performed manually or when those administering the system are not adequately trained. To be effective, the tester must know the exact configuration of the system-under-test. Configuration management also allows the tester to keep track of the many scripts and other files related to testing.

Problems found by testing typically require changes in code, which then result in a new product version. Tracking the test case version and the product version as part of the problem description eliminates confusion.

Lack of configuration control typically causes these types of problems:

- problems previously fixed suddenly reappear in newer product versions;
- changes made to older versions are lost;
- a special feature or file is missing from the product release.

For more information

The following authors describe software configuration management in significant detail: [Buckley96], [Humphrey89], [Leon00], [Mikkelson97], and [Pressman01]. [IEEE 828] is the IEEE standard on software configuration management.

9.2.4   Software quality assurance

Software Quality Assurance (SQA) provides management with appropriate visibility into the process being used by the software project and of the products being built [Paulk93]. This consists of a set of activities designed to evaluate the process by which products are developed or manufactured [IEEE 610.12]. SQA ensures that we use the right tools, procedures, and techniques for developing products all with the goal of producing high quality software by preventing defects or by detecting and removing them early. Early defect removal improves schedules by avoiding rework.

The following SQA activities apply throughout the entire development life-cycle:

- define quality plan;
- conduct software reviews;
- ensure methods exist for controlling changes to documents and to source code;
- audit software products for compliance to standards;
- collect software quality metrics;
- assess software development and test methods.

One SQA function is to conduct audits. An audit is an independent evaluation of project artifacts whose primary purpose is to ensure that product development conforms to approved standards and guidelines. Audits can be internal or external. Assessors internal to the company are part of the SQA organization. External audits are performed by auditors from a standards organization from whom the company has accreditation or even from the customer, when the software being developed is an actual component of the customer's own product.

Relevance to software testing

Some companies mistakenly equate SQA with software testing. SQA evaluates *process* quality with primary focus on defect prevention, as opposed to software testing, which evaluates *product* quality by focusing on error detection. SQA monitors the effectiveness of the test effort by reviewing test results and by collecting software quality metrics. An audit of software testing documents ascertains that the testing activities comply with established standards and guidelines.

For more information

[Humphrey89] and [Pressman01] describe SQA activities. [IEEE 730] defines the contents of a Software Quality Assurance Plan and [IEEE 1028] defines procedures for conducting audits.

9.2.5 Reviews and inspections

Reviews are one of the most effective ways of reducing problems and improving quality. The intent is to recognize and fix defects early, prior to writing code, by reviewing all artifacts as they are produced. This includes requirements, designs, code, test cases, and any other document pertinent to the project.

Reviewing and inspecting work products produced at every development phase helps to identify defects as early as possible and thus prevent these same defects from propagating to other development phases. According to [Boehm81], the biggest payback comes from inspecting requirements and design documents, because the cost of fixing a defect increases significantly if it is discovered later. Different types of reviews exist. These include:

Technical reviews which are typically peer group discussions with the purpose of commenting or approving a work product.

Walkthroughs often have the designer lead others through the document or code he has written. Thus, walkthroughs are a training tool for the rest of the group to learn about a specific product.

Software inspections are the most rigorous type of review. They follow a formal structured process that includes:

- using checklists to increase reviewers' effectiveness;
- assigning specific roles to participants;
- comparing the item-under-review to standards;
- conducting post-inspection follow-up;
- producing an inspection report;
- keeping records to highlight weak areas (both in the product and in the development process);
- keeping statistics to measure effectiveness of the inspection process.

Relevance to software testing

An inspection is a method of testing a document, whether it is a requirement, design, or other type of document. These documents become the source for defining test cases. Test documents are themselves prone to defects, so they too benefit from inspection.

Reviews find problems earlier than testing the code, because the documents exist before the source code is developed. Bugs found during a review are where you see them, whereas a bug found in testing provides no indication as to the exact source code location requiring modification. Testing finds defects that are either inserted after inspection or missed during the inspection.

For more information

Formal inspections are based on the work of Michael Fagan, which he describes in [Fagan86]. [IEEE 1028] defines procedures for conducting reviews. [Gilb93] provides a detailed description of the inspection process and includes case studies at actual companies. [Humphrey89] and [Kit95] provide inspection checklists. [Freedman90] includes checklists for reviewing test cases. [Marick95] contains checklists for code inspections.

9.3   Software testing environment

Creating the software testing environment is not a trivial task. Even some manual tests require special interfaces to communicate with the application. A driver is a special software utility that sends the tester's input to the application-under-test. This same driver, or another utility, can then capture the resulting outcome. Automated tests require the tester to program the test cases into a machine-readable form, known as scripts. An automated test environment sends the scripts to the application-under-test and then captures and evaluates the outcome.

Other factors to consider when setting up the testing environment are hardware, operating system, and third party utilities, the latter being vendor software that the application-under-test uses but that are not packaged or installed with the application.

Each phase of software development has a parallel testing activity as shown in Figure 9.1. The tester creates test cases from the documents produced at each development phase.

1. The requirements document provides input to defining system test cases and also drives the design phase.

2. The design phase consists of refining the design from high level down to a detailed level. Each design level defines a part of the system and thus requires integration tests to ensure that each component works as an incremental element.

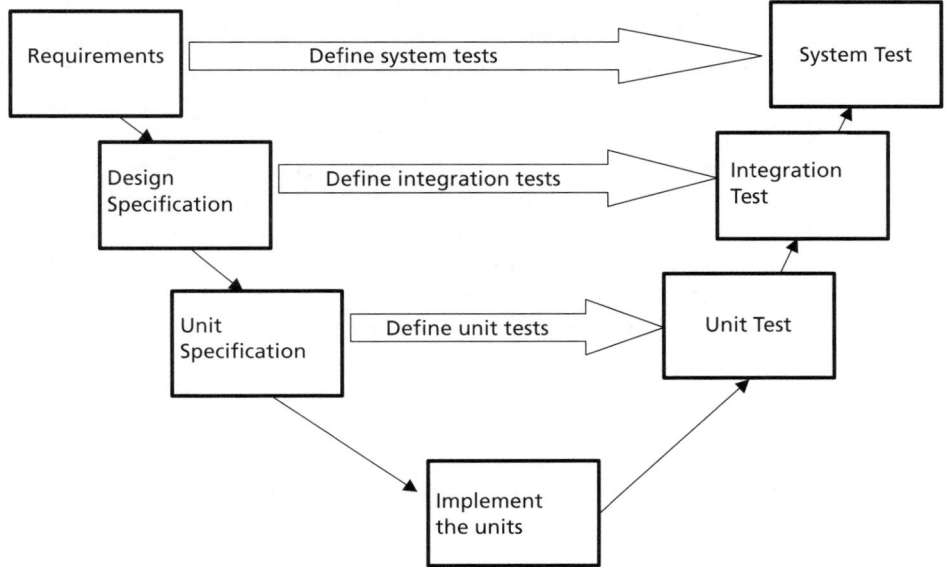

Figure 9.1 The relation between development phases and software testing levels

3. The unit phase provides the specifications and eventually the code for each unit. Unit specifications are used to define unit tests.

The tests are then executed when the corresponding software is available. These different testing levels each require an environment in which to execute tests. This can be the same environment or it can be totally different depending on how the tester defines the test strategy.

9.3.1 Unit testing

A unit is the smallest component that can be compiled. Unit testing consists of verifying each individual unit in isolation by running tests in an artificial environment. This requires the use of drivers and stubs. Drivers are test modules that invoke the unit-under-test. Stubs replace the missing components that are called by the unit. Stubs can:

- return to the unit without performing any other action;
- display a trace message and sometimes prompt the tester to continue;
- return a constant value or prompt the tester to enter a return value;
- perform a reduced implementation of the actual missing component replaced by the stub;
- simulate exceptions or abnormal conditions.

Many people divide unit tests into two categories: white box and black box. The tester uses the code's inner structure and control flow to construct white box tests. Black box tests derive from the requirements and other specifications, without any knowledge of the application's internal structure and control. Simply put: white box is based on the code's structure whereas black box is based on the functional or behavioral model. Black box and white box are techniques for designing test cases. They each generate sets of input and output conditions.

Although white box tests do find bugs, tests based on the code's internal structure pose the danger of verifying that the code works as written, without ensuring that the logic is correct. Black box techniques test the application against the requirements and ensure that specific inputs yield the correct expected outcome. According to lecture notes from Boris Beizer's "World of Testing" 5-day seminar, 1995, one effective approach for unit testing is to develop tests using a behavioral description of the unit and to use a coverage analyzer to ensure that the tests have achieved desired structural coverage criteria, whether it be 100% branch coverage, 100% condition coverage, or other coverage goal.

Prior chapters focus on constructing test cases based on the application's intended behavior. Thus, these tests are black box tests. For example, section 5.4.3 uses the source code to evaluate the effectiveness of tests, but it does NOT use the source code to construct the test cases.

Relevance to software quality

Unit testing is the first opportunity for exercising source code. By evaluating each unit in isolation, and ensuring that each works on its own, one can more easily pinpoint problems than if the unit were part of a larger system.

For more information

[IEEE 1008] is the IEEE Standard for Software Unit Testing. Strategies for devising tests, both white box and black box, are presented in [Beizer84], [Beizer95], [Kaner99], [Myers76], and [Myers79]. British Standard BS7925-2 describes black box and white box techniques for component (unit) testing.

9.3.2   Integration testing

A software integration strategy defines the order in which to merge individual units. Integration is a process that starts with a set of units each individually tested in isolation and ends when the entire application has been built. Integration testing verifies that the combined units function together correctly. This can facilitate finding problems that occur at interfaces or communication between the individual parts. When a problem does occur, it is easier to find the root cause, because at least in theory, the newly added component is suspect.

Four integration strategies exist, each with its own advantages and disadvantages. The terms bottom and top refer to the units' placement in the application's call graph or structure chart.

Bottom-up. Merge units and test from bottom-up. Unit test the lower level component, then have it called by a higher-level component. This method requires the use of drivers to invoke the unit-under-test.

Top-down. The high level routines become drivers for the rest of the units. This method requires stubs to simulate the behavior of lower level units.

Sandwich. This method combines top-down and bottom-up to eventually converge into a fully integrated system.

Big-bang. Integrate all units at once. Although this method requires no stubs and drivers, it is much more difficult to detect interface errors.

Relevance to software quality

Integrating software and integration testing typically are parallel activities. As a component is added to the growing system, tests verify that the interim configuration works as expected prior to adding more components.

For more information

Further discussions on integration strategies are found in [Beizer84], [Beizer90], [Binder00], [Hetzel88], and [Myers76].

9.3.3   System testing

System testing verifies the entire product, after having integrated all software and hardware components, and validates it according to the original project requirements. By having a fully integrated system, the tester can evaluate many attributes that could not be assessed at lower levels of testing. Some of the major categories of system testing include:

Compatibility testing. Assess how well the software performs in a particular environment defined by a specific version of hardware, software, operating system, network, etc.

Configuration testing. Use different software and hardware configurations (such as different peripherals, if applicable) that the system must support.

Functional testing. Verify that each feature complies with its requirements.

Install testing. Verify that installation procedures for full, partial, or upgrades work as documented; also test the uninstall processes.

Load testing. Expose the system to a typical user experience over a short period of time; the goal is to model real world interactions. Another definition is to test the application under a range of loads in order to determine at what point the system's response time degrades or fails.

Performance testing. Measure how long each task takes, under peak and normal conditions, to ensure that the system responds within the specified time constraints.

Recovery testing. Verify that the system can recover to a useable state after having experienced a crash, hardware failure, or similarly damaging problem.

Reliability testing. Verify that the system operates under stated conditions for a specified time period.

Security testing. Verify that only authorized users have access to allowable features.

Serviceability testing. Ensure that any internal maintenance information, such as traces and diagnostics messages, work as documented.

Stress testing. Force the system to operate under an unreasonable load while denying it the resources needed to process that load [Lecture notes from Boris Beizer's "World of Testing" 5-day seminar, 1995]. The goal is to push the system beyond the limits of its specified requirements to find potentially harmful bugs.

Usability testing. Assess the application's "user-friendliness" and identify operations that may be difficult for the users. This includes verifying manuals and other publications intended for the user.

Relevance to Software Quality

By evaluating the fully integrated system against its original requirements, the tester determines whether the final product functions properly. This often decides whether the final system is ready for release. When testing at the system level, the testing environment must be as close as possible to the deployment environment. Otherwise, the tester is not evaluating the final product.

For more information

[Beizer84], [Kaner99], and [Myers76] discuss system testing categories.

9.3.4   Regression testing

Regression testing consists of reusing a subset of previously executed tests on new versions of the application. The goal is to ensure that features that worked on previous versions still work as expected. Often, fixing a bug or adding a new feature can break something else that once worked.

Adding new features may invalidate old regression tests. Thus, the tester may need to purge or update existing tests to account for new product features.

Relevance to software quality

After the developer has fixed a defect, running a regression test re-checks the integrity of the modified application. In an ideal test environment, the tester re-executes regression tests every time the application changes. Just because a set of regression tests pass does not mean the application is free of defects. New tests are required to verify newly added features.

For more information

Publications that discuss regression testing include [Beizer90] and [Kaner99].

9.3.5   Acceptance testing

Acceptance testing validates the system against the user's requirements and ensures that the application is ready for operational use. This phase of testing occurs after completion of system testing. Acceptance tests consist of typical user scenarios focusing on major functional requirements. These tests are typically a subset of system test cases that are run in the real user's environment. Acceptance tests are often executed at the customer site for final handoff.

Relevance to software quality

Acceptance testing is the final checkpoint prior to delivery. The end user may often execute the acceptance tests, which are often a selected subset of system test cases that are run in the real environment. Executing acceptance tests in front of the customer is often a contractual requirement to demonstrate that the product satisfies the customer's needs.

For more information

Authors who write about acceptance testing include [Myers76] and [Hetzel88].

9.4 Software testing tasks

Software testing requires more than simply creating and executing tests. Before beginning to test, the tester must devise the overall test strategy, including how to record problems found during testing. Automation is a vital part of testing, yet it must be properly done to achieve significant benefits. At the end of a project, results from software testing activities are recorded in a final report.

9.4.1 Test planning

Ideally the tester creates a test plan at every level of testing, from system level, through integration, down to unit level testing. For many organizations, a test plan applies to the overall testing process.

A system test plan describes the requirements, resources, strategies, and schedule for testing an application. A good test plan defines the following:

- overview of schedule for test activities, which is used by project managers to produce the project schedule;
- approach to testing, including usage of testing tools;
- test tools, including how and when to obtain them;
- process by which to conduct tests and report results;
- system test entry and exit criteria;
- personnel required to design, develop, and execute tests;
- equipment resources – what machines and test benches are necessary;
- test coverage goals, where appropriate;
- special configurations of software and hardware needed for tests;

- strategies for testing the application;
- features that will and will not be tested;
- risks and contingency plans.

Integration and unit test plans contain much of the information listed for the system test plan, except that the scope is limited to integration and unit test activities respectively.

Relevance to software quality

The information contained in the test plan aides the tester in acquiring necessary resources for creating the test environment and in defining the approach for creating the tests. Once approved by managers, the plan defines the schedule for conducting testing activities and also establishes an understanding of the tester's scope of responsibilities.

For more information

The two standards [IEEE 829] and [IEEE 12207] list the contents of a test plan. Other references for test plans include [Beizer84], [Kaner99], and [Kit95]. [Humphrey89] provides a test plan review checklist.

9.4.2 Test automation

Automating parts of the testing process can provide long-term benefits to an organization, such as:

- reducing the amount of time it takes to execute a suite of tests;
- reducing the tester's involvement in executing tests;
- facilitating regression testing;
- allowing for the simulation of hundreds of users;
- avoiding human mistakes by having tools control repetitive and tedious tasks.

Test automation refers to two key testing activities: executing the tests and evaluating the output. Many commercial tools support these testing activities. Some of the more common tools include:

Capture-playback tools record events (including keystrokes, mouse activity, and display output) while the tester is running the application, and place the information into a script. In theory, the tool can then replay the script to exercise the application. In practice, captured tests have limited use, but well-structured execution scripts give significant benefits.

Comparators find differences between two sets of data and then determine whether the test passed or failed. The tester can often specify parts of the data to ignore. For example, ignoring a date/time field difference still results in a passed test if the rest of the data are correct.

Test execution tools establish an execution environment that initializes the application, sends the data to the application, captures the output, sends the output to a comparator for evaluation, and logs the results.

However, test automation is not free – significant work is required to achieve benefits. Just acquiring a test tool will not automate the testing process successfully. Test automation builds upon a good test process. Thus, if you have a chaotic environment, then you'll simply automate the existing chaos. Building a useful automated test environment takes time, and the cost benefits are achieved after several iterations of running the tests. These facts pertain to successful test automation:

1. Automated test tools do not define or create test scripts for you. Significant time is needed to program the tests.
2. Scripts are themselves programming languages. Thus, automating test execution requires programming experience.
3. Test tools do not select the right tests to automate.
4. Testers require training in how to use the tools.
5. Any new tool has a steep learning curve.
6. Configuration management is necessary to track the large number of files and test-related artifacts.
7. An automated test that fails to find bugs does not guarantee that no other bugs exist.
8. Maintaining the test suites may take a lot of time and effort.
9. New tests are always needed because they go stale over time. Existing tests have already caught the bugs they were designed to catch.
10. Test tools are themselves software; they have their own bugs.

Test automation is not for you if:

1. Tests rely on manual interaction, such as loading a disk.
2. You plan to run tests only once or very infrequently.
3. If test evaluation, which is easy for a person, is difficult to program. For example, determining whether the output format is readable or user-friendly.

Relevance to software quality

Test automation facilitates regression testing, by repeating previous tests as often as necessary and executes it in much shorter time than done by a human. Automated tests avoid errors caused by manual tests, because even the best-intentioned person makes typing mistakes. A tired tester may falsely interpret the generated output. Good test automation requires the skills of an experienced tester to define and select good test cases.

For more information

Two recent works dedicated to test automation are [Dustin99] and [Fewster99]. The latter gives real-life stories – both positive and negative – from actual projects. Browsing the websites of tool vendors can provide additional information in the form of demonstrations, papers, and tutorials on how to use their tools.

9.4.3 Problem reporting system

Problem reporting is a process for initiating bug fixes, enhancements, approvals, and for tracking the progress of change. This presents a method for managing change and for minimizing the impact of rework, which are essential for controlling quality. Depending on the organization's development environment, a problem reporting system may be combined with or be independent from the configuration management system.

Three activities help to control change:

● setting priorities for which changes to make;

● analyzing how a change in requirements affects work already completed;

● assigning one person responsible to make the change.

Many commercial problem reporting tools exist in today's market. These tools provide metrics and reports to identify deficiencies and to monitor test status.

Relevance to software quality

A problem reporting system is the primary means of communication between testers and developers. The tester records every problem found and provides detailed information for reproducing the problem, although some problems are not easily reproducible. Once the developer has fixed the problem and a new release is available for testing, the tester re-executes the associated test case to ensure that the problem has been fixed.

Managers gauge the testing effort by generating metrics from the problem reporting system. Comparing the rate of new problems found versus the number of problems closed helps to determine whether the application is ready for release. Bug statistics also help identify areas that generate the most problems.

For more information

Many books on software configuration management also address problem reporting, so refer to the list in section 9.2.3. Other books that discuss problem reporting and change control include [Kaner99] and [Wiegers96].

9.4.4   Test reporting

Although a test report can take on many forms, the primary goal is to describe what occurred during the test activities. Organization and audience needs determine which type of report is more appropriate. A typical test report identifies the configurations and test environment used, and then enumerates the tests executed and their results. A detailed test report often includes the test log, which lists every test case with its results and may also include a list of every problem report associated with failed tests. A test summary report, on the other hand, tallies the test results and lists the number of tests executed, passed, failed, re-tested, and types of problems found.

Relevance to software quality

This document provides an audit trail of what the tester accomplished while testing the application. Metrics derived from the test statistics help determine the application's readiness for use.

For more information

[IEEE 829] and [Humphrey89] address issues pertaining to problem reporting.

9.5   Summary

Key software engineering disciplines are vital for producing quality software and are necessary for effective testing.

1. Defining good requirements drives the development and testing activities.
2. Project management defines the resources and schedules for the project and tracks the actual development effort.
3. Software configuration management keeps track of changes throughout the development life cycle.
4. Software quality assurance ensures that products are developed according to established guidelines.
5. Reviews, as a general term, are a process by which people evaluate a piece of work. Other project members can learn about a product by attending a walk-through. Software inspections, a specific type of review, follow stringent rules.

The test environment requires significant setup in order to execute tests. Tests apply to all levels of software development, from unit tests, through integration test, finishing with system testing of the entire product. Regression tests consist of repeating existing tests to ensure that previous features still work as expected. Acceptance tests are the final checkpoint in which the end user requirements are assessed, often by the customer.

Creating and executing tests are only part of the entire testing picture. The test planning phase at the beginning defines the overall testing strategy. Test tools help to automate many of the testing tasks. The problem reporting system tracks the information from failed tests. A final report issued upon the conclusion of the testing activities summarizes the testing effort and its statistics.

10 Applying Software Standards to Test Documentation

10.1 Introduction

Earlier chapters of this book present methods for organizing product information for the purpose of writing test cases. Some of the resulting test descriptions are quite thorough while others are insufficient. For many organizations, just getting some test cases written down – even if imperfect – is a significant achievement. Although well-intentioned documentation is better than haphazardly defined tests, it's not enough for organizations that seek compliance with industry standards.

Many organizations use software standards as certification schemes, while others use assessment models as a basis for improvement. Regardless of the goal, the standards and models all emphasize practices that have been proven to produce good software. [Moore98] provides a brief description about each of the many software engineering standards available today. For simplicity, I'll use the generic term *standard* to refer to standards, models, and certification schemes.

Although few of the standards address software testing issues directly, it is possible to define software test procedures that meet compliance. Having a defined test process implies that uniform testing practices apply to all projects. This benefits the organization by freeing the tester from investing time in defining test practices and documentation contents for new projects. Naturally, modifications to the test process evolve as testers learn what aspects work well and which need improvement. Software process improvement is an area onto itself and is beyond the scope of this book.

This chapter provides guidelines for making test documentation conform to established industry practices. It is not a primer on the standards; rather it focuses on how each affects test case documentation. We will look at the following models and certification schemes commonly used by the software development community:

- ISO 9001.
- ISO/IEC 12207 and IEEE/EIA 12207.
- IEEE Software Engineering standards.
- Capability Maturity Model® for Software (SW-CMM®). (SW-CMM and Capability Maturity Model are registered in the US Patent and Trademark Office.)

The standards differentiate between what is required and what is recommended. A recommended step becomes an auditable requirement only when the organization mandates that step in its internal process. Because these standards address overlapping issues, it is possible to produce test case documents that fully comply with some or all of these standards. This chapter concludes with a test case template that identifies required and recommended contents.

 ## 10.2   Common elements

Most standards affecting software engineering address some of the same key elements. Every quality system requires configuration management and reviews, while others recommend various degrees of traceability. Chapter 9 provides a general overview of these concepts. The following sections suggest some ways of applying those concepts to test cases in order to comply with the standards.

10.2.1   Configuration management

From a tester's perspective, configuration management functions in several areas, including:

● the version of the test documentation;

● the version of the application-under-test;

● test environment management.

For test documentation, a version number can apply to an individual test case, to a table of test cases, or to a document containing a collection of test cases. Regardless of how test cases are packaged, the tester must be able to easily identify a test's version. Although it is acceptable for a tester to insert the version number into the test case description manually, the less error-prone technique is to use a commercial configuration management tool to track test case or document versions. Using a tool is more foolproof, because it does not rely on human memory and accuracy.

A new version number is assigned to each new build of the software application. The tester references this version number when executing tests and filing problem reports. Using a configuration management tool to build the software is the most effective means of controlling the many components that make up the application.

The test environment must be an adequate representation of the production environment, in order to properly test the delivered application. Configuration management helps to control the composition of the test environment, including operating system versions and system configurations. This allows the tester to report accurate and complete test results.

10.2.2   Reviews

Many of the standards require that test cases and test documentation undergo review, and that the outcome of the review be documented. As different standards emphasize reviews to various degrees, let's focus on the similarities, which are to find problems, find inconsistencies, document findings, and recommend improvements.

The important information to record includes the following:

- list of issues found;
- priority of each issue;
- review date;
- names of reviewers;
- approvals.

Since the tester often produces one document containing a collection of test cases, a single approval page that records the review information and approval signatures may be used. Several recording methods capture the outcome of a review, and the organization must decide which process to enforce. Possible methods of recording review information include:

1. Each reviewer must initial and date the document that contains a collection of test cases.
2. Each reviewer must initial and date every test case or table reviewed.
3. Use a review log sheet to record the date, items reviewed, the issues found, priority of issues, and the names of the reviewers.
4. Issue an e-mail that records the date, items reviewed, the issues found, priority of issues, and the names of the reviewers. Send this e-mail to the product team and archive it for future reference.

Once the individual reviews are complete, the tester should make the appropriate changes to the test case document, communicate the changes made to each of the reviewers, and place a copy of the new document into configuration management.

10.2.3   Requirements traceability

Some of the standards address traceability between requirements and test cases. We've already seen some examples of traceability in previous chapters. One example is a traceability matrix, as shown in Table 4.19 on p.109, which maps each requirement to one or more associated test cases. Using a traceability matrix is one of the easiest ways to achieve requirements traceability. Other methods consist of storing the traceability information within the test case and other design documents.

Some of the previous examples illustrate instances of *backward traceability*. The test cases in Table 3.1 on p. 61, which are derived from a test outline, reference the corresponding outline item that generates each test case. This traces the test case back to the test outline. Similarly, the test cases derived from the state tables (Tables 5.3 and 5.4, p. 118) reference the event associated with each test. These two examples provide traceability from the test cases back to the design document that specifies the test; this does NOT trace the test case back to the original requirements as called for by some of the standards. Listing the requirement validated by the test case on the actual test case form is another way to achieve backward traceability.

Table 3.7 on p. 70 shows the use of *forward traceability*. Each outline item references the test case that exercises the specified condition. If any changes are made to the outline, the tester can quickly determine which test cases are affected by the change. Forward traceability in this example links the test design to the resulting test case – not from the original requirement to the corresponding test case.

10.3 Industry standards

Let's look at how some of the more common standards affect software testing. Many of the test case examples from previous chapters have to change in order to comply with the specified requirements and recommendations.

10.3.1 ISO 9001

ISO 9001 is a standard based on quality management principles. Originally adopted by manufacturers, many industries now use ISO 9001. The ISO 9001 standard can also apply to software development. It covers product design, development, production, installation, and services.

ISO 9001 places great emphasis on documentation, control, traceability, measurement, and accountability. Corrective action and follow-through are also key themes. Not only is it important to log and report problems, but procedures must exist to assure that problems are resolved and that the cause is corrected.

ISO 9001 states *what* must be done to achieve a quality environment; it does not say *how* to do this. Definition of the actual procedures is left to each individual organization, with the goal that the procedures meet the customer's needs. In essence, the standard states key functional requirements for which you must "say what you do, do what you say, and be able to show what you've done". Implementations can vary among organizations. The guideline ISO 9000-3 and the British guide TickIT describe how to apply the ISO 9001 standard to the software development environment.

Effect on software testing

Since each organization seeking ISO 9001 compliance defines its own software testing procedures, the level of rigor will vary. An auditor trained in software testing principles will look for these activities:

- test documentation that conforms to company defined standards;
- existence of a test plan;
- control of all test environments;
- verification of design;
- defined audit and sign-off procedures for final test activities;
- evidence that problems are logged and tracked to resolution;
- maintenance of quality records;
- performance of internal quality system audits.

Organizations can implement accountability and traceability by defining the following procedures:

- maintaining test cases under configuration control;
- documenting or otherwise defining traceability between requirements and test cases;
- reviewing the test cases;
- recording who reviewed and who approved the test cases;
- archiving test cases;
- documenting failed test cases in such a way that the failures are reproducible;
- recording and resolving problems.

Changes to previous examples

The test case examples from previous chapters are themselves compliant with ISO 9001, provided that these conform to the organization's documented procedures.

Suggested references

The most recent release of the international standard [ISO 9001:2000] supersedes the prior version [ISO 9001:1994]. [ISO 9000-3] is the guideline for applying ISO 9001 to the software development environment.

Publications that address how to implement ISO 9001 in a software environment include: [Bamford97], [Kehoe96], and [Schmauch94]. Comparisons of ISO 9001 to the Capability Maturity Model® for software are available from [Bamford93], [Bamford98], and [Paulk94].

For the latest information on TickIT, go to the website www.tickit.org

10.3.2 ISO/IEC 12207 and IEEE/EIA 12207

ISO/IEC 12207 is an international standard jointly developed by the International Organization for Standardization (ISO) and the International Electrotechnical Commission (IEC). It offers a framework for software life-cycle processes from concept through retirement. This standard is compatible with the ISO 9001 approach to quality systems, quality management, and quality assurance. IEEE/EIA 12207 is the US adaptation of ISO/IEC 12207.

ISO/IEC 12207 describes the following life-cycle processes:

- Primary processes: Acquisition, Supply, Development, Operation, and Maintenance.
- Supporting processes: Documentation, Configuration Management, Quality Assurance, Verification, Validation, Joint Review, Audit, and Problem Resolution.
- Organization processes: Management, Infrastructure, Improvement, and Training.

ISO/IEC 12207 does not dictate a particular life-cycle model or software development method nor does it specify the details of the development process or of the format and content of documentation. Therefore, organizations seeking to apply ISO/IEC 12207 may want to use additional standards, such as one of the IEEE Software Engineering standards to specify the activities that comprise the process.

ISO/IEC 12207 and IEEE/EIA 12207 call for several levels of software testing, which include:

- software coding and testing: develop and document test procedures and data for testing each software unit;
- software integration and testing: develop an integration plan that integrates the software units and tests them as the aggregates are developed;
- software qualification testing: ensure that each software unit meets its requirements prior to integration;
- system qualification testing: ensure that the product is ready for delivery.

In addition, the standards call for the following support activities:

- configuration management;
- quality assurance;
- validation and verification;
- reviews;
- audits;
- problem resolution process.

Effect on software testing

To comply with ISO/IEC 12207 or IEEE/EIA 12207, the following test documentation is required. The standards also specify the content of each of these documents:

- software quality assurance plan;
- test plan;
- test procedure;
- test results report.

ISO/IEC 12207 and IEEE/EIA 12207 require that test procedures contain the following information:

- author;
- test configuration;
- objectives and rationale;
- test preparation, including hardware and software;
- test identifier;
- requirements addressed and requirements traceability;
- prerequisite conditions;
- test coverage criteria, or other methods of assuring sufficiency of testing;
- test input;
- procedures and data for testing each software unit and database;
- expected test results;
- criteria for evaluating results;
- instructions for conducting procedures.

To comply with either ISO/IEC 12207 or IEEE/EIA 12207, the organization must conduct configuration management and reviews of test documents, and it must provide a problem resolution process.

Changes to previous examples

The test cases in previous chapters incorporate many, but not all, of the components required by ISO/IEC 12207 and IEEE/EIA 12207. Adding the following information to the test case document will satisfy the standards:

- test case author;
- test objective and rationale;
- requirements addressed, unless you refer to the requirements matrix;
- criteria for evaluating results;
- instructions for conducting procedures.

Suggested references

[ISO 12207] is the international standard.

[IEEE 12207], the US equivalent, consists of a three-volume set:

- IEEE/EIA12207.0 – ISO 12207 with a US introduction and six additional appendices. This document wraps US material around the full text of ISO/IEC 12207.
- IEEE/EIA12207.1 – A summarization of the contents of each type of document.
- IEEE/EIA12207.2 – Guidebook with additions, alternatives, and implementation approaches to many of the activities and tasks of ISO 12207.

[Shoemaker99] provides an overview of how to use ISO/IEC 12207.

10.3.3 IEEE software engineering standards

The Institute of Electrical and Electronics Engineers (IEEE) issues a collection of standards that pertain to software engineering. Each individual standard describes a particular aspect of software development and provides specific directions on performing that task. Of all the standards presented in this chapter, the IEEE Software Engineering standards most directly describe *how* to perform software testing activities.

The IEEE Software Engineering standards emphasize many of the same key infrastructure principles as the other standards. Those relevant to software testing include:

- well-defined requirements;
- configuration management;
- reviews and audits;
- requirements traceability.

Effect on software testing

We will look at the following three IEEE standards that most directly deal with software testing:

- ANSI/IEEE Std 829-1998, IEEE standard for software test documentation.
- ANSI/IEEE Std 1008-1987 (R1993), IEEE standard for software unit testing.
- ANSI/IEEE Std 730-1998, IEEE standard for software quality assurance plans.

[IEEE 829] defines the format and specifies the contents for the following types of documents.

1. Test plan: addresses planning issues such as scope of work, scheduling, staffing, and what features will and will *not* be tested.

2. Test design specification: specifies the approach used to test the application.

3. Test case specification: defines a test case identified by the test design.

4. Test procedure specification: specifies the steps needed to execute a set of tests.

5. Test item transmittal report: identifies the item to be tested by specifying the item's location, delivery medium, and the person responsible to test that item.

6. Test log: records relevant details about test execution. Many of the tables shown in earlier chapters contain test execution information.

7. Test incident report: documents events discovered during testing that require further investigation. A Problem Reporting System is one such means to record this information.

8. Test summary report: provides an overall evaluation of the testing effort.

This book presents many principles of test design, test case, and test procedure specifications. The test descriptions from prior chapters contain many of the elements required by [IEEE 829], such as:

● test identifier;
● special requirements necessary to run test;
● description of input;
● description of output;
● dependency on other tests;
● definition of pass/fail.

[IEEE 1008] lists various tasks necessary for conducting unit testing. Those relevant to test case documentation include:

● identifying risk areas to be addressed by testing;
● identifying resources needed for testing;
● selecting features to be tested;
● designing the tests;
● identifying input and output data characteristics;
● reviewing and approving all test cases;
● using configuration management for all test cases and test documents;
● using code coverage tools to monitor test effectiveness.

[IEEE 730] emphasizes the following activities that affect test case documents:

● following a defined process for configuration management;
● conducting reviews and audits;
● following a defined process for reporting, tracking, and resolving problems.

In addition to specifying test documentation and unit testing procedures, separate IEEE standards exist for configuration management, reviews, audits, and requirements specifications.

Changes to previous examples

The sample test cases contain many of the components called for in [IEEE 829]. To comply with this standard, the tester must provide the following additional information:

- list of what features will be tested and which will *not* be tested;
- definition of what criteria constitutes pass and fail;
- information necessary to set up and execute the tests;
- unambiguous description of test input;
- unambiguous description of expected output;
- for failed tests, provide the associated problem report number.

The test outlines and test tables presented in earlier chapters are vital additions to the test documentation, because they help identify the features to test. Depending on how this information is used, the tester can include the outlines and tables either in the test plan or in the test design document. An outline or table that helps determine the testing tasks can be used as the test plan's "list of testing tasks" section. A test table that dictates the test cases can be part of the test design document. Of course, when shortcuts are used and no other information exists, the outline and tables function both as test design and test case document. The best directive is for the tester to include outline and tables in whatever test document uses this information as input.

Suggested references

The standards described above are [IEEE 730], [IEEE 829], and [IEEE 1008].

[Kit95] provides a brief description of the various IEEE software engineering standards. [Schmidt00] provides general information on how to use the IEEE software engineering standards.

10.3.4   Capability Maturity Model® for software

The Capability Maturity Model® for Software (SW-CMM®), produced by the Software Engineering Institute, focuses primarily on management issues. The model assigns a maturity level designation of 1 through 5 based on the capability demonstrated by an organization. The core principles of the SW-CMM® include:

- well-defined steps for performing each task;
- proper training for each person to perform his or her job;
- existence of management support for all efforts performed;
- measurement of all steps performed.

The five SW-CMM® levels are:

Level 1   Initial: Process is informal and ad hoc.

Level 2   Repeatable: Project management practices are institutionalized.

Level 3   Defined: Technical practices are integrated with management practices and institutionalized.

Level 4   Managed: Product and process are quantitatively controlled.

Level 5   Optimizing: Process improvement is institutionalized.

A higher maturity level indicates that an organization follows a more rigorous process than one at a lower level. As companies move from one level to the next, they increase productivity and quality, while lowering the risk of failed projects and lost revenue.

The SW-CMM® does not provide much guidance on the subject of software testing, however, level 3 addresses some testing-related issues. To achieve level 3, the organization must already have been assessed at level 2 by having demonstrated proficiency in the following areas:

- requirements management;
- software configuration management;
- software quality assurance;
- software subcontractor management;
- software project planning;
- software project tracking and oversight.

Effect on software testing

Provisions for the SW-CMM® have more affect on the testing and development environment than on the actual test case documents. Implementation of the testing-related tasks under the software product engineering key process area addresses the following activities:

- defined process for performing software testing;
- peer reviews for test plans, test procedures, and test cases;
- configuration management for test plans, test procedures, and test cases;
- testing activities that are clearly identified in the project plans and schedules;
- traceability of product requirements from software requirements through design, code, and test cases;
- adequate resources and funding for performing software testing tasks;
- use and availability of tools;
- adequate training for software testers to perform their tasks;
- test readiness criteria established for unit, integration, system, and acceptance testing;
- use of test coverage to determine adequacy of testing;
- problem tracking procedures.

Changes to previous examples

The sample test cases can comply with the SW-CMM® provided that they are developed according to the process defined by the organization. If the process dictates that test cases must provide detailed input and other information, then the tester must change the test case documents accordingly. Ideally, the organization's process should require that test cases be reviewed and placed under configuration management.

Suggested references

The reference for the SW-CMM® is [Paulk93]. [Humphrey89] describes the SW-CMM® in further detail. [Bamford93], [Bamford98], and [Paulk94] compare ISO 9001 to the SW-CMM®.

The Software Engineering Institute ·has created other models, which are based on similar concepts. These include the Systems Engineering Capability Maturity Model® and the Capability Maturity Model Integration[SM]. All documents produced by the Software Engineering Institute are available from their website: www.sei.cmu.edu

10.4   Complying with the standards

It is possible to create one test case format that complies with multiple standards. Table 10.1 lists the possible contents of a test case. The required or recommend fields vary according to each standard. The structure of this table is as follows:

- Column 1 lists the test case field name.
- Column 2 provides a brief description about the field content.
- Columns 3 though 6 indicate which fields are required (a ✓ check mark) or recommended (an * asterisk) by the corresponding standard.
- Column 7, the last column, identifies information that can be stored separately from the actual test case. More on that later.

Each organization defines its own internal process and decides on the format of test cases. This includes deciding which, if any, of the recommended information to include in the test case documentation. Table 10.1 marks a field as recommended (identified by an * asterisk) if the corresponding standard addresses this information, either directly or in reference. How to handle the recommended fields depends on how one interprets and applies each standard.

ISO 9001 does not explicitly state what information to record in test documents. Table 10.1 lists recommended fields based on what the standard emphasizes. In terms of testing, ISO 9001 states the need for verification, and so we can surmise that test cases must have the basic components of input and output descriptions. ISO 9001 also addresses configuration management and problem tracking; however, the standard does not specify *how* to implement these tasks. Therefore, it

seems reasonable to record information about component versions and to associate a failed test with the corresponding problem report number.

ISO/IEC 12207 lists specific information to document in a test case. The standard requires configuration management and reviews, thus related fields might
also be part of the test documentation. The standard also requires a list of problems encountered during testing, and so the tester can either cross-reference this
information by including the problem report number in the test case or by having
a problem reporting tool reference the failed test.

IEEE 829 defines the contents of test plan, test case, and test procedure specifications. These contents, collectively, appear as required fields in Table 10.1. Strict
implementation of IEEE 829 requires creating the test documents as specified.
Testers following a loose interpretation of this standard can provide the same
information, although not necessarily in the stated test documents. If the organization decides to implement the IEEE standards on software reviews and
configuration management, then the related information (marked as recommended
in Table 10.1) should also be recorded.

The SW-CMM® does not define the contents of test cases, although we assume
that well-structured test cases are called for. An organization working on level 3
has, by definition, achieved proficiency in level 2 activities. Level 2 addresses
such issues as configuration management and traceability, whereas level 3
addresses reviews. It follows that the related information may be part of the test
documents.

Part of customizing a software testing process involves first defining what
information to track and then deciding how to record the selected information.
Ideally, a tool facilitates tracking much of the information. Regardless of how the
information is stored, the key principle is that it be available upon demand.

Test case format

Unless dictated by existing company procedures, the tester determines the actual
test case format. This format varies from one organization to another. Some organizations document test cases as tables or spreadsheets, others create detailed test
cases similar to that shown in Figures 4.4 on p. 88 and 5.3 on p. 132, while still
others rely on a test tool to capture and store test case information.

A major influence on test documentation format depends on whether the test
cases are manual or automated. Manual test cases require human intervention.
The corresponding test documentation should list the steps that the tester must
follow with enough detail so that the tester can execute the test as intended. The
tester records the results either on the test case form or in a special log file.

Automated tests require less human intervention. Testers must define, debug,
and in some cases initiate tests under control of a test tool. On completion, the
tester inspects an output log file to see which tests have passed and failed.
Automated test tools store test case information in a specialized file that can be
viewed by the tester. In such situations, there is no real test case documentation,
per se. A good tool provides this information readily and generates printed copies

Table 10.1 Test case contents

Test case field	Description	ISO 9001	ISO/IEC 12207	SW-CMM®	IEEE 829	External Reference
Test description						
Test identifier	unique test case identifier	*	✓	*	✓	
Requirements traceability	identify the requirement being tested	*	✓		*	requirements matrix
Objective/Test items	brief description of features to be tested		✓		✓	
Test case dependencies	list other test cases that must be executed prior to running this test; identify prerequisite conditions		✓		✓	
System configuration						
Application version	version of the software build or application	*	*	*	*	CM tool
Operating system version	version of the operating system used to run the application-under-test	*	*	*	*	CM tool
Hardware version	version of the hardware on which the application is running	*	*	*	*	CM tool
Test Tool version	version of test tool used to execute test (if a test tool is being used)	*	*	*	*	CM tool
Test environment and input information						
Environmental needs	list the required software, hardware, data, files, etc.	*	✓	*	✓	test plan
Initial setup	list the steps that the tester must perform prior to executing this test	*	✓	*	✓	
Special procedural requirements	describe any special operator intervention, outcome determination procedures, or other necessary procedures	*	✓	*	✓	
Input specification	list the input sequence and data that the tester must enter	*	✓	*	✓	

Table 10.1 *continued*

Test case field	Description	ISO 9001	ISO/IEC 12207	SW-CMM®	IEEE 829	External Reference
Results information						
Expected results	specify all output, including (if appropriate) response time and tolerances for expected values	*	✓	*	✓	
Evaluation criteria	criteria used to determine whether test passed or failed		✓		✓	test plan
Actual results	after having executed the test, record how the application responded	*	✓	*	✓	test log
Test execution record						
Date of test	date this test was executed		✓		✓	test log
Name of tester	name or initials of person executing this test				✓	test log
Results: ___ Pass ___ Fail	indicate whether this test executed successfully or unsuccessfully	*	✓	*	✓	test log
Problem report number: ___	if the test failed, enter the problem report number here	*	*	*	✓	test log or PR system
Test case history						
Test case version	version number of this test case	*	*	*	*	CM tool
Test creation date	date this test was created	*	*	*	*	CM tool
Test author	name of person who wrote the test case	*	*	*	*	CM tool
Reviewed by	name(s) of person(s) who reviewed this test case	*	*	*	*	review log
Review date	date on which this test was reviewed	*	*	*	*	review log
Approved by	name of person who signed off on this test case	*		*		review log

of the test cases when necessary. There are several instances which require printed copies of test case contents:

1. Contractual obligations with a customer can require that test cases be published and delivered to the customer.
2. Printed copies of test cases facilitate reviewing the actual tests.
3. Printed copies of test cases facilitate debugging. (Yes, the tester will have to debug the tests!)

When defining the format of a test case, the tester must balance the amount of required information. Test cases with too many fields run the risk of being incomplete and incorrect. Unless procedures are in place to assure complete test case descriptions, a tester under tight deadline may resort to leaving some fields empty or fail to provide correct information. In some circumstances, a tool can fill in some of the information.

External information

To keep the size of the test case manageable, some of the information can be stored separately from the actual test case document, provided that the information is available regardless of its location. Information that can be stored elsewhere relate to test case history, configuration management, requirements traceability, reviews, test results, or problem reporting. The column labeled "external reference" in Table 10.1 suggests the following alternate locations for recording this information:

CM tool	Use a configuration management tool to track versions of all components.
PR system	Record information about failed tests in the problem reporting system.
Requirements matrix	Use a matrix that maps the traceability between requirements and test cases.
Review log	Have the review process record relevant information in the review log.
Test log	Use a test log to track execution and results information.
Test plan	Have the test plan define information that pertains to a set of test cases.

Some of this information can apply to an entire suite of tests. One documentation approach is to use a test case table that separates the general information from the test-specific. Table 10.2 lists information relating to configuration and reviews separately from the individual test cases. Note that this table does not include all the fields listed in Table 10.1.

Table 10.2 Recording general information separately from the test cases

Application Version   _____   Required Equipment   _____

Test Tool Version   _____   Test Cases Reviewed By   _____

Operating System Version   _____   Date Reviewed   _____

Hardware Version   _____   Test Cases Approved By   _____

Test case ID	Requirement addressed	Input	Expected results	Actual results	Pass / Fail	Test machine	Problem report number	Date test created	Test case author	Date test executed	Tester's name

10.5 Summary

Although most of the test cases produced throughout this book have been adequate, many need additional information to comply with the standards. This additional information pertains to ensuring that the test environment, configurations, input conditions, results, and post-test information are all well documented.

The standards specify some information that test cases must contain and also recommend other information that the organization might want to record. They also address various levels of configuration management, reviews, and requirements traceability. An organization will define its own internal process and what type of information to track as part of a test case. A test case can be structured to comply with the requirements of several standards. A tool can provide and track most, if not all, of the test case fields. The tester can also store some of the information separately from the actual test case document, provided that the relevant information is easily accessible.

11 Appendices

Appendix A

This appendix contains the following outlines referenced by Chapter 2. The shaded portions of each outline indicate items added relative to the prior iteration.

Appendix A1   first iteration of the test outline.

Appendix A2   second iteration of the test outline.

Appendix A3   third iteration of the test outline.

Appendix A4   fourth iteration of the outline.

Chapter 3 references the following test case information:

Appendix A5   test cases derived from the test outline.

Appendix A6   shortcut using the outline as a test case checklist.

Appendix A1

Outline iteration 1

1   Oven temperature
   1.1   [R-1] Boundaries 200–500° F
   1.2   [R-1] Multiples of 5° F
   1.3   [R-5] Default to 350° F
2   [R-3] Manual mode
   2.1   [R-4] Cooking temperature
   2.2   [R-8] Start command
   2.3   [R-10] Stop command
3   [R-3] Automatic mode
   3.1   [R-4] Cooking temperature
   3.2   [R-6] Start time
   3.3   [R-6] Stop time
   3.4   [R-7] Start command
   3.5   [R-11] Stop cooking
      3.5.1   [R-11] Elapsed time
      3.5.2   [R-11] Stop command

Appendix A2

Outline iteration 2

1   [R-3] Manual mode
   1.1   [R-4] Cooking temperature
      1.1.1   [R-1] Boundaries 200–500° F
      1.1.2   [R-1] Multiples of 5° F
      1.1.3   [R-5] Default to 350° F
   1.2   [R-8] Start command
   1.3   [R-10] Stop command
2   [R-3] Automatic mode
   2.1   [R-4] Cooking temperature
      2.1.1   [R-1] Boundaries 200–500° F
      2.1.2   [R-1] Multiples of 5° F
      2.1.3   [R-5] Default to 350° F
   2.2   [R-6] Start time
   2.3   [R-6] Stop time
   2.4   [R-7] Start command
   2.5   [R-11] Stop cooking
      2.5.1   [R-11] Elapsed time
      2.5.2   [R-11] Stop command

Appendix A3

Outline iteration 3

1   [R-3] Manual mode
   1.1   [R-4] Cooking temperature
      1.1.1   [R-1] Boundaries 200–500° F
      1.1.2   [R-1] Multiples of 5° F
      1.1.3   [R-5] Default to 350° F
      1.1.4   Enter twice
      1.1.5   Valid data
      1.1.6   Invalid data
   1.2   [R-8] Start command
      1.2.1   No data / default
      1.2.2   Enter twice
   1.3   [R-10] Stop command
      1.3.1   No data / default
      1.3.2   Enter twice
   1.4   Abort command
   1.5   Power loss
   1.6   Stress the system

2   [R-3] Automatic mode
   2.1   [R-4] Cooking temperature
      2.1.1   [R-1] Boundaries 200–500° F
      2.1.2   [R-1] Multiples of 5° F
      2.1.3   [R-5] Default to 350° F
      2.1.4   Enter twice
      2.1.5   Valid data
      2.1.6   Invalid data
   2.2   [R-6] Start time
      2.2.1   No data / default
      2.2.2   Enter twice
      2.2.3   Valid data
      2.2.4   Invalid data
      2.2.5   Relative to current time
         2.2.5.1   current time < start time
         2.2.5.2   current time = start time
         2.2.5.3   current time > start time
      2.2.6   Relative to entering stop time
         2.2.6.1   Start time specified after stop time
         2.2.6.2   Specify start time, then stop time, then start time
   2.3   [R-6] Stop time
      2.3.1   No data /default
      2.3.2   Enter twice
      2.3.3   Valid data
      2.3.4   Invalid data
      2.3.5   Relative to start time
         2.3.5.1   start time < stop time
         2.3.5.2   start time = stop time
         2.3.5.3   start time > stop time
      2.3.6   Relative to current time
         2.3.6.1   current time < stop time
         2.3.6.2   current time = stop time
         2.3.6.3   current time > stop time
   2.4   [R-7] Start command
      2.4.1   No data /default
      2.4.2   Enter twice
   2.5   [R-11] Stop cooking
      2.5.1   [R-11] Elapsed time
      2.5.2   [R-11] Stop command
         2.5.2.1   No data / default
         2.5.2.2   Enter twice
   2.6   Abort command
   2.7   Power loss
   2.8   Stress the system

Appendix A4

Outline iteration 4

1   [R-3] Manual mode
    1.1   [R-4] Cooking temperature
        1.1.1   [R-1] Boundaries 200–500° F / Multiples of 5° F
            1.1.1.1   199 / 200 / 201
            1.1.1.2   195 / 200 / 205
            1.1.1.3   499 / 500 / 501
            1.1.1.4   495 / 500 / 505
        1.1.2   [R-5] Default to 350° F
        1.1.3   Enter twice
            1.1.3.1   oven is idle
            1.1.3.2   oven is heating
        1.1.4   Valid data
            1.1.4.1   410
        1.1.5   Invalid data
            1.1.5.1   0
            1.1.5.2   000
            1.1.5.3   0410
            1.1.5.4   non-multiple of 5
            1.1.5.5   negative value (**Note**: cannot enter a negative value with this design)
            1.1.5.6   alphabetic character (**Note**: cannot enter a character with this design)
            1.1.5.7   other key (**Note**: no other key exists with this design)
    1.2   [R-8] Start command
        1.2.1   No data / default
            1.2.1.1   oven is idle
            1.2.1.2   oven is heating
        1.2.2   Enter twice
            1.2.2.1   oven is idle
            1.2.2.2   oven is heating
    1.3   [R-10] Stop command (Cancel key)
        1.3.1   No data / default
            1.3.1.1   oven is idle
            1.3.1.2   oven is heating
        1.3.2   Enter twice
            1.3.2.1   oven is idle
            1.3.2.2   oven is heating
2   [R-3] Automatic mode
    2.1   [R-4] Cooking temperature
        2.1.1   [R-1] Boundaries 200–500° F / Multiples of 5° F

2.1.1.1   199 / 200 / 201
2.1.1.2   195 / 200 / 205
2.1.1.3   499 / 500 / 501
2.1.1.4   495 / 500 / 505
2.1.2   [R-5] Default to 350° F
2.1.3   Enter twice
2.1.3.1   oven is idle
2.1.3.2   oven is heating
2.1.4   Valid data
2.1.4.1   350
2.1.5   Invalid data
2.1.5.1   0
2.1.5.2   000
2.1.5.3   035
2.1.5.4   non-multiple of 5
2.1.5.5   negative value (**Note**: cannot enter a negative value with this design)
2.1.5.6   alphabetic character (**Note**: cannot enter a character with this design)
2.1.5.7   other key (**Note**: no other key exists with this design)
2.2   [R-6] Start time
2.2.1   No data /default
2.2.1.1   No number given (Start Time key followed by a key listed below)
2.2.1.1.1   Hit Enter key
2.2.1.1.2   Hit Stop Time key
2.2.1.1.3   Hit Start key
2.2.1.1.4   Hit Cancel key
2.2.1.2   Number typed but not followed by Enter key
(Start Time key + number + a key listed below. This aborts the Start Time command, whereas hitting the Enter key accepts the start time value.)
2.2.1.2.1   Hit Stop Time key
2.2.1.2.2   Hit Start key
2.2.1.2.3   Hit Cancel key
2.2.2   Enter twice
2.2.2.1   oven is idle
2.2.2.2   oven is heating
2.2.3   Valid data
2.2.3.1   0000 (lower bound)
2.2.3.2   2359 (upper bound)
2.2.4   Invalid data
2.2.4.1   410
2.2.4.2   negative value (**Note**: cannot enter a negative value with this design)

2.3.6.2   current time = stop time

2.3.6.3   current time > stop time

2.4   [R-7] Start command

2.4.1   No data / default

2.4.1.1   oven is idle (**Note**: can only have "no data" when in manual mode)

2.4.1.2   oven is heating

2.4.2   Enter twice

2.4.2.1   oven is idle

2.4.2.2   oven is heating

2.5   [R-11] Stop cooking

2.5.1   [R-11] Elapsed time

2.5.1.1   start time specified

2.5.1.2   start time not specified

2.5.1.3   cancel automatic mode, prior to start of heating

2.5.2   [R-11] Stop command (Cancel key)

2.5.2.1   No data / default

2.5.2.1.1   oven is idle (Oven cannot be both idle and in automatic mode)

2.5.2.1.2   oven is heating

2.5.2.2   Enter twice

2.5.2.2.1   oven is idle (Oven cannot be both idle and in automatic mode)

2.5.2.2.2   oven is heating

Appendix A5

Test cases derived from the test outline

Test case ID	Test outline	Prior state	Input	Expected results	Actual results
T-1	1.1.1.1	(idle)	199 Enter key	Display: TEMP ERROR	
T-2	1.1.1.1 1.1.1.2	(idle)	200 Enter key Start key	Oven turns on and heats to 200° within 4 minutes. Temperature in range 198°–202°. Display: BAKE when heating is on	
T-3	1.1.1.1	(idle)	201 Enter key	Display: TEMP ERROR	
T-4	1.1.1.2	(idle)	195 Enter key	Display: TEMP ERROR	
T-5	1.1.1.2	(idle)	205 Enter key Start key	Oven turns on and heats to 205° within 4 minutes. Temperature in range 203°–207°. Display: BAKE when heating is on	

Test case ID	Test outline	Prior state	Input	Expected results	Actual results
T-6	1.1.1.3 1.1.5.4	(idle)	499 Enter key	Display: TEMP ERROR	
T-7	1.1.1.3 1.1.1.4	(idle)	500 Enter key Start key	Oven turns on and heats to 500° within 6 minutes. Temperature in range 498°–502°. Display: BAKE when heating is on	
T-8	1.1.1.3	(idle)	501 Enter key	Display: TEMP ERROR	
T-9	1.1.1.4	(idle)	495 Enter key Start key	Oven turns on and heats to 495° within 6 minutes. Temperature in range 493°–497°. Display: BAKE when heating is on	
T-10	1.1.1.4	(idle)	505 Enter key	Display: TEMP ERROR	
T-11	1.1.2 1.2.1.1 2.4.1.1	(idle)	Start key	Oven turns on and heats to 350° within 5 minutes. Temperature in range 348°–352°. Display: BAKE when heating is on	
T-12	1.1.3.1	(idle)	250 Enter key 405 Enter key Start key	Oven turns on and heats to 405° within 6 minutes. Temperature in range 403°–407°. Display: BAKE when heating is on	
T-13	1.1.3.2	run T-5	2 minutes after heating starts in T-5, hit 450 Enter key Start key	Oven heats to 450° in less than 6 minutes. New temperature in range 448°–452°. Display: BAKE when heating is on	
T-14	1.1.4.1	(idle)	410 Enter key Start key	Oven turns on and heats to 410° within 6 minutes. Temperature in range 408°–412°. Display: BAKE when heating is on	
T-15	1.1.5.1	(idle)	0 Enter key	Display: TEMP ERROR	
T-16	1.1.5.2	(idle)	000 Enter key	Display: TEMP ERROR	
T-17	1.1.5.3	(idle)	0410 Enter key	Display: TEMP ERROR	
T-18	1.2.1.2	run T-9	one minute after heating starts in T-9, hit Start key	No change in oven behavior. T-9 continues to operate as expected.	
T-19	1.2.2.1	(idle)	Start key Start key	Oven turns on and heats to 350° within 5 minutes. Temperature in range 348°–352°. Display: BAKE when heating is on	

Test case ID	Test outline	Prior state	Input	Expected results	Actual results
T-20	1.2.2.2	run T-11	one minute after heating starts in T-11, hit Start key Start key	No change in oven behavior. T-11 continues to operate as expected.	
T-21	1.3.1.1	(idle)	Cancel key	No action. Oven remains idle. Display: <empty>	
T-22	1.3.1.2	run T-2	20 seconds after heating starts in T-2, hit Cancel key	Oven stops heating and shuts off. Display: <empty>	
T-23	1.3.2.1	(idle)	Cancel key Cancel key	No action. Oven remains idle. Display: <empty>	
T-24	1.3.2.2	run T-5	20 seconds after heating starts in T-5, hit Cancel key Cancel key	Oven stops heating and shuts off. Display: <empty>	
T-25	2.1.1.1	(idle) current time must be before 14:30	Start Time key 1430 Enter key 199 Enter key	Display: TEMP ERROR	
T-26	2.1.1.1 2.1.1.2	(idle) current time must be before 14:32	Start Time key 1432 Enter key 200 Enter key Start key	When time reaches 14:32, oven turns on and heats to 200° within 4 minutes. Temperature in range 198°–202°. Display: BAKE when heating is on	
T-27	2.1.1.1	(idle) current time must be before 13:30	Start Time key 1330 Enter key 201 Enter key	Display: TEMP ERROR	
T-28	2.1.1.2	(idle) current time must be before 14:30	Start Time key 1430 Enter key 195 Enter key	Display: TEMP ERROR	
T-29	2.1.1.2	(idle) current time must be before 15:06	Start Time key 1506 Enter key 205 Enter key Start key	When time reaches 15:06, oven turns on and heats to 205° within 4 minutes. Temperature in range 203°–207°. Display: BAKE when heating is on	

Test case ID	Test outline	Prior state	Input	Expected results	Actual results
T-30	2.1.1.3 2.1.5.4	(idle) current time must be before 04:30	Start Time key 0430 Enter key 499 Enter key Start key	Display: TEMP ERROR	
T-31	2.1.1.3 2.1.1.4	(idle) current time must be before 09:30	Start Time key 0930 Enter key 500 Enter key Start key	When time reaches 09:30, oven turns on and heats to 500° within 6 minutes. Temperature in range 498°–502°. Display: BAKE when heating is on	
T-32	2.1.1.3	(idle) current time must be before 14:30	Start Time key 1430 Enter key 501 Enter key	Display: TEMP ERROR	
T-33	2.1.1.4	(idle) current time must be before 20:10	Start Time key 2010 Enter key 495 Enter key Start key	When time reaches 20:10, oven turns on and heats to 495° within 6 minutes. Temperature in range 493°–497°. Display: BAKE when heating is on	
T-34	2.1.1.4	(idle) current time must be before 16:00	Start Time key 1600 Enter key 505 Enter key	Display: TEMP ERROR	
T-35	2.1.2	(idle) current time must be before 14:05	Start Time key 1405 Enter key Start key	When time reaches 14:05, oven turns on and heats to 350° within 5 minutes. Temperature in range 348°–352°. Display: BAKE when heating is on	
T-36	2.1.3.1 2.2.5.1	(idle) current time is 11:20	310 Enter key Start Time key 1130 Enter key 455 Enter key Start key	When time reaches 11:30, oven turns on and heats to 455° within 6 minutes. Temperature in range 453°–457°. Display: BAKE when heating is on	
T-37	2.1.3.2	run T-35	At 14:15, when oven has reached 350°, hit 325 Enter key Start key	Oven cools down to 325°. Display: <empty> when cooling Then maintain temperature in range 323°–327°. Display: BAKE when heating is on	

Test case ID	Test outline	Prior state	Input	Expected results	Actual results
T-38	2.1.4.1 2.5.1.2	(idle) current time is 09:07	350 Enter key Stop Time key 1215 Enter key Start key	Oven turns on and heats to 350° within 5 minutes. Temperature in range 348°–352°. Display: timer countdown, starting from 03:08:00 Oven shuts off at 12:15 (when timer = 00:00:00) and sounds buzzer Display: <empty>	
T-39	2.1.5.1	(idle) current time must be before 05:00	Start Time key 0500 Enter key 0 Enter key	Display: TEMP ERROR	
T-40	2.1.5.2	(idle) current time must be before 02:41	Start Time key 0241 Enter key 000 Enter key	Display: TEMP ERROR	
T-41	2.1.5.3	(idle) current time must be before 15:00	Start Time key 1500 Enter key 035 Enter key	Display: TEMP ERROR	
T-42	2.2.1.1.1	(idle)	Start Time key Enter key Start key	Oven turns on and heats to 350° within 5 minutes. Temperature in range 348°–352°. Display: BAKE when heating is on	
T-43	2.2.1.1.2	(idle)	Start Time key Stop Time key Start key	Oven turns on and heats to 350° within 5 minutes. Temperature in range 348°–352°. Display: BAKE when heating is on	
T-44	2.2.1.1.3	(idle)	Start Time key Start key	Oven turns on and heats to 350° within 5 minutes. Temperature in range 348°–352°. Display: BAKE when heating is on	
T-45	2.2.1.1.4	(idle)	Start Time key Cancel key	No action. Oven remains idle. Display: <empty>	
T-46	2.2.1.2.1	(idle)	Start Time key 1122 Stop Time key	Display: TIME ERROR	
T-47	2.2.1.2.2	(idle)	Start Time key 0805 Start key	Display: TIME ERROR	
T-48	2.2.1.2.3	(idle)	Start Time key 400 Cancel key	No action. Oven remains idle. Display: <empty>	

Test case ID	Test outline	Prior state	Input	Expected results	Actual results
T-49	2.2.2.1	(idle) current time is 07:00	Start Time key 0725 Enter key Start Time key 0720 Enter key Start key	When time reaches 07:20, oven turns on and heats to 350° within 5 minutes. Temperature in range 348°–352°. Display: BAKE when heating is on	
T-50	2.2.2.2	run T-49	30 seconds after heating starts in T-49, hit Start Time key 0840 Enter key Start Time key 1200 Enter key	No change in oven behavior. T-49 continues to operate as expected.	
T-51	2.2.3.1 2.2.5.2	(idle) current time is 00:00	Start Time key 0000 Enter key Start key	Oven turns on and heats to 350° within 5 minutes. Temperature in range 348°–352°. Display: BAKE when heating is on	
T-52	2.2.3.2 2.2.5.1	(idle) current time is 23:58	Start Time key 2359 Enter key Start key	When time reaches 23:59, oven turns on and heats to 350° within 5 minutes. Temperature in range 348°–352°. Display: BAKE when heating is on	
T-53	2.2.4.1	(idle) current time must be before 04:10	Start Time key 410 Enter key Start key	Display: TIME ERROR	
T-54	2.2.5.2	(idle) current time is 19:30	Start Time key 1930 Enter key Start key	Oven turns on and heats to 350° within 5 minutes. Temperature in range 348°–352°. Display: BAKE when heating is on	
T-55	2.2.5.2 2.3.3.2 2.3.5.1 2.5.1.1	(idle) current time is 19:30	Start Time key 1930 Enter key Stop Time key 2359 Enter key Start key	Oven turns on and heats to 350° within 5 minutes. Temperature in range 348°–352°. Display: timer countdown, starting from 04:29:00 Oven shuts off at 23:59 (when timer = 00:00:00) and sounds buzzer Display: <empty>	
T-56	2.2.5.3	(idle) current time is 10:57	Start Time key 1056 Enter key Start key	No action. Oven remains idle. Display: <empty>	

Test case ID	Test outline	Prior state	Input	Expected results	Actual results
T-57	2.2.6.1	(idle) current time is 16:40	Stop Time key 1740 Enter key Start Time key 1730 Enter key Start key	When time reaches 17:30, oven turns on and heats to 350° within 5 minutes. Temperature in range 348°–352°. Display: timer countdown, starting from 00:10:00 Oven shuts off at 17:40 (when timer = 00:00:00) and sounds buzzer Display: <empty>	
T-58	2.2.6.2	(idle) current time is 16:40	Start Time key 1852 Enter key Stop Time key 1900 Enter key Start Time key 1858 Enter key Start key	When time reaches 18:58, oven turns on and starts to heat to 350°. Display: timer countdown, starting from 00:02:00 Oven shuts off at 19:00 (when timer = 00:00:00) and sounds buzzer Display: <empty>	
T-59	2.3.1.1.1	(idle)	Stop Time key Enter key Start key	Oven turns on and heats to 350° within 5 minutes. Temperature in range 348°–352°. Display: BAKE when heating is on	
T-60	2.3.1.1.2	(idle)	Stop Time key Start Time key Start key	Oven turns on and heats to 350° within 5 minutes. Temperature in range 348°–352°. Display: BAKE when heating is on	
T-61	2.3.1.1.3	(idle)	Stop Time key Start key	Oven turns on and heats to 350° within 5 minutes. Temperature in range 348°–352°. Display: BAKE when heating is on	
T-62	2.3.1.1.4	(idle)	Stop Time key Cancel key	No action. Oven remains idle. Display: <empty>	
T-63	2.3.1.2.1	(idle)	Stop Time key 2010 Start Time key	Display: TIME ERROR	
T-64	2.3.1.2.2	(idle)	Stop Time key 1745 Start key	Display: TIME ERROR	
T-65	2.3.1.2.3	(idle)	Stop Time key 400 Cancel key	No action. Oven remains idle. Display: <empty>	
T-66	2.3.2.1	(idle) current time is 16:00	Stop Time key 1605 Enter key Stop Time key 1705 Enter key Start key	Oven turns on and heats to 350° within 5 minutes. Temperature in range 348°–352°. Display: timer countdown, starting from 01:05:00 Oven shuts off at 17:05 (when timer = 00:00:00) and sounds buzzer Display: <empty	

Test case ID	Test outline	Prior state	Input	Expected results	Actual results
T-67	2.3.2.2	run T-31	At 9:31(after heating starts), hit Stop Time key 1010 Enter key Stop Time key	No change in oven behavior. T-31 continues to operate as expected.	
T-68	2.3.3.1	(idle) current time is 00:00	Stop Time key 0001 Enter key Start key	Oven turns on and starts to heat to 350°. Display: timer countdown, starting from 00:01:00 Oven shuts off at 00:01 (when timer = 00:00:00) and sounds buzzer Display: <empty>	
T-69	2.3.4.1	(idle)	Stop Time key 0000 Enter key	Display: TIME ERROR	
T-70	2.3.4.2	(idle)	Stop Time key 930 Enter key	Display: TIME ERROR	
T-71	2.3.5.2	(idle) current time is 14:00	Start Time key 1647 Enter key 375 Enter key Stop Time key 1647 Enter key Start key	No action. Oven remains idle. Display: <empty>	
T-72	2.3.5.3	(idle) current time is 14:00	Start Time key 1648 Enter key Stop Time key 1647 Enter key Start key	No action. Oven remains idle. Display: <empty>	
T-73	2.3.6.1	(idle) current time is 14:00	Stop Time key 1401 Enter key Start key	Oven turns on and starts to heat to 350°. Display: timer countdown, starting from 00:01:00 Oven shuts off at 14:01 (when timer = 00:00:00) and sounds buzzer Display: <empty>	
T-74	2.3.6.2	(idle) current time is 14:00	Stop Time key 1400 Enter key Start key	No action. Oven remains idle. Display: <empty>	
T-75	2.3.6.3	(idle) current time is 14:01	Stop Time key 1400 Enter key Start key	No action. Oven remains idle. Display: <empty>	

Test case ID	Test outline	Prior state	Input	Expected results	Actual results
T-76	2.4.1.2	run T-55	20 seconds after heating starts in T-55, hit Start key	No change in oven behavior. T-55 continues to operate as expected.	
T-77	2.4.2.1	(idle) current time is 12:00	Stop Time 13:00 Enter Start key Start key	Oven turns on and heat to 350° within 5 minutes. Temperature in range 348°–352°. Display: timer countdown, starting from 01:00:00 Oven shuts off at 13:00 (when timer = 00:00:00) and sounds buzzer Display: <empty>	
T-78	2.4.2.2	run T-38	20 seconds after heating starts in T-38, hit Start key Start key	No change in oven behavior. T-38 continues to operate as expected.	
T-79	2.5.1.3	(idle) current time is 13:00	Start Time key 1400 Enter key Start key Wait 10 minutes, then hit Cancel key	No action. Oven remains idle, even when the oven is waiting to start heating at 14:00. Display: <empty>	
T-80	2.5.2.1.2	run T-38	2 minutes after heating starts in T-38, hit Cancel key	Oven stops heating and shuts off. Display: <empty>	
T-81	2.5.2.2.2	run T-55	1 minute after heating starts in T-55, hit Cancel key Cancel key	Oven stops heating and shuts off. Display: <empty>	

Appendix A6

Test case checklist with separate columns for priority code, input data, and test result

Priority	Test case outline	Data	Results
	1 [R-3] Manual mode		
	1.1 [R-4] Cooking temperature		
	1.1.1 [R-1] Boundaries 200–500° F / Multiples of 5° F		
	1.1.1.1 199 / 200 / 201		
2	1.1.1.2 195 / 200 / 205	195	✓
2	1.1.1.3 499 / 500 / 501	499	✗
	1.1.1.4 495 / 500 / 505		
1	1.1.2 [R-5] Default to 350° F		✓
2	1.1.3 Enter twice	*see sublist*	✓
	1.1.3.1 oven is idle	250, 405	✓
	1.1.3.2 oven is heating	205, 450	✓
1	1.1.4 Valid data	345	✓
1	1.1.4.1 410		✓
	1.1.5 Invalid data		
	1.1.5.1 0		
1	1.1.5.2 000		✗
	1.1.5.3 0410		
	1.1.5.4 non-multiple of 5		
2	1.1.5.5 negative value	can't be done	n/a
	1.1.5.6 alphabetic character		
	1.1.5.7 other key		
	1.2 [R-8] Start command		
	1.2.1 No data / default		
	1.2.1.1 oven is idle		
	1.2.1.2 oven is heating		
	1.2.2 Enter twice		
	1.2.2.1 oven is idle		
	1.2.2.2 oven is heating		
	1.3 [R-10] Stop command (Cancel key)		
	1.3.1 No data / default		
	1.3.1.1 oven is idle		
	1.3.1.2 oven is heating		
	1.3.2 Enter twice		
	1.3.2.1 oven is idle		
	1.3.2.2 oven is heating		

Priority	Test case outline	Data	Results
	2 [R-3] Automatic mode		
	2.1 [R-4] Cooking temperature		
	2.1.1 [R-1] Boundaries 200–500° F / Multiples of 5° F		
	2.1.1.1 199 / 200 / 201		
1	2.1.1.2 195 / 200 / 205	195, 205	✓
	2.1.1.3 499 / 500 / 501		
	2.1.1.4 495 / 500 / 505		
1	2.1.2 [R-5] Default to 350° F		✓
	2.1.3 Enter twice		
	2.1.3.1 oven is idle		
	2.1.3.2 oven is heating		
	2.1.4 Valid data		
	2.1.4.1 350		
	2.1.5 Invalid data		
	2.1.5.1 0		
	2.1.5.2 000		
	2.1.5.3 035		
	2.1.5.4 non-multiple of 5		
	2.1.5.5 negative value		
2	2.1.5.6 alphabetic character	can't be done	n/a
	2.1.5.7 other key		
	2.2 [R-6] Start time		
	2.2.1 No data /default		
	2.2.1.1 No number given		
2	2.2.1.1.1 Hit Enter key		✓
2	2.2.1.1.2 Hit Stop Time key		✗
2	2.2.1.1.3 Hit Start key		✓
	2.2.1.1.4 Hit Cancel key		
	2.2.1.2 Number typed but not followed by Enter key		
	2.2.1.2.1 Hit Stop Time key		
	2.2.1.2.2 Hit Start key		
	2.2.1.2.3 Hit Cancel key		
	2.2.2 Enter twice		
1	2.2.2.1 oven is idle	0725, 0720	✓
	2.2.2.2 oven is heating		
	2.2.3 Valid data		
	2.2.3.1 0000 (lower bound)		
	2.2.3.2 2359 (upper bound)		
	2.2.4 Invalid data		
	2.2.4.1 410		
	2.2.4.2 negative value		

Priority	Test case outline	Data	Results
	2.2.4.3 alphabetic character		
	2.2.4.4 other key		
	2.2.5 Relative to current time		
1	2.2.5.1 current time < start time	current= 23:58 start= 23:59	✓
1	2.2.5.2 current time = start time	current= 19:30 start= 19:30	✓
2	2.2.5.3 current time > start time	current= 10:57 start= 10:56	✓
	2.2.6 Relative to entering stop time		
	2.2.6.1 Start time specified after stop time		
	2.2.6.2 Specify start time, then stop time, then start time		
	2.3 [R-6] Stop time		
	2.3.1 No data /default		
	2.3.1.1 No number given		
	2.3.1.1.1 Hit Enter key		
	2.3.1.1.2 Hit Start Time key		
	2.3.1.1.3 Hit Start key		
	2.3.1.1.4 Hit Cancel key		
	2.3.1.2 Number typed but not followed by Enter key		
	2.3.1.2.1 Hit Start Time key		
	2.3.1.2.2 Hit Start key		
	2.3.1.2.3 Hit Cancel key		
	2.3.2 Enter twice		
	2.3.2.1 oven is idle		
1	2.3.2.2 oven is heating		✗
	2.3.3 Valid data		
	2.3.3.1 0001 (lower bound)		
1	2.3.3.2 2359 (upper bound)		✓
	2.3.4 Invalid data		
	2.3.4.1 0000		
	2.3.4.2 930		
	2.3.4.3 negative value		
	2.3.4.4 alphabetic character		
	2.3.4.5 other key		
	2.3.5 Relative to start time		
2	2.3.5.1 start time < stop time	start= 19:30 stop= 23:59	✓
1	2.3.5.2 start time = stop time	start= 16:47 stop= 16:47	✓
2	2.3.5.3 start time > stop time	start= 16:48 stop= 16:47	✓

Priority	Test case outline	Data	Results
	2.3.6 Relative to current time		
	2.3.6.1 current time < stop time		
	2.3.6.2 current time = stop time		
	2.3.6.3 current time > stop time		
	2.4 [R-7] Start command		
	2.4.1 No data / default		
	2.4.1.1 oven is idle		
	2.4.1.2 oven is heating		
	2.4.2 Enter twice		
	2.4.2.1 oven is idle		
	2.4.2.2 oven is heating		
	2.5 [R-11] Stop cooking		
	2.5.1 [R-11] Elapsed time		
1	2.5.1.1 start time specified		✓
	2.5.1.2 start time not specified		
	2.5.1.3 cancel automatic mode, prior to start of heating		
	2.5.2 [R-11] Stop command (Cancel key)		
	2.5.2.1 No data / default		
	2.5.2.1.1 oven is idle		
	2.5.2.1.2 oven is heating		
	2.5.2.2 Enter twice		
	2.5.2.2.1 oven is idle		
	2.5.2.2.2 oven is heating		

Appendix B

Appendix B1

Test cases derived from the shopper commands outline

Test case ID	Test source	Input	Expected results	Actual results
MG-1	1.1.1	From main menu: select "Women's clothes"	The list of stores screen appears and lists 3 women's clothes stores.	
MG-2	1.1.2	From main menu: select "Men's clothes"	The list of stores screen appears and lists 2 men's clothes stores.	
MG-3	1.1.3	From main menu: select "Children's clothes"	The list of stores screen appears and lists 4 children's clothes stores.	
MG-4	1.1.4	From main menu: select "Women's shoes"	The list of stores screen appears and lists 2 women's shoes stores.	
MG-5	1.1.5	From main menu: select "Men's shoes"	The list of stores screen appears and lists 2 men's shoes stores.	
MG-6	1.1.6	From main menu: select "Flowers"	The list of stores screen appears and lists 1 flower store.	
MG-7	1.1.7	From main menu: select "Gifts"	The list of stores screen appears and lists 2 gift stores.	
MG-8	1.1.8	From main menu: select "Restaurants"	The list of stores screen appears and lists 5 restaurants.	
MG-9	1.2.1	From main menu: (a) hit map key (b) hit print key	(a) Get a map of the mall posted on the screen. (b) Get a printed copy of the map.	
MG-10	1.2.2	From main menu: (a) hit map key (b) hit "return to previous screen" key	(a) Get a map of the mall posted on the screen. (b) Return to main menu.	
MG-11	1.2.3	From main menu: (a) hit map key (b) hit "main menu" key	(a) Get a map of the mall posted on the screen. (b) Return to main menu.	
MG-12	1.2.4.1	From main menu: (a) hit map key (b) hit help key (c) hit "return to previous screen" key	(a) Get a map of the mall posted on the screen. (b) Get the help screen providing information about the map menu. (c) Return to map menu.	
MG-13	1.2.4.2	From main menu: (a) hit map key (b) hit help key (c) hit "main menu" key	(a) Get a map of the mall posted on the screen. (b) Get the help screen providing information about the map menu. (c) Return to main menu.	

Test case ID	Test source	Input	Expected results	Actual results
MG-14	1.3.1	From main menu: (a) hit help key (b) hit "return to previous screen" key	(a) Get the help screen providing information about the main menu. (b) Return to main menu.	
MG-15	1.3.2	From main menu: (a) hit help key (b) hit "main menu" key	(a) Get the help screen providing information about the main menu. (b) Return to main menu.	
MG-16	2.1.1	From main menu: (a) select "Women's clothes" (b) select the first store name from the list (c) hit print key	(a) The list of stores screen appears and lists 3 women's clothes stores. (b) Get a map to this store posted on the screen. (c) Get a printed copy of the map.	
MG-17	2.1.2	From main menu: (a) select "Men's clothes" (b) select the second store name from the list (c) hit "return to previous screen" key	(a) The list of stores screen appears and lists 2 men's clothes stores. (b) Get a map to this store posted on the screen. (c) Return to list of stores screen listing 2 men's clothes stores.	
MG-18	2.1.3	From main menu: (a) select "Children's clothes (b) select the fourth store name from the list (c) hit "main menu" key	(a) The list of stores screen appears and lists 4 children's clothes stores. (b) Get a map to this store posted on the screen. (c) Return to main menu.	
MG-19	2.1.4.1	From main menu: (a) select "Women's shoes" (b) select the first store name from the list (c) hit help key (d) hit "return to previous screen" key	(a) The list of stores screen appears and lists 2 women's shoes store. (b) Get a map to this store posted on the screen. (c) Get the help screen providing information about the map menu. (d) Return to screen with map of store.	
MG-20	2.1.4.2	From main menu: (a) select "Men's shoes" (b) select the second store name from the list (c) hit help key (d) hit "main menu" key	(a) The list of stores screen appears and lists 2 men's shoes stores. (b) Get a map to this store posted on the screen. (c) Get the help screen providing information about the map menu. (d) Return to main menu.	
MG-21	2.2	From main menu: (a) select "Flowers" (b) hit "main menu" key	(a) The list of stores screen appears and lists 1 flower store. (b) Return to main menu.	
MG-22	2.3.1	From main menu: (a) select "Gifts" (b) hit help key (c) hit "return to previous screen" key	(a) The list of stores screen appears and lists 2 gift stores. (b) Get the help screen providing information about the list of stores menu. (c) Return to list of stores screen listing 2 gift stores.	
MG-23	2.3.2	From main menu: (a) select "Restaurants" (b) hit help key (c) hit "main menu" key	(a) The list of stores screen appears and lists 5 restaurants. (b) Get the help screen providing information about the list of stores menu. (c) Return to main menu.	

Appendix B2

Test cases derived from the use cases

Test case ID	Test source	Initial system state	Input	Expected results	Actual results
u1-1	use case #1	Start test from the main menu.	(a) select "Men's clothes" (b) select the first store name from the list. (c) hit print key	(a) The list of stores screen appears and lists 2 men's clothes stores. (b) Get a map to this store posted on the screen. (c) Get a printed copy of the map.	
u1-2	use case #1 extension 1a	Start test from the main menu.	(a) hit help key (b) hit "return to previous screen" key	(a) Get the help screen providing information about the main menu. (b) Return to main menu.	
u1-3	use case #1 extension 1b	Start test from the main menu.	[No input: Shopper wants to find a book store].	Main menu does not list books as a store category.	
u1-4	use case #1 extension 2a	Start test from the main menu.	(a) select "Restaurants" (b) hit help key	(a) The list of stores screen appears and lists 5 restaurants. (b) Get the help screen providing information about the list of stores menu.	
u1-5	use case #1 extension 2b	"Lorna's Shoes" is not a valid store name. Start test from the main menu.	Select "Women's shoes"	The list of stores screen appears and lists 2 women's shoes stores, but "Lorna's Shoes" is not included.	
u2-1	use case #2	Gifts stores listed are "Collectibles" and "The Gift Box". Start test from the main menu.	1. select "Gifts" 2. select "Collectibles" 3. hit print key 4. hit "return to previous screen" key 5. select "The Gift Box" 6. hit print key	1. The list of stores screen appears and lists 2 gift stores. 2. Get a map showing the location of "Collectibles". 3. Get a printed copy of the map. 4. Return to list of stores screen listing 2 gift stores. 5. Get a map showing the location of "The Gift Box". 6. Get a printed copy of this map.	

Test case ID	Test source	Initial system state	Input	Expected results	Actual results
u3-1	use case #3	Start test from the administrator menu.	1. select "Men's clothes" 2. type in "The Cave" 3. enter location of store onto map 4. run test #u1-1 to verify addition of new store	1. List containing 2 store names appears. 2. System accepts the store name. 3. Map updated. 4. Get list of 3 stores, including new name; get map showing new store location.	
u3-2	use case #3 extension 1a	Start test from the administrator menu.	1. create new store category "Books" 2. add new store "The Reading Room" to the books category 3. enter location of store onto map 4. use Shopper interface to confirm addition of new store	1. New category created. 2. System accepts the store name. 3. Map updated. 4. New book category contains the new store name; get map showing new store location.	
u3-3	use case #3 extension 2a	Gifts stores listed are "Collectibles" and "The Gift Box". Start test from the administrator menu.	1. select the Gifts category 2. type in "Collectibles"	1. List containing 2 store names appears. 2. Get error: name already exists.	
u3-4	use case #3 extension 3a	"Red Roses" is the one flower store listed. Start test from the administrator menu.	1. select "Flowers" 2. type in "Flower Shoppe" 3. specify the location currently occupied by "Red Roses"	1. List containing 1 store name appears. 2. System accepts the store name. 3. Get error: location already occupied.	

References

[Bach] Bach, J. 'What is Exploratory Testing? And How it Differs from Scripted Testing'. Article available at http://www.satisfice.com/articles/what_is_et.htm

[Bamford93] Bamford, R. and Deibler, W.J. (1993) 'Comparing, Contrasting ISO 9001 and the SEI Capability Maturity Model' in *COMPUTER*, IEEE Computer Society, Vol. 26, No. 10, October.

[Bamford97] Bamford, R. and Deibler, W.J. (1997) 'The Application of ISO 9001 to Software Development', in *The ISO 9000 Handbook* (third edition) (R.W. Peach, ed.), McGraw-Hill.

[Bamford98] Bamford, R. and Deibler, W.J. (1998) 'Hybrid Multi-Model Assessment – When the CMM Meets ISO 9001', in *CROSSTALK – The Journal of Defense Software Engineering*, Vol. 11, No. 9, September.

[Beizer84] Beizer, B. (1984) *Software System Testing and Quality Assurance*, Van Nostrand Reinhold Company.

[Beizer90] Beizer, B. (1990) *Software Testing Techniques* (second edition), Van Nostrand Reinhold. Inc.

[Beizer95] Beizer, B. (1995) *Black Box Testing*, John Wiley.

[Binder00] Binder, R.V. (2000) *Testing Object-Oriented Systems: Models, Patterns, and Tools*, Addison-Wesley.

[Black99] Black, R. (1999) *Managing the Testing Process*, Microsoft Press.

[Boehm81] Boehm, B. (1981) *Software Engineering Economics*, Prentice-Hall.

[Buckley96] Buckley, F.J. (1996) *Implementing Configuration Management: Hardware, Software, and Firmware* (second edition), IEEE Computer Society Press.

[Cockburn01] Cockburn, A. (2001) *Writing Effective Use Cases*, Addison-Wesley.

[Cohen97] Cohen, D.M., Dalal, S.R., Fredman, M. L., and Patton, G.C. (1997) 'The AETG System: An Approach to Testing Based on Combinatorial Design' in *IEEE Transactions on Software Engineering*, Vol. 23, No. 7, July.

[Dumas99] Dumas, J.S. and Redish, J. (1999) *A Practical Guide to Usability Testing* (revised edition), Ablex.

[Dustin99] Dustin, E., Rashka, J. and Paul, J. (1999) *Automated Software Testing: Introduction, Management, and Performance*, Addison-Wesley.

[Fagan86] Fagan, M.E. (1986) 'Advances in Software Inspections,' in *IEEE Transactions on Software Engineering*, Vol. SE–12, No. 7, July.

[Fewster99] Fewster, M. and Graham, D. (1999). *Software Test Automation: Effective Use of Test Execution Tools*, Addison-Wesley.

[Freedman90] Freedman, D.P. and Weinberg, G.M. (1990). *Handbook of Walkthroughs, Inspections, and Technical Reviews, Evaluating Programs, Projects, and Products* (third edition), Dorset House Publishing.

[Gause89] Gause, D. and Weinberg, G. (1989). *Exploring Requirements, Quality Before Design*, Dorset House Publishing.

[Gilb93] Gilb, T. and Graham, D. (1993) *Software Inspection*, Addison-Wesley.

[Hamlet01] Hamlet, D. and Maybee, J. (2001) *The Engineering of Software*, Addison-Wesley.

[Hetzel88] Hetzel, B. (1988), *The Complete Guide to Software Testing* (second edition), John Wiley.

[Humphrey89] Humphrey, W.S. (1989) *Managing the Software Process*, Addison-Wesley.

[IEEE 610.12] ANSI/IEEE Std 610.12–1990, (1990) 'IEEE Standard Glossary of Software Engineering Terminology', IEEE Computer Society Press.

[IEEE 730] ANSI/IEEE Std 730–1998 (1998) 'IEEE Standard for Software Quality Assurance Plans', IEEE Computer Society Press.

[IEEE 828] ANSI/IEEE Std 828–1998 (1998) 'IEEE Standard for Software Configuration Management Plans', IEEE Computer Society Press.

[IEEE 829] ANSI/IEEE Std 829–1998 (1998) 'IEEE Standard for Software Test Documentation', IEEE Computer Society Press.

[IEEE 830] ANSI/IEEE Std 830–1998 (1998) 'IEEE Recommended Practice for Software Requirements Specifications,' IEEE Computer Society Press.

[IEEE 1008] ANSI/IEEE Std 1008–1987 (R1993) 'IEEE Standard for Software Unit Testing', IEEE Computer Society Press.

[IEEE 1028] ANSI/IEEE Std 1028–1997, (1997) 'IEEE Standard for Software Reviews', IEEE Computer Society Press.

[IEEE 1058] ANSI/IEEE Std 1058–1998 (1998) 'IEEE Standard for Software Project Management Plans', IEEE Computer Society Press.

[IEEE 1233] ANSI/IEEE Std 1233–1998 (1998) 'IEEE Guide for Developing of System Requirements Specifications', IEEE Computer Society Press.

[IEEE 12207] IEEE/EIA 12207 (1998) Industry Implementation of International Standard ISO/IEC 12207:1995 (ISO/IEC) Standard for Information Technology.

[ISO 9000–3] ISO 9000–3 (1991) *Quality management and quality assurance standards – Part3: Guidelines for the application of ISO 9001 to the development, supply and maintenance of software*, International Organization for Standardization (ISO).

[ISO 9001:1994] ISO 9001 (1994). *Quality systems – Model for quality assurance in design, development, production, installation and servicing* (second edition), International Organization for Standardization (ISO).

[ISO 9001:2000] ISO 9001 (2000) *Quality management systems – Requirements*, International Organization for Standardization (ISO).

[ISO 12207] International Organization for Standardization & International Electrotechnical Commission (1995). *Information Technology: Software Life Cycle Processes (ISO 12207)*, International Organization for Standardization/ International Electrotechnical Commission.

[Kaner99] Kaner, C., Falk, J. and Nguyen, H.Q (1999). *Testing Computer Software* (second edition), John Wiley.

[Kehoe96] Kehoe, R. and Jarvis, A. (1996) *ISO 9000–3: A Tool for Software Product and Process Improvement*, Springer.

[Kit95] Kit, E. (1995) *Software Testing in the Real World: Improving the Process*, Addison-Wesley.

[Leon00] Leon, A. (2000) *A Guide to Software Configuration Management*, Artech House.

[Leveson95] Leveson, N.G. (1995) *Safeware: System Safety and Computers*, Addison-Wesley.

[Marick95] Marick, B. (1995) *The Craft of Software Testing: Subsystems Testing Including Object-Based and Object-Oriented Testing*, Prentice-Hall.

[McCabe82] McCabe, T.J. (1982) *Structured Testing: A Software Testing Methodology Using the Cyclomatic Complexity Metric*, National Bureau of Standards Special Publication 500–99.

[McConnell98] McConnell, S. (1998) *Software Project Survival Guide*, Microsoft Press.

[McGregor01] McGregor, J.D. and Sykes, D.A. (2001) *Practical Guide to Testing Object-Oriented Software,* Addison-Wesley.

[Mikkelson97] Mikkelson, T. and Pherigo, S. (1997) *Practical Software Configuration Management*, Prentice-Hall.

[Moore98] Moore, J.W. (1998) *Software Engineering Standards: A User's Road Map*, IEEE Computer Society.

[Myers76] Myers, G.J. (1976) *Software Reliability, Principles and Practices*, John Wiley.

[Myers79] Myers, G.J. (1979) *The Art of Software Testing*, John Wiley.

[Nguyen01] Nguyen, H.Q. (2001) *Testing Applications on the Web: Test Planning for Internet-Based Systems*, John Wiley.

[Paulk93] Paulk, M.C., Curtis, B., Chrissis, M.B. and Weber, C.V. (1993) *Capability Maturity Model for Software, Version 1.1*, (CMU/SEI-93-TR-24), Carnegie Mellon University.

[Paulk94] Paulk, M.C. (1994) *A Comparison of ISO 9001 and the Capability Maturity Model for Software*, (CMU/SEI-94-TR-12), Carnegie Mellon University.

[Pfleeger01] Pfleeger, S.L. (2001) *Software Engineering Theory and Practice* (second edition), Prentice-Hall.

[Pressman01] Pressman, R.S. (2001) *Software Engineering: A Practitioner's Approach* (fifth edition), McGraw-Hill.

[Robertson99] Robertson, S. and Robertson, J. (1999) *Mastering the Requirements Process*, Addison-Wesley.

[Rothman99] Rothman, J. and Lawrence, B. (1999) 'Testing in the Dark', in *Software Testing and Quality Engineering*, March/April 1999. Article available at: http://www.jrothman.com/Papers/Pragmaticstrategies.html

[Rubin94] Rubin, J. (1994) *Handbook of Usability Testing: How to Plan, Design, and Conduct Effective Tests*, John Wiley.

[Schmauch94] Schmauch, C.H. (1994) *ISO 9000 for Software Developers*, ASQC Press.

[Schmidt00] Schmidt, M.E.C. (2000) *Implementing the IEEE Software Engineering Standards*, SAMS.

[Segue00] Segue Software (2000) *Gain eConfidence: The e-Business Reliability Survival Guide*, Segue Software.

[Shoemaker99] Shoemaker, D. and Jovanovic, V. (1999) *Engineering a Better Software Organization*, Quest Publishing House.

[Splaine01] Splaine, S., Jaskiel, S.P. and Savoia, A. (2001) *The Web Testing Handbook*, Software Quality Engineering.

[Wiegers96] Wiegers, K.E. (1996) *Creating A Software Engineering Culture*, Dorset House Publishing.

[Wiegers99] Wiegers, K.E. (1999) *Software Requirements*, Microsoft Press.

Index